The Process-
Centered School

This trilogy is dedicated to all children whose natural giftedness is not recognized under our current educational structure. Within each one of them lie the beauty and wisdom of the whole world, and so we are choosing to honor their unique and diverse strengths—their spiritual essence. They have touched our hearts and filled us with love. They are the individual stars that together form the galaxies. We invite them to fill our lives with their special light and help us learn from and appreciate the kaleidoscopic world in which we live.

The Process-Centered School

Sustaining a Renaissance Community

Editors

Arthur L. Costa
Rosemarie M. Liebmann

CORWIN PRESS, INC.
A Sage Publications Company
Thousand Oaks, California

For information address:

Corwin Press, Inc.
A Sage Publications Company
2455 Teller Road
Thousand Oaks, California 91320
E-mail: order@corwin.sagepub.com

SAGE Publications Ltd.
6 Bonhill Street
London EC2A 4PU
United Kingdom

SAGE Publications India Pvt. Ltd.
M-32 Market
Greater Kailash I
New Delhi 110 048 India

Printed in the United States of America

Library of Congress Cataloging-in-Publication Data

Main entry under title:

The process-centered school: sustaining a renaissance community /
    editors, Arthur L. Costa, Rosemarie M. Liebmann.
        p.   cm.
    Includes bibliographical references and index.
    ISBN 0-8039-6313-0 (cloth: acid-free paper).—ISBN
    0-8039-6314-9 (pbk.: acid-free paper)
        1. School management and organization—United States.
    2. Curriculum planning—United States. 3. Educational change—
    United States. I. Costa, Arthur L.   II. Liebmann, Rosemarie M.
    LB2805.P923 1996
    371.2′00973—dc20   96-35631

97 98 99 00 01 02 03 10 9 8 7 6 5 4 3 2 1

Editorial Assistant:	Kristen L. Green
Production Editor:	Michèle Lingre
Production Assistant:	Karen Wiley
Typesetter & Designer:	Andrea Swanson
Indexer:	Cristina Haley
Cover Designer:	Marcia R. Finlayson

Contents

Foreword

Peter M. Senge

The Tragedy of Our Times

Gordon Brown, former dean of the MIT School of Engineering, used to say, "To be a great teacher is to be a prophet—for you need to prepare young people not for today, but for 30 years into the future."

At few times in history has this admonition been more true than today. Yet if we look at the process, content, and achievements of public education, can any of us be confident that we are preparing young people well for the future in which they will live? Are we contributing to the capabilities of a 21st-century society to govern itself wisely, to prosper economically and culturally, and to generate insight into pressing problems and build consensus for change?

We stand poised at a turning point in history, with unprecedented challenges, some of which are literally unique in our history as a species. For the first time in our evolution, human beings have the power to fundamentally alter the natural environment within which we all live. No generation has ever had to face problems such as global warming (or cooling) and deterioration of the ozone layer. We are now the first species in the history of life on this planet that systematically destroys other species. No generation has ever had to confront the prospect of human activities that literally alter the gene pool and the evolutionary process. The nuclear arms race, now 50 years old, has entered a new, potentially more dangerous stage, with many nations involved. No generation before has ever had to live with the prospect of nuclear terrorism.

Within the United States, we are faced with uncontrollable government deficits and an unprecedented breakdown of the traditional family structure. No generation in America has ever had to confront such wholesale mortgaging of the future—simultaneously borrowing from future generations to support our current standard of living and leaving "no one at home" to raise that generation.

The common denominator of all the problems above is that they are *systemic* problems. The destruction of the environment, the arms race, and the erosion of community and family structures are not isolated problems with singular causes. They arise from the interactions, often during long periods, of diverse forces of change worldwide—forces such as technological progress, shifting societal values, global economics, and continuing population growth. Such problems cannot be understood by breaking them apart into components, and they will only be exacerbated by the "business as usual" politics of polarization and special interest groups. There are no villains to blame, no simple problems to fix. As the cartoon character "Pogo"—the first systems thinker in popular U.S. culture—said, "We have met the enemy and he is us."

A system of public education inevitably rests on public consensus regarding the skills, knowledge, and attitudes that will be needed by future citizens. Today, I believe our traditional consensus regarding the goals and process of public education leaves us dangerously vulnerable in a world of expanding interdependence. We have all been taught to analyze complex problems and to fix the pieces. Our traditional education process—indeed our theory of knowledge in the West—is based on reductionism, fragmenting complex phenomena into components and building up specialized knowledge of the parts. Moreover, our traditional educational process is based on competition and individual learning. This educational process, founded on fragmentation and rivalry, starts in elementary school and continues right through university, getting worse and worse the further one "progresses" in higher education. Literally, to be an "expert" in our society is to know a lot about a little. Such an educational process can never lay a solid foundation for understanding interdependency and for fostering genuine dialogue that integrates diverse points of view.

Concerns today with public education focus on achievement relative to traditional standards. But the real problem lies with the relevance of the traditional standards themselves. Preparing citizens for the future with the skills of the past has always been the bane of public education. Today, it could be the tragedy of our times.

A Leading Edge of Change

Given the profound changes that are unfolding all about us, it is not surprising that we are witnessing a massive deterioration of traditional institutions worldwide. In a world of rapid change and growing interdependence, large, centrally controlled organizations have become virtually ungovernable. The former Soviet Union, General Motors, and IBM, one-time paragons of power and control, all suffered massive breakdowns of their central nervous systems in the 1980s. The fundamental problem became the management system itself—the inability to effectively coordinate and adapt in an increasingly dynamic world, the inability to push decision making to "front lines," and the inability to neutralize traditional political power blocks committed to self-interest over common interest.

The failure in our traditional system of management is driving extraordinary change in the institution in which I spend most of my time—large business enterprises. Perhaps no sector has been forced to confront the startling changes of an interdependent world more rapidly than business. Because businesses literally compete against one another around the world, if one company or one part of the world makes significant headway in developing new skills and capabilities for a dynamic, interdependent world, it quickly gains advantage. Others will have to play catch-up or go out of business.

This is precisely what began to happen in the 1960s and 1970s, first with the Japanese, followed in rapid succession by the Koreans, Taiwanese, Singaporeans, and the other "Asian tigers"—what eventually became known as the total quality management (TQM) revolution. TQM represented, in the words of the Japanese TQM pioneer Ishikawa, "a thought revolution in management," based on such "radical" notions as "continuous improvement" (i.e, continuous learning) and focusing on "processes," not just products—how we are doing things, not just measuring the results of what we have done. TQM included a principle that everyone is part of a larger system, and the question should be not "What is my job description?" but "Whom do I serve?" Extended to the enterprise as a whole, this principle implied that everyone in the enterprise needs to understand whom the enterprise intends to serve—its "customers."

But TQM was merely the first wave of far more sweeping changes in traditional, centrally controlled bureaucratic organizations. Today, process-oriented management is being extended beyond basic manufacturing processes, the traditional focus of TQM, to thinking of everything an organization does as processes and to considering major reengineering of processes as well as continuous improvement. This is leading to new ideas about organization design—decentralization and network organizations, and even "virtual corporations," in which large numbers of highly autonomous operators interact, in effect, to create the scale of a large enterprise. Clearly, effective knowledge workers, whether they operate in networks of smaller enterprises or "networked," process-oriented larger enterprises, will need new skills and capabilities to understand complexity, communicate in ways that integrate diverse points of view, and build shared aspirations and mental models. In fact, without such new skills and capabilities, these new organizational forms may never come into being because they rely as much on the "soft technologies" of reflective conversation and systems thinking as they do on the "hard technologies" of information systems and telecommunications. In addition, in my view, running below the surface of these diverse changes may be a return to some guiding ideas from traditional management wisdom, ideas lost in the drive to reduce the art of management to a purely rational, quantifiable, mechanical model. These include ideas such as that an enterprise should exist to serve society, to contribute in some important way, and that this alone is their basis for sustaining a profit; that there is no substitute for passion, personal vision, excitement, and belief in what one is doing; and that profits when they are earned are more like oxygen than an end in and of themselves—they enable the enterprise to stay in the game and continue to generate and contribute.[1]

This whole cluster of changes in guiding ideas, core capabilities, management focus, and organization design represents a fundamental shift in our entire system of management and the overarching ethos of organizations, from "controlling organizations" to "learning organizations." This is the only ethos that seems compatible with organizational health in a world of growing interdependence and change.

The basic problem with all of this is that it is not easy. It takes years to develop the skills and knowledge to understand complex human systems, to learn how to think and learn together across cultural boundaries, to reverse years of conditioning in authoritarian organizations in which everyone "looks upward" for direction, and to build genuinely shared visions and promote "looking sideways" to see the larger systems of which each is a part. Equally challenging are the patience, perseverance, and extraordinary commitment required to develop these skills and understandings in the context of corporate environments still dominated by authoritarian, control-oriented cultures.

A Lagging Edge of Change

The more people understand the skills, knowledge, and beliefs needed to succeed in an interdependent world, the more we see the folly of thinking that we can focus exclusively on our system of management and ignore our system of education. Probably no one became more identified with the early stages of the quality management revolution than the American Dr. W. Edwards Deming. Shortly before Dr. Deming passed away in December 1993, I had an opportunity to ask him, "Dr. Deming, could the system of management you propound ever be widely implemented in the United States in our business enterprises if it is not implemented in our schools?" His simple answer was "no."

Having worked now for 20 years at developing the particular capabilities that seem vital to "learning organizations" in business organizations, it becomes clear that Deming was right. Isn't it silly to begin developing systems thinking capabilities in 35-year-olds who have spent the preceding 30 years becoming master reductionists? Isn't it grossly inefficient to begin developing reflectiveness, the ability to recognize and challenge one's own mental models, with successful adults—who to be successful in school and work had to become masters at solving problems rather than thinking about the thinking that generated the problems? Isn't it naive to think that we as adults can suddenly master collaborative learning, when so much of our lives has been devoted to win-lose competition and proving that we are better than each other? Shouldn't *personal mastery*, the discipline of fostering personal vision and working with "creative tension," be a cornerstone of schooling? Educators often speak of the ideal of lifelong learners—people with a keen sense of purposefulness, who are self-directed and good at objective self-assessment. Isn't it hypocritical to espouse personal vision and mature self-assessment when so much of traditional schooling is devoted to learning what *someone else* says we should learn and then convincing *them* we've learned it?

Increasingly, business people are recognizing the tragic neglect of fundamental innovation in public education. And they are moving from corporate contributions and public relations to action. For example, Electronic Data Systems (EDS) has a corporate policy that allows any employee to take time off each week with pay to volunteer in public schools. Intel employees have worked to start new public schools in Arizona and in statewide educational reform movements in Oregon and New Mexico. Ford employees are teaching systems thinking and mental models in community colleges in Detroit. Motorola has started its own "summer camp," teaching basic science and technology for children of Motorola employees.

But little is likely to take hold, spread, and grow from such isolated experiments until there is a widespread revolution in professional *and* public thinking about the nature and goals of public education for the 21st century. How will the traditional skill set of the industrial era have to be expanded for successful workers and citizens in the knowledge era? How must the traditional education process be transformed? How must traditional ideas of what constitutes "school" give way as more and more of the content of traditional education becomes available over the Internet? What will educational institutions commensurate with the knowledge era actually look like?

There will be no easy answers to such questions. My guess is that two cornerstones to the new system of education will be elevating the learning process to comparable standing with the content of what is learned and making high-level thinking and learning skills, such as systems thinking and collaborative learning, as important as traditional skills of reductionistic thinking and individual problem solving. These could indeed be two elements of a thought revolution in education.

Who Will Lead the Transformation?

Recently, my wife and I attended an awards assembly at our teenage son's school. Our 5-year old son, Ian, was with us. When the winner of the first award was announced, Ian turned to Diane and asked, "Mommy, is only one child getting an award? So, the other kids don't get a reward?"

What does a 5-year-old see that the sophisticated educators do not see? Why can he see the system as a whole—all the kids—and the educators see only the pieces, the "exceptional" kids? Maybe it's simply because the professional educators have spent their whole lives in schools. Maybe, despite their knowledge about learning theory and research, they also have the hardest time seeing beyond "the way it's always been done." Maybe the leadership that will be needed must come from all of us.

In 1994-1995, I participated in a series of satellite broadcasts on learning organizations.[2] One of these shows involved three kids from the Orange Grove Middle School in Tucson, Arizona, a school that has been integrating systems thinking and learner-directed learning throughout its curriculum and management practices for more than 5 years. The clarity, articulateness, and composure of these young people (ages 13 and 14) deeply impressed the other participants, mostly corporate managers doing the same types of work within their businesses. As the program went on, many of the most penetrating insights were offered by the young people. When the moderator asked who would like to offer any closing remarks, Kristi Jipson, an eighth-grade student at Orange Grove, said,

> I'd really like to say to those parents who say that "a book and a ruler is what it's all about," that you really need to talk to kids. If you talk to us, you'll see that we are really excited about what we are learning now. Before, you only needed to learn the "book and ruler" stuff. But now, as this program shows, businesses are changing, and by the time we get there this is what will be going on, and we'll need to know it.

One of the most forceful voices for innovation in the Catalina Foothills District, in which Orange Grove is located, has been a group of senior "citizen champions," many in their 70s and older, who in the words of Luise Hayden, became "enrolled in a revolution." They formed the Ideals Foundation with a vision of "entire curricula" organized around

> demonstrating how the parts relate to the whole. The foundation should benefit all children who are capable of learning, quickening their academic growth and enlarging their future aspirations and opportunities for school and career success, regardless of their present level of achievement. It should be a search for methods whereby students can use their own learning advances to help another, in a sustained and mutually supportive relationship.

The profound rethinking of public education required today cannot be led by any one constituency or professional group. The future is the responsibility of us all. And *all* includes those who have seen most of the past and those who will see the most of the future. All must participate, and all must lead.

Notes

1. Such ideas may seem naively idealistic, but that is only because of widely shared mental models about business, not because of any careful study of successful enterprises historically. For example, Royal-Dutch Shell's study of long-lived companies—business enterprises that have survived for more than 100 years—found virtually exactly these characteristics (see deGeus, 1995).

2. The broadcasts were a series of three programs on *Applying the Principles of the Learning Organization* (1994-1995), sponsored by a learning partnership of the Associated Equipment Distributors (AED) Foundation, the Association for Supervision and Curriculum Development (ASCD), The Learning Circle (TLC), and the PBS Adult Learning Services. The programs were coproduced by The Learning Circle and N.A.K. Production Associates.

References

deGeus, A. P. (1995, January). *Companies: What are they?* [Speech delivered to the Royal Society of the Arts]. Available from the MIT Center for Organizational Learning, Cambridge.

The Learning Circle and N.A.K. Production Associates (Coproducers). (1994-1995). *Applying the principles of the learning organization* [Satellite broadcasts]. Sudbury, MA: The Learning Circle.

Preface to the Trilogy

Arthur L. Costa
Rosemarie M. Liebmann

When we no longer know what to do we have come to our real work and when we no longer know which way to go we have begun our real journey. The mind that is not baffled is not employed. The impeded stream is the one that sings.

Wendell Berry

Each new journey begins with a quest, a yearning to move beyond present limits. As we tried to envision the future needs of our learners, we were taken aback by how little we actually know about the world in which they will live. Numerous studies guided our way, but in reality, these are only predictions of a time we cannot fathom. Change is with us, and it seems to be invading our lives at an ever more rapid rate. Not only are we feeling the personal transitions, but organizational change, which has been traditionally slow, is responding to a faster and more demanding society.

This trilogy provides educators with a bold but responsive perspective on curriculum intended to serve learners well into the 21st century. In today's complex and intelligence-intensive world economy, organizations can no longer rely exclusively on the intelligence of those few at the top of the pyramid. The amount of clear thinking required to meet the demands for speed, flexibility, quality, service, and innovation means that everyone in the organization must be involved. The organization must engage the acumen, business judgment, and systemwide responsibility of all its members.

Processes for the Workplace

Students entering the marketplace must come fully equipped with the skills that enable them to be lifelong learners. They must bring into the workplace their ability to think for themselves—to be self-initiating, self-modifying, and self-directing. They must acquire the capacity to learn and change consciously, continuously, and quickly.

The members of future organizations will require skills beyond that of content knowledge. The new employees must possess process skills. As Peter Senge addresses in the foreword, community members will be and are expected to go beyond just fixing problems to anticipating what might happen and to searching continuously for more creative solutions.

Societal Processes

The development of such a learning society depends on people's willingness to define the relationships between the individual and the community. The collective nurturing and understanding of our interdependence is essential if we wish to ensure our survival on this earth. More and more facets of society are beginning to challenge the traditionally held views of reductionist thinking. We are recognizing the need to see the world not only through the eyes of the individual but also as a part of a greater system in which connections are as important as differences.

Our society further recognizes a growing need for informed, skilled, and compassionate citizens who value truth, openness, creativity, and love, as well as the search for personal and spiritual freedom. We hear statements about community, interdependence, a balance in all areas of one's life, and making work an arena for self-discovery. This implies that the school's curriculum must be open enough to accept an androgynous perspective.

In an age in which self outweighs all other considerations, popular society is responding to the media because they appeal to the senses, not thoughts. The advertising industry is geared to selling the sizzle to the senses, not the steak to the cerebrum. An Anheuser-Busch commercial delivers the following message: "Why ask why? Drink Bud Dry." Or simply put, don't think, just drink! The media deliver the message that image is everything and substance is nothing. A recent Mazda commercial advocates, "Buy the car because it feels right." And Nike T-shirts are emblazoned with the statement, "Just Do It," which sends a message that impulsivity, rather than deliberation, is valued in this popular society.

Many persons are currently concerned with the increasing violence in schools, communities, and the world. Yet the media send a message that rules are unacceptable—"On Planet Reebok there are no rules!" The effect of the media as forces in learning cannot be underestimated. Education, therefore, must begin to help learners understand that not every opinion is worthwhile and that experts should be consulted. Educators must assist the young in moving away from the episodic grasp of reality created by the media.

These are not new thoughts but rather part of the continual quest for meaning as humans increase their knowledge base. Our desire to improve the current educational system has been founded on the erroneous belief that more of the same techniques and strategies will make all the difference. Yet if we consider the following quotes and their accompanying dates (from *Newsletter of the Curriculum and Supervisors Association,* 1994), one is left thinking that more of the same may in fact not hold the answers:

> More than eleven-twelfths of all the children in the reading classes in our schools do not understand the meaning of the words they read. —Horace Mann, 1838
>
> It is the opinion of high school teachers that from one fourth to one half the pupils are not greatly benefited by their course of study. These students lack interest, industry, effort, purpose, and are feebly endowed. —A Boston School Official, 1874
>
> A "despairing teacher" sent the *New York Times* samples of students' atrocious writing. —1911
>
> The president of the Carnegie Foundation complained, "In a large number of institutions the teaching has become enormously diluted." —1923
>
> The *Elementary School Journal* reported a "chronic problem facing American schools: a significant proportion of children were practically unable to learn to read under the prevailing methods of instruction." —1929
>
> The New York Committee on Delinquency in the Secondary Schools reported a "wide array of reckless, irresponsible, and anti-social behavior, with instances of violence, extortion, gang fights, and threats of bodily harm. There was vandalism against school property, private property, and pupils' personal possessions; there was theft, forgery, obscenity and vulgarity." —Early 1950s (p. 1)

The current education problems are the result of business as usual.

The re-visioning of education now required is so profound that it reaches far beyond the questions of budget, class size, teacher pay, and the traditional conflicts over the curriculum. In truth, the current industrial model of education is largely obsolete.

Processes of Meaning Making

Educators, in conjunction with other stakeholders, must begin to address the purpose behind the content. They must ask themselves the question, "Why do we do what we do at all?"

The exploding array of information makes it more impractical than ever to cover content at the expense of in-depth treatment. We are on the verge of a paradigm shift—content will become the mechanism by which we teach process. This shift will embrace the child's natural love of learning. As Senge (1990) has stated,

> Children come fully equipped with an insatiable drive to explore and experiment. Unfortunately the primary institutions of our society are oriented predominantly toward controlling rather than learning, rewarding individuals for performing for others rather than cultivating their natural curiosity and impulse to learn. (p. 7)

Content can no longer be the end in and of itself but the tool by which people learn to make meaning for themselves or to solve the problems for which they do not have answers.

In the past, educators have considered knowledge as static. This concept has influenced how we view a student's ability to learn. Valued is the possession of information, thus excluding the dynamic processes by which information is acquired and applied to authentic challenges. In the words of Deepak Chopra (1994), we "have become obsessed with the child's weaknesses, hiring tutors to make up for his [her] deficiencies, instead of looking at his [her] strengths and nurturing the natural talents." Not all children can be mathematicians, scientists, artists, authors, poets, musicians, historians, and so forth. Children come for a purpose unique to who they are, a purpose appropriate to the overall mosaic of life. It is time educators value individuals for their natural skills and talents, instead of trying to create clones, all possessing the same abilities.

Each human being has an inestimable potential for higher-order thought. As a result, we believe processes should be at the center of education. According to Chopra (1994),

> We think of the human body basically as a physical machine that has learned to think. Consciousness becomes the by-product of matter. The reality is that your physical body is not a frozen anatomical structure, but literally a river of intelligence and energy that's constantly renewing itself every second of your existence.
>
> I'd like to propose that we are not physical machines that have learned how to think. Perhaps it's the other way around: We are thoughts (and impulses, consciousness, feelings, emotions, desires, and dreams) that have learned how to create physical bodies; that what we call our physical body is just a place that our memories call home for the time being.
>
> Understanding that consciousness is the creator of the mind and body, I think, is really necessary for us to survive and create a new reality. Not only is the body a field of ideas, but so is the physical universe we inhabit.

Curriculum: A Shared Purpose

All institutions are changing as the relationships between employee and employer, woman and man, offspring and parent, and student and teacher alter in deep and permanent ways in response to the need for all to contribute their intelligence, creativity, and responsibility to society.

The dilemma of what to teach and how best to teach dates from early colonial times. In the present controversy, educators and those outside education wrestle with basic skills, which can be seen as quantifiable measures of the success of education, versus intellectual skills, which are essentially qualitative and require authentic forms of assessment.

The importance of establishing a shared purpose for education in a culturally diverse country needs to be understood. As one corporate executive stated,

> Schools have no alignment on purpose. It is as if someone blows the whistle and starts the football game but forgets the goalposts and the markings on the ground. The players are simply running around and the game keeps going on, but we have no idea if we are winning.

To be effective, an organization must have a clear vision or shared purpose, clear insights into current reality, and a willingness to work at closing the gap between the two. Until schools begin to recognize the changes in society, focus on new visions for students that are congruent with these changes, and come to grips with the current state of reality, the industrial model of education will be perpetuated in an intellectual, community-modeled learning society. As the old smokestacks of the industrial era vanish from the horizon, so must the industrial model of education. We need to reawaken in our students the joy of learning to use and develop their intellects.

Toward a Process Curriculum

Tomorrow's workplaces will require the following characteristics: flexible and customized production that meets the needs of the consumer, decentralized control, flexible automation, on-line quality control, work teams of multiskilled workers, delegation of authority to workers, labor-management cooperation, a screening procedure for basic skills abilities, a realization that the workforce is an investment, a limited internal labor market, advancement by certified skills rather than by seniority, a recognition that everyone requires continuing training, and employees with broader skills as opposed to specialists. Therefore, education needs to focus on

- The development of thinking skills
- Self-assessment integral to learning
- Opportunities for students to actively construct knowledge for themselves
- Learning environments that develop cooperative problem solving
- Skills that are learned in the context of real problems
- Learner-centered, teacher-directed management
- Outcomes that ensure all students have learned to think

Anthony Gregorc (1985) expresses this focus well:

The intent of education is to aid the student in realizing that he/she is a thinking person equipped with a personal knowledge bank and a decision-making instrument called a mind. Each student is expected to realize that he/she has a personal set of truths, opinions, biases, and blind spots which guide attitudes and actions. The educational process is intended to demonstrate how the student uses his/her thinking mind, how he/she learns from others and how he/she is affected by the environment. (pp. 98-99)

Ernest Boyer (1993) of the Carnegie Foundation saw the need for the following outcomes for students: being well-informed, acting wisely, continuing to learn, going beyond isolated facts to larger context and thereby discovering the connection of things, and seeing patterns and relationships that bring intellectual or aesthetic satisfaction.

We believe that the purpose of education is to enhance and develop the natural tendency of human beings as meaning makers. Humans' curiosity is aroused as we search for the meaning behind ambiguous principles and concepts. It is this continual search that promotes technological as well as personal advancements. When engaged in this search, we experience moments of illumination and moments of total change of heart. Educators need to return to learners their willingness to be playful, courageous, trusting, and risk taking. We need to invite them to reach for their outermost limits at all times. We need to create environments that allow students to practice freely without fear. We need to build not only strength of body but strength of character and strength of mind.

Where are we now? Csikszentmihalyi (1990) states,

In the past few thousand years—a mere split second in evolutionary time—humanity has achieved incredible advances in the differentiation of consciousness. We have developed a realization that mankind is separate from other forms of life. We have conceived of individual human beings as separate from one another. We have invented abstraction and analysis—the ability to separate dimensions of objects and processes from each other, such as the velocity of a falling object from its weight and its mass. It is this differentiation that has produced science, technology, and the unprecedented power of mankind to build up and to destroy its environment.

But complexity consists of integration as well as differentiation. The task of the next decades and centuries is to realize this under-developed component of the mind. Just as we have learned to separate ourselves from each other and from the environment, we now need to learn how to reunite ourselves with other entities around us without losing our hard-won individuality. The most promising faith for the future might be based on the realization that the entire universe is a system related by common laws and that it makes no sense to impose our dreams and desires on nature without taking them into account. Recognizing the limitations of human will, accepting a cooperative rather than a ruling role in the universe, we should feel the relief of the exile who is finally returning home. The problem of meaning will then be resolved as the individual's purpose merges with the universal flow. (p. 41)

For what should educators strive? Many of the answers lie in the chapters of these books. We need to develop holonomous thinkers—people who understand their individuality as well as their interdependence. We need to equip every member of society with the skills to survive in and contribute to a chaotic universe that is in constant change. All members need the strength and courage to live their lives to the fullest by giving their unique gifts back to the universe. Perhaps it is time that we as educators found the courage to open Pandora's box and release the butterfly inside.

The solution which I am urging is to eradicate the fatal disconnection of subjects which kills the vitality of our modern curriculum. There is only one subject-matter for education, and that is Life in all its manifestations.

Alfred North Whitehead

References

Boyer, E. (1993, March). *Keynote address.* Address presented at the national conference of the Association for Supervision and Curriculum Development, Washington, DC.

Chopra, D. (1994, September). *Ageless body, timeless mind.* Presentation given at the Boundless Energy Retreat, Somerset, NJ.

Csikszentmihalyi, M. (1990). *Flow: The psychology of optimal experience.* New York: Harper & Row.

Gregorc, A. (1985, Fall/Winter). Toward a redefinition of teaching, instructing, educating, and training. *Curriculum in Context,* 97-100.

Newsletter of the Curriculum and Supervisors Association (1994, June), p. 1.

Senge, P. (1990). The leader's new work: Building learning organizations. *Sloan Management Review, 32*(1), 7-22.

Preface to
The Process-Centered School

Arthur L. Costa
Rosemarie M. Liebmann

New frameworks are like climbing a mountain—the larger view encompasses, rather than rejects the earlier more restricted view.

Albert Einstein

We must never forget that any new journey will bring expectancy, eagerness, playfulness, resistance, hesitancy, and concern. There will also be times of great joy, as well as moments when we question our goals. The human spirit on which the envisioned reform is based requires a passionate commitment by the leader and his or her followers.

This third volume of the trilogy offers suggestions and strategies for those embarking on the journey of transforming education into a process-oriented paradigm. Contributions from researchers, theoreticians, and practitioners suggest practical ways to involve and enlist the support of a wide range of school community members—parents, boards of education, businesses, administrators, teachers, and students. Teacher education and staff development are explored in depth, the administrative resources and tools are addressed, and the resulting implications for teachers are reviewed.

Keenly aware of our society's need to monitor the progress of its educational systems, we have chosen to conclude with a section that speaks to the issue of assessment of progress toward achieving process as content. We present selected topics that serve to provide evidence of process as content. These include alignment and reevaluation of the curriculum, better problem solvers and finders, a sense of wonderment and curiosity, a willingness to take risks and raise questions, an appreciation for divergent thinking and diversity, an openness to new thoughts and ideas, the use of feedback spirals, and a continual development of and refinement of indicators of growth both from within and from outside the learning organization.

The Process as Content trilogy invites a new vision of education and literacy. As we enter a world in which knowledge doubles in less than 5 years (and is projected to double every 73 days by the year 2020), it is no longer feasible to anticipate the future information requirements of individuals. We must look differently, and with greater depth, at what learning is of most worth. We need, in the words of Michael Fullan (1993), to take a "quantum leap" (p. 5) in how we think about and develop curriculum.

Because of increased knowledge on how the brain learns, because of paradigm shifts from the new sciences, and because of societal needs to engage in systems thinking, the time has come to shift our focus from the *what* of knowledge (content) to the *how* of learning (processes)—from, as Seymour Papert (1991) states, "instructionism to constructionism" (p. 24). We need to nurture the skills, operations, and dispositions that will enable individuals to solve problems when answers are *not* readily known. Educators need to embark on radical reforms that shift away from content to process and to value the collective intelligence of the group, as well as the intelligence of each learner.

We are not suggesting that content be devalued. We are suggesting that content be viewed from the perspective of how it enhances and accomplishes the development of processes. As we began to collect the authors for this trilogy, repeated concern over our vision surfaced, namely, were we reversing the dichotomy from content being highly valued and prized—so much so that process has almost been excluded—to process being the primary emphasis and content forgotten? The answer to this question is a firm, resounding "No!" We, as editors and authors, believe strongly in the duality that both are required and must be intertwined. It is not a dichotomy of inclusion versus exclusion but rather an interaction.

> Process—the cluster of diverse procedures which surround the acquisition of knowledge—is, in fact, the highest form of content and the most appropriate base for curriculum change. It is in the teaching of process that we can best portray learning as a perpetual endeavor and not something which terminates with the end of school. Through process, we can employ knowledge, not merely as a composite of information but, as a system for learning. (Parker & Rubin, 1966, p. 1)

We propose that when humans operate at their peaks of efficacy, there is a congruence between what they are thinking, feeling, and doing. This concept is supported by Thomas Moore (1992), who states,

> An eternal question about children is, how should we educate them? Politicians and educators consider more school days in a year, more science and math, the use of computers and other technology in the classroom, more exams and tests, more certifications for teachers, and

less money for art. All of these responses come from the place where we want to make the child into the best adult possible, not from the ancient Greek sense of virtuous and wise, but in the sense of one is an efficient part of the machinery of society.

If we accept that there is currently a shift away from the industrial model of society to a learning society, then the focus of education needs to also shift. The change will require a movement away from a content driven curriculum to a curriculum which provides individuals with the skills necessary to engage in life-long learning. (p. 53)

Simultaneously, the role of the educator needs to shift from information provider to that of a catalyst, coach, innovator, researcher, and collaborator with the learner throughout the learning process. The development of the learner's unique abilities becomes the central focus of the learning environment.

The intent of this book is to influence curriculum decision makers at all levels—teachers, administrators, school board members, test constructors, textbook authors, legislators, parents—and to support them in thinking anew about the role of restructuring the curriculum in the school.

We believe that the most critical, but least understood, component of restructuring in the school reform movement is the restructuring of curriculum. Curriculum in the broadest sense is everything that influences the learning of the students both overtly and covertly, inside and outside the school. Curriculum is the heart, the pulse of the school; it is what drives everything else. Curriculum is the currency through which teachers exchange thoughts and ideas with students and the school community. It is the passion that binds the organization together.

Current reform movements are being driven by national, state, and local mandates, reorganization of time concerning the school day or the school year, redistribution of the power of decision-making processes, investing in technology, and recombining interdisciplinary teams and subjects. These and other such reforms constitute the *how* of delivery, not the sum and substance of what we are all about. When we begin to address the very heart of the organization, the driving component—curriculum—then all other reform efforts will fall into place. We have been building new reform structures around old-fashioned curriculum. Therefore, this book offers a bold proposal: Redesign the curriculum as the main component of re-visioning the school.

Such radical shifts in our current thinking require a clear articulation of process education. The first book in this trilogy, *Envisioning Process As Content: Toward a Renaissance Curriculum*, addressed what is meant by processes and what some of these processes are. We presented supportive literature from the new sciences and the expectations of performance from America's corporations to underscore why the time is right for such a shift in thinking about how we educate.

The second book, *Supporting the Spirit of Learning: When Process Is Content*, explores organizational questions: What would instruction, assessment, curriculum, and staff development be like if process were the content?

Numerous changes and shifts in paradigms are offered to those who embark on the journey. The third book of the trilogy, *The Process-Centered School:*

Sustaining a Renaissance Community, offers suggestions and strategies for those embarking on the journey of transforming education into a process-oriented paradigm. This book presents techniques and strategies designed to help the adventuresome get started.

We invite you, the reader, to play with these visions, thoughts, and ideas—to elaborate, change, or modify them in ways that best meet the needs of your learning organization. They are offered to you as a way to stimulate your own growth and learning. Process, by its very nature, enables a dynamic response to the environment that surrounds us.

As people continue to recognize that knowledge speaks to us not in a single voice but with many, we will simultaneously accept that there are multiple ways of thinking and understanding. As Marvin Minsky (1987) has stated,

> Everyone can benefit from multiple ways of thinking about things. Understanding something in just one way is a rather fragile kind of understanding. You need to understand something at least two different ways in order to really understand it. Each way of thinking about something strengthens and deepens each of the other ways of thinking about it. Understanding something in several different ways produces an overall understanding that is richer and of a different nature than any one way of understanding. (p. 103)

We invite you to consider curriculum in a different way—to enter a world of learning that permits greater freedom, greater control, and, in the end, more thoughtful learners. From this increased freedom, we will generate eager, autonomous, interdependent, lifelong learners.

References

Fullan, M. (1993). *Change forces: Probing the depths of educational reform.* Bristol, PA: Falmer.

Minsky, M. (1987). *The society of mind.* New York: Simon & Schuster.

Moore, T. (1992). *Care of the soul.* New York: HarperCollins.

Papert, S. (1991). Situating constructionism. In I. Harel & S. Papert (Eds.), *Constructionism.* Norwood, NJ: Ablex.

Parker, J. C., & Rubin, L. J. (1966). *Process as content: Curriculum design and the application of knowledge.* Chicago: Rand McNally.

Acknowledgments

We wish to acknowledge the valuable contributions of each of the contributors to this volume and this trilogy. Their contributions represent a vast and diverse range of points of view and, at the same time, reflect a common focus, dedication, and commitment to promoting process-oriented education. They have been patient with our prodding, agreeable to our edits, and supportive of our mission. For their time, energies, and talents, we are forever grateful.

We also wish to acknowledge Alice Foster of Corwin Press, whose encouragement and support sustained us through the 3-year duration of this project. We also wish to express our thanks to the editors at Corwin Press who assisted us greatly with refining the manuscript.

Arthur L. Costa
Rosemarie M. Liebmann

About the Authors

William Baker is Co-Director of Group Dynamics Associates and is Senior Associate with the Institute for Intelligent Behavior, Berkeley, California. An educator for 45 years, he has been an instrumental and vocal music teacher, an elementary schoolteacher and principal, a research associate, a college instructor, and an educational consultant. He retired from the Alameda (California) County Office of Education after serving 19 years as a coordinator in the curriculum and instruction division. In retirement, he presents Cognitive Coaching Foundation seminars, coordinates activities for the Institute for Intelligent Behavior, and works with school faculties to promote facilitative participation (i.e., learning to speak with and attend to each other with sensitivity and candor).

Arthur L. Costa is Emeritus Professor of Education at California State University at Sacramento and Co-Director of the Institute for Intelligent Behavior in Berkeley, California. He has served as a classroom teacher, a curriculum consultant, and an assistant superintendent for instruction and as the Director of Educational Programs for the National Aeronautics and Space Administration. He has made presentations and conducted workshops in all 50 states and in Mexico, Central and South America, Canada, Australia, New Zealand, Africa, Europe, Asia, and the islands of the South Pacific. Author of numerous journal articles, he edited *Developing Minds: A Resource Book for Teaching Thinking* and authored *The Enabling Behaviors, Teaching for Intelligent Behaviors,* and *The School as a Home for the Mind.* He is coauthor of *Cognitive Coaching: A Foundation for Renaissance Schools* and coeditor of *The Role of Assessment in the Learning Organization: Shifting the Paradigm* and *If Minds Matter.* Active in many professional organizations, he served as President of the California Association for Supervision and Curriculum Development and was the National President of ASCD from 1988 to 1989.

Robert J. Garmston, Emeritus Professor of Educational Administration at California State University, Sacramento, is Executive Director at Facilitation Associates, an educational consulting firm specializing in leadership, learning, and personal and organizational development. He is codeveloper of Cognitive Coaching and Co-Director of the Institute for Intelligent Behavior. He is the author of numerous publications on leadership, supervision, and staff development. He conducts seminars throughout the United States and in Canada, Europe, Asia, and the Middle East. Formerly a teacher and administrator, he is active in many professional organizations. He is Past President of the California Association for Supervision and Curriculum Development and formerly a member of the Executive Council for ASCD.

Charles Lavaroni has been an active California teacher and administrator in both public and independent education since 1949. He has served as an elementary school principal, an assistant superintendent at the district and intermediate levels, and a superintendent. At the college level, he functioned as the Director of Teacher Education, Dean of Admissions and Financial Aid, and Director of the Educational Administration Program, all at the Dominican College of San Rafael, California. Since 1965, he has taught short courses, workshops, and summer sessions at several colleges and universities throughout the United States and Canada. He has served as a consultant to many state departments of education, professional organizations, school districts, and schools throughout the world. Currently, although partially retired, he is actively writing and consulting. He is Director for Innovative Assessment, a California corporation, and serves as Curriculum Coordinator for the Kittredge School, a small independent school in San Francisco.

Rosemarie M. Liebmann is Director of the Institute for Continuous Learning Systems, a private consulting firm; Director of Curriculum and Instruction, Livingston School District, Livingston, New Jersey; and Adjunct Professor at Seton Hall University, South Orange, New Jersey. She attained her Ed.D. from Seton Hall University and has done extensive work in the field of human resource development. Her doctoral thesis probed the holonomous skills required of a literate society. This research has led her to a recognition of the need for society to return to valuing personal and interpersonal spirituality. She has extensively researched the ancient art of shamanism as well as feminist spirituality. Having served in the educational field for 25 years as a teacher and administrator, she seeks to help others through the use of Cognitive Coaching. In her work as lecturer, workshop leader, educator, and author, she aspires to model for others that our minds will blossom only when we permit the buds to open. The richness of learning and experiencing the world around us is the nutrients for the soil of our spirits.

Laura Lipton is Director of Educational Consulting Services, a New York-based human development firm specializing in a systems approach to change for individuals and organizations. She is a Senior Associate with the Institute for Intelligent Behavior (Berkeley, California), codirected by Arthur Costa and Robert Garmston. She engages with schools and school districts to build capacity for growth, designing and conducting workshops on learner-centered instruction, integrated curriculum, and authentic assessment. She facilitates organizational adaptivity and learning through training and development in shared leadership, action research, group dialogue, and Cognitive Coaching. She pursues personal growth opportunities through her study and research in the fields of organizational culture, change, and cognitive science. Her recent publications include *Supporting the Learning Organization: A Model for Congruent System-Wide Renewal* (with Ruth Greenblatt) and *Shifting Rules, Shifting Roles: Transforming the Work Environment to Support Learning* (with Arthur Costa and Bruce Wellman).

Robert Melamede is Assistant Professor in the Department of Microbiology and Molecular Genetics at the University of Vermont in Burlington. His research and publications center on DNA repair and molecular immunology. Both these fields examine basic homeostatic molecular mechanisms by which cells and organisms interact with their environment. His dominant intellectual focus is on applying concepts of nonequilibrium thermodynamics not only to his research interests but also to life in general. In particular, he believes that the science that underlies growth, creativity, and cooperativity provides a model that promotes healthy individuals forming a healthy society.

Michael A. Pennella has served as the president of technology and marketing businesses and is the founder of Shared Learning, located in Branchburg, New Jersey, a group that specializes in workforce and workplace effectiveness issues. In these capacities, he has contributed to change initiatives in such diverse organizations as health care, government, and service and manufacturing industries, as well as school districts and colleges. Prior to entering the private sector, he held the positions of director of education and secondary school principal. While he was serving as Principal of Ridge High School in Bernards Township, New Jersey, the school was recognized by the Secretary of Education as a "Select School" for "Excellence in Education." Pennella has also served as a consultant to the U.S. Department of Education, conducting on-site evaluations of public and private schools within Los Angeles County, California. He holds a Ph.D. from New York University.

Alison Preece is Associate Professor with the Education Faculty at the University of Victoria, British Columbia, Canada. A former elementary school teacher, she is coauthor of two books, *Evaluating Literacy* (with Terry Johnson, Norma Mickelson, and Robert Anthony) and *Young Writers in the Making* (with Diane Cowden). Her research on young children's narratives won the 1987 IRA Dissertation of the Year Award. Her interests include integrated approaches to language and literacy, play and language, gender issues relevant to classroom practice, and evaluation. A staunch advocate of involving students and parents in evaluation, she has been privileged to work with teachers throughout Canada, the United States, and Australia to support reform of evaluative practices.

Louis Rubin is Professor of Curriculum and Instruction at the University of Illinois, Champaign-Urbana. He has taught at Stanford University, the University of California at Berkeley, the University of Nebraska, and Emery University, as well as Simon Fraser University and the University of British Columbia in Canada. He has published an extensive array of articles dating from 1960 and is the author/editor of 11 books, including a two-volume *Handbook of Curriculum, Facts and Feelings in the Classroom* and *The Future of Education: Frontiers in Leadership and Artistry in Teaching*. He was formerly the Director of the Communications Coalition for Educational Change in Washington, D.C., and Director of the Center for Coordinated Education in Santa Barbara, California. He has served as a consultant to UNESCO, the U.S. Department of Education, the Ford and Kettering Foundations, and numerous state departments of education and several foreign nations. A frequent speaker, he has lectured in Europe, Asia, Africa, and South America.

Joseph M. Saban, a practicing educator of 26 years, has 15 years of teaching experience at the elementary, middle school, and high school levels. He currently serves on a number of professional boards, teaches for the Illinois Administrator Academy, and is an Affiliate Professor at Northern Illinois University in the College of Education. He is Superintendent of Schools for Community High School District 155, Crystal Lake, Illinois. The district is a suburban Chicago system composed of four high schools (Crystal Lake Central, Crystal Lake South, Cary Grove, and an alternative school, The Annex). Prairie Ridge High School, under construction, is scheduled to open in 1997 as the district's fifth site. A lifelong learner, he holds a bachelor's degree in biology (chemistry minor), a master's degree in microbiology, advanced degrees in school administration and school business management, and a doctorate in curriculum and instruction.

Peter M. Senge is a Faculty Member of the Massachusetts Institute of Technology and Director of the Center for Organizational Learning at MIT's Sloan School of Management, a consortium of corporations that work together to advance methods and knowledge for building learning organizations. He is author of *The Fifth Discipline: The Art and Practice of the Learning Organization* and is coauthor (with colleagues Charlotte Roberts, Rick Ross, Bryan Smith, and Art Kleiner) of *The Fifth Discipline Fieldbook: Strategies and Tools for Building a Learning Organization*. He is also a founding partner of the management, consulting, and training firm Innovative Associates. He has lectured extensively throughout the world, translating the abstract ideas of systems theory into tools for better understanding economic and organizational change. His special interests and expertise focus on decentralizing the role of leadership in an organization to enhance the capacity of all people to work productively toward common goals. His work articulates a cornerstone position of human values in the workplace, namely, that vision, purpose, alignment, and systems thinking are essential if organizations are to truly realize their potentials. He has worked with leaders in business, education, health care, and government. He works collaboratively with organizations such as Ford, Federal Express, Motorola, AT&T, Intel, Electronic Data Systems (EDS), Harley-Davidson, Hewlett Packard, and Royal/Dutch Shell. He received a B.S. in engineering from Stanford University, an M.S. in social systems modeling, and a Ph.D. in management from MIT.

Stanley Shalit is Curriculum and Instruction Coordinator for Alameda County Office of Education, Hayward, California. He is responsible for countywide coordination of restructuring, schoolwide planning and school accountability, and history-social science instruction. He recently managed the county's homeless children's education project and has also codirected the Bay Area Administrator Assessment Center. In addition to having consulted or worked with almost all of Alameda County's schools, he has facilitated districtwide planning and a variety of districtwide committees. He has consulted and trained staff from hundreds of schools and districts in California, Illinois, Nevada, and New Jersey. For 4 years, he developed and coordinated the California Association for Supervision and Curriculum Development's symposia for district and school leadership teams on new assessment practices, schoolwide planning, and restructuring. His private consulting company is Group Dynamics Associates. His main emphases are designing more efficient procedures for involving staff, community, and students in renegotiating school cultures so that fewer students slip through the cracks; translating state initiatives into workable approaches to enable more students to succeed; and training administrators and teachers in self-assessment techniques, especially Cognitive Coaching, in collaboration with Art Costa and Bob Garmston.

Gloria Appelt Slick is Associate Professor in the Department of Curriculum and Instruction and Director of the Office of Educational Field Experiences at the University of Southern Mississippi at Hattiesburg. She has been an educator for more than 25 years. Her professional experiences include classroom teacher, curriculum coordinator, federal program director, education specialist (Region VI Service Center, Texas), principal, assistant superintendent, professor, and administrator. Throughout her career, she has focused on teacher preparation and professional development of practicing teachers. As Director of the Federal Teaching Strategies Program, she began researching information about and developing strategies for effective instructional processes. Her ultimate goal is implementing process learning in the field experiences programs in undergraduate teacher preparation. Process learning fits her philosophy of learner participation at higher levels of cognitive involvement.

Bruce Wellman is Director of Science Resources (Guilford, Vermont) and Senior Associate with the Institute for Intelligent Behavior (Berkeley, California). He consults with school systems, professional groups, and organizations throughout the United States and Canada, presenting workshops and courses for teachers and administrators on teaching methods and materials in science, thinking skills development, Cognitive Coaching, presentation skills, and facilitating collaborative groups. He is the author and coauthor of numerous publications related to organization and professional development, quality teaching, and improving science curriculum and instruction practices. He has served as a classroom teacher, curriculum coordinator, and staff developer in public schools in Oberlin, Ohio, and Concord, Massachusetts.

Fred H. Wood is Professor of Education in the Department of Educational Leadership at the University of Oklahoma in Norman. He received his bachelor's at Western Michigan University, where he became certified as a secondary social studies teacher. He received a master's at Western Michigan University in educational administration. He earned a doctorate in curriculum instruction at the University of Missouri. He has been an elementary, junior high, and high school teacher and a school administrator in rural and suburban school districts. In addition, he has held positions of Associate and full Professor at the University of Nebraska and Pennsylvania State University. Prior to assuming the position of Dean at the University of Oklahoma, he served 9 years as Division Head of Curriculum and Instruction at Pennsylvania State University. His special research interests are in the areas of continuing professional education and the improvement of the preparation of public school administrators. His scholarly activities include more than 50 referenced publications and an extensive record of national presentations and workshops on continuing professional development.

Diane P. Zimmerman is an Elementary Principal in Davis, California. She is Senior Associate with the Institute for Intelligent Behavior (Berkeley, California). She also serves as a consultant to school districts in both the United States and Canada. During her 21 years in education, she has worked as a speech therapist, classroom teacher, and administrator of special education. She is featured in the Association for Supervision and Curriculum Development video *Another Set of Eyes: Conferencing Skills.* In this 1-hour video, she coaches a sixth-grade teacher before and after her lesson. She coauthored the book *The Constructivist Leader* and is pursuing a doctorate in organizational development from the Fielding Institute in Santa Barbara, California. Her dissertation will study school change from a systems perspective.

1

Constructing the
Metaphors for Process

Diane P. Zimmerman

The clause "when process is content" haunts the rational mind. The juxtaposition of the words—*process* and *content*—confuses the boundaries of meaning. To understand this clause, each word must be thought of in the context of the other—as if they were oscillators, each reflecting the other. Coupled oscillators start out as separate and distinct, and as they move into synchrony, they gain a collective identity that can be as simple as a tuning fork or as complex as a thousand fireflies creating an orchestra of light. Considering the two words in tandem creates a synchrony in which new meanings and understandings about a larger context for learning and knowing become evident. Understanding this flexible interdependence allows one to generate the meaning needed to finish the sentence. This chapter explores how metaphor can finish the sentence in the context of a learning community.

The pairing of process and content invites new metaphors for learning and adapting. Metaphors from both the arts and the sciences will be drawn on to explore the relationship of process to content in community. In the arts, process learning is dependent on production for full expression. The artist improvises to explore new mediums and to produce something that speaks from the inner self. Improvisation cannot be understood without attention to process. For most art, the process defines the content. The first part of this chapter explores how the process of improvisation creates the content.

Metaphors from quantum physics have turned the rational mind on its head. Instead of neat Newtonian containers created by the logic of *either/or*, concepts viewed in relationship require the logic of *both/and*. The wave-particle duality and nonlocal correlations provide analogs for a multiplex view of reality—a way of considering process as content in complex organizational systems. In the quantum world, words once considered distinct can no longer be considered in isolation. Finally, the notion of process as content suggests a new way of considering concepts often taken for granted. Synectic instructional strategies have taught that when dissimilar words are juxtaposed, a creative tension arises, generating a rich mix of information. Complexity theorists have joined together to study exactly what happens when rich pools of information reach the edge of chaos. It is the optimal state of creative growth and adaptation. The conclusion of this chapter explores ways in which practitioners might operate in this new world of *both/and* to find the creative potential needed in an adaptive organization.

Assumptions

First, it is appropriate to review some of the assumptions about the construction of meaning and the use of metaphor that underlie this work. The process of understanding or meaning making finds its epistemological roots in constructivist theories about learning and knowing. Piaget (1952), who described himself as a genetic epistemologist, concerned himself with how the child constructs cognitive structures on a developmental continuum. The development of cognitive structures comes from a child's quest for equilibrium when confronted with contradictions. Vygotsky (1978) defined the ways in which knowledge is as much a social construction as a personal construction. Later, Chomsky (1977) and Bruner (1986) reinforced the theory that language and experience are closely associated with the construction of new structures and understandings. Kegan (1982) extended Piaget's stage theory to adults through the integration of meaning making and social development as essential elements in the development of later stages. Kegan states that "meaning is, in its origins, a physical activity (grasping, seeing), a social activity (it requires another), a survival activity (in doing it, we live). Meaning understood in this way, is the primary human motion, irreducible" (pp. 18-19). In other words, meaning making is process, and it is through process that one comes to understand content. Mikhail Bakhtin, a great Russian cultural theorist, redefined the relationship of self and others in the process of coming to know. Watson (1993) explains this redefinition as follows: "Self and others cannot be divided or separated, they can only be distinguished or pointed out, and even then only with great difficulty, because they are so intertwined within the community" (p. 8). This description is not unlike quantum theorists' explanation of the wave-particle duality discussed later in this chapter. The underlying assumption in this chapter is that coming to know through language is a socially constructed process.

Barnes and Todd (1977) describe the phenomenon of coming to know as cycles of utterances, suggesting that meaning is created in cycles through time.

Pierce and Gilles (1993) extended the concept of cycles of meaning to the conversation that individuals and groups create through time as they discuss rich text. A premise of this chapter is that to create rich systems of learning in an organization, the conversations must be analogous to Pierce and Gilles's discussions of rich text. It is the process of discussing substantive issues or concepts that reshapes them into something new and maintains a fluidity about this learning that promotes adaptation.

Linguistic moves and language choices bring fluid form to the meaning-making process (Zimmerman, 1995). The field created by the conversation (not unlike Pierce & Gilles's [1993] cycles of meaning) serves as the medium for the reciprocal process of communicating. A few elegant linguistic moves can frame, deepen, and move the conversation to facilitate the construction of meaning. Learning to inquire and to respond to the meaning created by the group is an essential skill for the constructivist leader—a leader in process.

Inquiry has important historical roots in Western tradition. Pedagogical experience has taught that verbs are where the action is. Bloom, Engelhart, Furst, Hill, and Krathwohl (1956) are credited with developing the first verb list that has become known as Bloom's taxonomy. The genius of this list was that it created a process strategy to be used by teachers for the construction of different logical levels of meaning. Others have followed with their own lists that when used to frame questions, create new understandings (Costa & Garmston, 1994; Dilts, 1992; Taba, 1957). Asking questions from a field of information is the essence of process as content.

Responding behaviors in daily conversations are more often questions or data provided from the speaker's point of view. Summarizing or highlighting another's message is a skill not often practiced in the casual conversation. In conversations that create meaning, however, it is an essential element. The paraphrase is a linguistic skill that has received little attention in the professional literature. Costa and Garmston (1994) identify the paraphrase as an important response strategy in coaching others. Through coaching work with others, they have found the paraphrase a powerful tool for building meaning. It is through the paraphrase that ideas are amplified, redirected, or bounded.

When applying the above assumptions to group learning, one must consider the implications of constructivist views in the context of group learning and leading. Lambert (1995) has defined constructivist leadership as "the reciprocal processes which enable participants in an educational community to construct meanings which lead toward a common purpose about schooling" (p. 32). Learning communities must develop members' ability to operate in process as an essential action of a constructivist leader.

Finally, Drath and Palus (1994) define meaning making as a process of "naming, interpreting and making commitments to actions, to other people, and to values" (p. 9). They define leadership as the act of making this process happen in conjunction with practice. They identify communities of practice as groups who know how to create shared knowledge and shared ways of knowing that commit them to action.

Although metaphor or story has been used to construct and interpret reality since mythic times, the understanding of how metaphor affects meaning making has gained great popularity through the work of Lakoff. "The essence of metaphor is understanding and experiencing one kind of thinking in terms of another" (Lakoff & Johnson, 1980, p. 5). In this landmark work, tacit metaphors are deconstructed to demonstrate how the structure of understanding is embedded in metaphor. In a later work, Lakoff (1987) extends his thinking about metaphor beyond the classical categories taken for granted in semantics. Instead, he advocates for a more natural system that he calls *radial*. His analysis of category structure finds that categories do not have hierarchical structures with a limited number of essential attributes as in classical studies but rather have a radial structure learned through social conventions. Category structure is a complicated network of resemblances, rather than defined similarities. This loose structure for meaning explains why meaning making is a fluid process. The mind can create resemblances between widely disparate things. Viewing process as content frees individuals from the defined similarities and differences and allows for the discovery of nuance and deep understanding. The first metaphor to consider in the construction of meaning for process as content comes from the arts.

Improvisation: When Process Is the Conversation

The act of speaking is an improvisational act. Bateson (1989) describes the speaker's improvisational role as follows: "Each speaker learns to combine and vary familiar components to say something new to fit a particular context and evoke a particular response, sometimes something of a very great beauty or significance, but always improvisational and always adaptive" (p. 3). Improvisation is the recombining of the partly familiar in new ways. In jazz, modern dance, and conversation, the process creates the content. The musician, the dancer, and the conversationalist allow the process to ebb and flow in relationship. Even when clumsy or poorly executed, there is a sense of coherence and wholeness.

The value of the conversation to the adaptive organization is well documented (Bohm, 1990; Senge, 1990; Stacey, 1992). Whether to understand mental models, to reflect on past actions, or to generate a new idea, each of these theorists stresses process over content. The improvisational spirit of dialogue is to discover something that is yet unknown to the self or to the group, just as jazz musicians strive to find an undiscovered set of sounds. Nachmanovitch (1990) reminds us, "Every conversation is a form of jazz" (p. 17). To embark on a dialogue with no ready answers requires a spirit of improvisation. Through a process of coaching others, Costa and Garmston (1994) have learned that the skills of questioning and paraphrasing are two process skills that allow groups to improvise in a way that builds coherence. When these skills are used together with an intention to establish rapport, a powerful bond occurs in which ideas meld together and are mutually generated. The linguistic skills of generating, summarizing, and inquiring about the field become the choreography.

The way groups interact within these linguistic fields distinguishes a meaning-making community from others. Senge (1990) describes most organizations as communities of advocacy in which individuals articulate their own views and learn little from each other. This is improvisation without attention to context and response. It loses its generative potency and is not what I am referring to as the artistic act of improvisation.

An organization that is rich in process provides a different culture than one that is not. In a process-rich organization, ambiguity and information are sought. In contrast, an organization weak in process seeks to remove ambiguity and to control information. In describing improvisation, Nachmanovitch (1990) states, "We know what might happen in the next day or minute, but we cannot know what *will* happen" (p. 21). Improvisation reminds us that a leader's job is to manage the unknowable. An example from this past school year describes this improvisational state.

When our school was 2 years old, my colleagues and I generated mission and vision statements as part of building a school culture. Being a graduate student in organizational development, I thought I knew what these words meant. Much to my surprise, however, I could find no consistent framework for putting meaning to the words *vision* and *mission*. Just when I thought I understood each word, I discovered that I could not describe the relationship of these two words to each other. Some readers may be a bit perplexed, thinking that I am making this much too complicated. The problem is not so much in the definitions but rather in the process that one goes through to arrive at the finished product—in other words, how the improvisation is staged. I found that when trying to describe the content, I could not do so without also considering the process. It is the process that creates the meaning for these words. This is an extremely important concept in mission and vision building that is rarely understood in the professional literature. Many an office has a neatly framed statement that was written in process, treated as content, and left to be forgotten on an office wall. I learned this more clearly as I began to work with teachers and parents to make the vision come alive. Each member of the school community needed to improvise his or her personal meanings to make it come alive. We needed many conversations and many chances for improvisation. What I thought was a simple issue of content, understanding the labels, was a mirage.

Stacey (1992) eloquently describes my discovery:

> Instead of intention to secure something relatively known and fixed, it becomes intention to discover what, why, and how to achieve [in my case, a vision]. Such intention arises not from what managers foresee but from what they have experienced and now understand. It is the intention to be creative and deal with what comes, not intention to achieve some particular future state. (p. 146)

This is improvisation at its finest.

Both Process and Content

Bateson (1989) states that a composite thinker "poses the recurring riddle of what the parts have in common" (p. 15). The concept of relationship was extended when quantum physicists realized that particles and waves must be considered in the context of the other. Viewed from a quantum perspective, language learning and production are both process and content.

Traditional views of language establish categories and rules, creating a duality not unlike the quantum physicist dilemma of the wave-particle duality. In a quantum world, the observer finds that when trying to measure, she or he can measure only a wave or only a particle. The observer can never fully realize both and yet must consider both. Furthermore, the wave is not fixed but appears to be smeared, making it indeterminate. Content has the illusion of being fixed, or fully defined; process as meaning making is not fixed, and its boundaries are difficult to define. To understand meaning as motion, one must transcend the traditional notion of content as a separate entity. In *The Quantum Society*, Zohar and Marshall (1994) state that things are both determinant and indeterminate at the same time. When taken to extremes, the indeterminate loses its shape and meaning; likewise, the determinant becomes fixed and narrow at the extreme. The goal in organizations becomes one of finding the creative tension that is generated with just the right amounts of determinacy and indeterminacy. Groups who work well together understand this intuitively. Consider the following example.

A group of colleagues and I worked to re-create a ballot initiative that, if successful, would bring $1.5 million into the district for specialized programs. Initially, we started with containers—special reading, class size, additional offerings for secondary students, and so on. This brainstorming session created the tension needed to discover the shape of our thinking in new ways. We no longer were living in the boxes but rather were beginning to see multiple linkages that crisscrossed like the spokes on a spider web. In this conversation, the amount of ambiguity must be balanced—too much would have made the conversation lose shape; too little would have made it lose the design of multiplicity. Process defined the content.

Scientists have begun to reconcile that in an either/or world, concepts are fragmented and held in isolation, even when it is evident they belong to a larger system. Fullan (1994) suggests that the critical crisis of the postmodern world is the lack of coherence and the increase of fragmentation. The fallacy of specialization has led to this fragmentation. In an either/or world, meanings are considered as discrete containers, not moving mosaics of nuance. The gift of constructivism is the reminder that labels are nothing without social process for shared meaning. In workshops, I often query audiences as to what they think about when they think of something as routine in schools as report cards. The varied responses are never the same. The richness of human experience extends well beyond the dictionary definition. At least one third of most adult groups have strong emotional experiences that inform their thinking about this word. Some feel proud; others sad or angry. Some feel the burden of the responsibility in judging and affecting another person's future. Each one of these internal experiences generates a different nuance about the word. The parent who has negative memories responds differently than does a parent with positive memories. A teacher with negative memories might avoid grading altogether. What matters is that meanings must be considered in a myriad of contexts. Contradictory views are considered an important part of a multiplex system. In a both/and organization, process defines the content, requiring continuing conversations to achieve this end.

Nonlocal Synchrony: Process as Content

Einstein's theory of relativity was based on the premise that nothing traveled faster than light. One of the great paradoxical events pondered by Einstein was that scientists were finding multiple examples of instantaneous connections. Within the context of relativity, there can be no such thing as instantaneous causal influence. This paradoxical phenomenon has been labeled correlation in the absence of any force or "nonlocality." These correlations can be positive, negative, or zero. Positive correlation is eidetic, negative is one of opposites, and zero is the absence of any correlation. These correlations create emergent properties that come into existence only in relation with another and create an identity that can exist only in relationship. Both the French artist Victor Vasarely and the Dutch artist M. C. Escher understood this phenomenon. These artists painted shapes and repeated them over and over on a canvas using correlations of light and dark or changing hues of color. From a constructivist viewpoint, these nonlocal correlations would be co-constructive. This metaphor suggests that the interpretation of meaning ought to be a co-constructive process. The topic of this book, process as content, demands co-construction. Co-construction is the reflexive process that creates the domains of both instruction and organizational culture.

Although Jung (1958) did not use the word *co-construction,* he thought of it in a paradoxical frame. He believed that wholeness was possible only through the coexistence of opposites and that meaning was found in this coexistence. Quantum theory extends the notion of co-construction to complex levels. Again, the art of M. C. Escher creates ambiguity in visual image. Instead of simple paired opposites, his canvases contain multiple levels of correlation with contrasts in dark and light, tricks to the eye in which background becomes foreground or up is down. All the elements are dependent on co-construction for their meaning, and they communicate an order that is neither linear nor hierarchical. In a world in which content is dominant, hierarchical systems are important. Ideas and concepts are organized as if they were building blocks, one stacked on the other. In contrast, in a world in which process is dominant, probabilities and relationships make for complex systems that are generative, resourceful, and rich in possibilities. Shepherd (1993) states, "Seeing the workings of the world as cyclic and interactive, rather than simply linear and hierarchical, prompts us to develop a different value system—to value the process rather than seek only the end result" (p. 153). The distinction made here is to value the process as a process of co-construction.

The Edge of Chaos:
Process Is Content in the Learning Organization

In the 1980s, a group of scientists joined together at the Santa Fe Institute to study complex systems, which they defined as anything with strongly interacting parts (Waldrop, 1992). A visual metaphor developed by Chris Langton as reported by Lewin (1992) helps to describe the edge of chaos. He described driving at the edge of the continental shelf, where the light blue, crystal-clear water turns to dark blue. As he looked over the edge, he found a slope that was teaming with life for as far as he could see into the darkness. Lewin states, "Chris' image was indeed powerful. And it turns out to be more than mere iconography, because there is good evidence that evolution is particularly innovative in such waters, poised between the chaos of the near shore and the frigid stability of the deep ocean" (p. 187). Organizations that have learned to live at the edge of chaos embrace process because they know that it will provide them a rich mixture of information. It is the process that brings order out of chaos and pushes the organization to learn and adapt. They understand that it is through the conversation that this is possible. These organizations have evolved well beyond what Senge (1990) describes as communities of advocacy. They have learned to balance inquiry with advocacy as well as how to reflect on their own thinking.

The pattern of innovation at the point of change is one of the critical features that scientists first noticed in complex systems. Physicists call the shift from one level to another *phase transitions,* biologists call them *punctuations,* and archaeologists call them *hinge points.* Complexity theorists describe this phenomenon within the context *the edge of chaos.* In adaptive organizations, groups seek out these same transitions. Members describe them as the "Ah, ha!" that comes from a shift in perception or from deeper understanding. The ability to consistently find this juncture allows organizations to become adaptive. Learning organizations know when to push themselves to the edge of chaos and when to remain stable. A volleyball coach from Winnipeg describes this phenomenon when explaining how he manages the team energy. When his team members become overconfident and loose and sloppy in their plays, the coach interacts in ways that increase the tension and increase creative coherence. When the team loses confidence and starts to panic, the plays become rigid and inflexible, requiring him to interact in ways that decrease the tension and help the players find a more optimal energy level. He goes on to say that the magic comes when the members of the group become self-organizing. In those magical moments, the team takes on a life of its own and becomes invincible. His team has won the division championship for the past 4 years.

The challenge for those of us in organizations is to learn to influence the energy of the organization. The conversation provides the space in which the interactions occur. When tensions get too high, group members use paraphrasing and inquiring to decrease the tension; when the group is low in energy and bored, the group members know how to use generative strategies and advocacy to provide new information into the system.

When metaphors are from art or science, the message is clear. In this complex world, neat compartmentalized realities are no longer relevant. Instead, process is needed to allow what was once fixed to become a moving mosaic. When this happens, process is content.

References

Barnes, D., & Todd, F. (1977). *Communication and learning in small groups.* London: Routledge & Kegan Paul.

Bateson, M. C. (1989). *Composing a life*. New York: Penguin.

Bohm, D. (1990). *On dialogue*. Ojai, CA: David Bohm Seminars.

Bloom, B., Engelhart, M., Furst, E., Hill, W., & Krathwohl, D. (1956). *Taxonomy of educational objectives: Handbook I. Cognitive domain*. New York: David McKay.

Bruner, J. (1986). *Actual minds, possible world*. Cambridge, MA: Harvard University Press.

Chomsky, N. (1977). *Language and responsibility*. New York: Pantheon.

Costa, A., & Garmston, R. (1994). *Cognitive coaching: A foundation for renaissance schools*. Norwood, MA: Christopher-Gordon.

Dilts, R. (1992). *Changing belief systems with NLP*. Cupertino, CA: Meta.

Drath, W. H., & Palus, C. J. (1994). *Making common sense: Leadership as meaning-making in a community of practice*. Greensboro, NC: Center for Creative Leadership.

Fullan, M. (1994). *Turning systemic thinking on its head*. Unpublished manuscript for the U.S. Department of Education, Washington, DC.

Jung, C. (1958). *Answer to job*. Princeton, NJ: Princeton University Press.

Kegan, R. (1982). *The evolving self*. Cambridge, MA: Harvard University Press.

Lakoff, G. (1987). *Women, fire, and dangerous things*. Chicago: University of Chicago Press.

Lakoff, G., & Johnson, M. (1980). *Metaphors we live by*. Chicago: University of Chicago Press.

Lambert, L. (1995). Towards a theory of constructivist leadership. In L. Lambert, D. Walker, D. P. Zimmerman, J. E. Cooper, M. D. Lambert, M. E. Gardner, & P. J. Ford Slack (Eds.), *The constructivist leader*. New York: Teacher's College Press.

Lewin, R. (1992). *Complexity: Life at the edge of chaos*. New York: Macmillan.

Nachmanovitch, S. (1990). *Free play: Improvisation in life and art*. Los Angeles: Jeremy P. Tarcher.

Piaget, J. (1952). *The origins of intelligence in children*. New York: International Universities Press.

Pierce, K. M., & Gilles, C. J. (1993). *Cycles of meaning: Exploring the potential of talk in learning communities*. Portsmouth, NH: Heinemann.

Senge, P. (1990). *The fifth discipline*. New York: Doubleday/Currency.

Shepherd, L. J. (1993). *Lifting the veil: The feminine face of science*. Boston: Shambhala.

Stacey, R. (1992). *Managing the unknowable*. San Francisco: Jossey-Bass.

Taba, H. (1957). *Teachers' handbook for elementary social studies*. Reading, MA: Addison-Wesley.

Vygotsky, L. (1978). *Mind in society* (L. Cole, V. John-Steiner, S. Scribner, & E. Souberman, Eds.). Cambridge, MA: Harvard University Press.

Waldrop, M. M. (1992). *Complexity: The emerging science at the edge of order and chaos*. New York: Simon & Schuster.

Watson, D. (1993). Community meaning: Personal knowing within a social place. In K. M. Pierce & C. J. Gilles (Eds.), *Cycles of meaning: Exploring the potential of talk in learning communities*. Portsmouth, NH: Heinemann.

Zimmerman, D. P. (1995). The linguistics of leadership. In L. Lambert, D. Walker, D. P. Zimmerman, J. E. Cooper, M. D. Lambert, M. E. Gardner, & P. J. Ford Slack (Eds.), *The constructivist leader*. New York: Teacher's College Press.

Zohar, D., & Marshall, I. (1994). *The quantum society*. New York: William Morrow.

2

Spreading the Good Word

Communicating With the School Community to Support Change

Alison Preece

The changes we envision for our schools cannot happen without genuine communication, shared commitment, and informed, sustained support.

Schools are *not* what they used to be—and there are many who deserve thanks for that. Schools are attempting more, for more, and, in many respects, achieving more than ever before (Barlow & Robertson, 1994; Graham, 1992). Public anxiety about the effectiveness of the public schools, however, appears to be at a cyclical high. Criticisms and unflattering comparisons abound, fingers of blame are freely pointed, and motives are suspect. It's almost impossible to open a newspaper or tune into a talk show without being confronted with claims that standards are slipping and educationally implicated economic crises are looming, if not already here. Simplistic and nostalgic solutions are offered with missionary zeal and professed good intentions. Although we could debate at length whether the reality matches or warrants its media portrayal, it's clear that parents and the general public have many questions, concerns, and misunderstandings about what goes on in our classrooms. This gap must be bridged; such (mis)perceptions have power to destroy.

Obviously, schools and their public—students, parents, and the communities they serve—need to find better ways of communicating with each other. We are desperately in need of dialogue—not diatribes. It falls to those of us involved with schools to find more open, accessible, invitational, respectful, responsive, and *effective* ways of communicating what it is we are about, what we are working to change, and why. Communication lies at the heart of understanding. Understanding precedes support. If change efforts are to have any hope of succeeding, support is crucial. If our schools are to become as good as they need to be, then those connected and touched by them must understand, have input into, and support what has to be done—*and what is already being done*—to make needed reforms reality. Communication lies at the heart of community. Curriculum change of the sort envisioned in this book requires both communication *and* community. This chapter looks at some ways we might go about contributing to both as we construct the process centered school.

The ever escalating expectations placed on schools can never be realized—or even realistically attempted—unless schools create genuine connections and alliances with the people they're designed to serve (Fiske, 1991). Finding ways to talk with each other—about program and long-range goals, about "new" and controversial instructional approaches, about changes occurring within and outside the school buildings, about concerns, and about our hopes and fears for the future our children face—is an essential first step. To debate whose responsibility it is to open these communication lines is to waste energy needed for other things; schools must take the initiative because they are best positioned to do so. Too much is at stake to risk the consequences of not reaching out.

Finding ways to bridge the gap can loom as an overwhelming and unwelcome task that can intimidate already overburdened educators, unless approached, as most ambitious undertakings actually are, piece by piece, person by person, one step at a time—each in his or her own way, each in his or her arena. To this end, this chapter will look at what "reaching out" and "communicating with the community" mean from the perspective of the classroom—and the communities inherent in classrooms and touched by them. Some practical strategies will be suggested for creating opportunities for significant contact that operate with respect, reciprocity, and genuine exchange as their hallmarks. Four themes will underpin the suggestions presented: (a) the need for teachers to make what is usually implicit about their practice explicit and then "public"; (b) the need for schools to take the initiative in establishing dialogue with the home; (c) the need to invite input and response from parents in a variety of ways so that information is shared, rather than simply distributed; and (d) the need for advocacy, so that the promise and potential of the public schools will not be undermined, deflected, or defeated.

The *Whys* of the Ways of School: Letting Students In

In his compelling synthesis of research on the change process, Fullan (1991) remarks that "we hardly know anything about what students think about educational change because no one ever asks them" (p. 182). Decrying the fact, he concludes that "students are rarely treated as if their opinion mattered"

(p. 186). To extend his complaint, students are all too rarely *told* about the rationale behind educational change, either—they simply experience the results of our efforts to implement and cope with it. Sarason (1971) outlines the omission succinctly:

> It appears that children know relatively little about how a teacher thinks about the classroom, that is what he takes into account, the alternatives he thinks about, the things that puzzle him about children, and about learning, and what he does when he is not sure of what he should do, how he feels when he does something wrong. (p. 185)

Such talk about the *why*s as well as the logic behind the *what*s of our practice could help students make sense of aspects of schooling that may very well strike them as arbitrary. Relevance, strategy, and values not always evident to students can be made plain. More pragmatically, if students are to have a useful role in conveying to their parents and families why things at school are being approached as they are, then we need to let them in on what we are striving to achieve, the ends to which we aspire, and the aims behind the activities and materials with which we attempt to engage them. Research indicates that open discussions of this sort are rare events in classrooms at any level of the system (Fullan, 1991; Katz, 1993); they need to be commonplace.

This is one area in which small shifts can cause significant ripple effects. Nothing major is required other than recognition of the need to routinely inform our students about our planning and purposes. This is particularly important when introducing something unfamiliar or something new that's being tried out or tried on. A brief explanation when introducing a topic, unit, strategy, activity, or new approach about *why* it was selected and what is hoped will be achieved through it can go a long way to helping students perceive the point of what they're asked to do and learn. Better yet is to get into the habit of eliciting this information from them and then taking time to discuss it with them:

> Why do *you* think I ask you to record and share the strategies you've used, and not just your solutions? What do you think is hoped you will learn as a result of our "Review and Reflect" sessions? Is that happening for you? What's the purpose of my requirement that you justify your portfolio selections? What value do you think there is in keeping a learning journal? How could it be made into a more useful tool for you?

Obviously, responses can turn into a superficial parroting of what students think their teachers want to hear unless students are shown that their views are taken seriously and that they are quite free to point out where activities or our agendas fall short for them, without fear of consequences for voicing criticism.

Once students are clear about what various "new" approaches, techniques, and activities "are for," they frequently are able to offer astute suggestions for improving them. Some become eloquent advocates. Recognizing this and that "communication is everything," teachers at one elementary school in Colorado, as part of their strategy for building support for a new performance-based report card they had developed (and which students much preferred to the old one), "trained students as ambassadors to explain the new report cards to their parents" (Kenney & Perry, 1994, p. 24). Parental acceptance of these reports can be attributed, in part at least, to the role played by the students. Recently, I attended a conference session in Winnipeg, Manitoba, on techniques for encouraging reluctant readers. The speakers were a panel of secondary school students. All were self-described as former and recently converted "reluctant readers." They provided the conference participants with compelling testimony about their experiences as readers, perceptive analyses of the instructional techniques that have defeated or supported them, and a persuasive lobby for access, choice, and open-ended response—the conditions provided by their teacher, Syd Korsunsky, whom they credited with their changed attitudes toward reading. The students' articulate commitment powerfully illustrated the value of sharing the goals behind our strategies with those they're designed to support.

It's not entirely honest to claim that "nothing major is required," however. Obviously, before we can talk frankly with our students about the rationale undergirding the techniques and trappings of our teaching, we must first clarify that rationale for ourselves. This isn't something all of us do as a matter of course—in the grinding bustle of the day-to-day, it's easier to get on with the job than to examine the logic, merits, and consequences of how we go about it. Such self-scrutiny can be an unsettling business; some of our most taken-for-granted practices will turn out to be difficult to justify, and some of our best efforts at implementing highly touted new ones can fall far short of what was promised for them. *There is no way, however, that we can communicate and convincingly endorse the **whys** that drive and guide our practice if we haven't first clarified them for ourselves.* Once we have, though, much is to be gained from sharing our insights about intentions and methods with our students and, *just as important,* with their parents.

I clearly remember how touched and impressed I was on receiving from my daughter's fourth-grade teacher, Yves Parizeau, a letter addressed to all the parents of his class in which, with an endearing and rather brave frankness, he outlined what he hoped to achieve for our children, how he planned to go about it, and what teaching meant to him. What struck me at the time was that he was willing to risk revealing his professional self in a way that stepped outside the usual carefully couched, noncommittal prose of home-school communications. It was a small gesture—but one that earned my deep respect, and one that, by its difference, inadvertently demonstrated for me the anemic quality of what all too commonly passes for teacher-parent contact.

Letting our students—and their parents—in on how we go about evaluating their progress can efficiently illustrate and clarify for them "what counts" and what is being aimed for. Evaluation is one of the litmus tests of change: If advocated goals and practices aren't evident in the way evaluation is handled, then those changes haven't fully happened. As we strive to bring our evaluative practices into closer alignment with our educational goals, genuine gains have been made in rendering those practices more open, more inclusive, and more informing (Anthony, Johnson, Mickelson, & Preece, 1991; Johnston, 1992). Even so, far too many students at all levels of the system still report having little or no idea about how their grades, marks, and report card ratings are determined nor any understanding of the criteria by which the judgments are made. After reviewing undergraduate students' experiences of grading practices, Raths, Wojtaszek-Healy, and Kubo Della-Piana (1987) conclude that most problems "are rooted, in some large measure, in communication failures between instructor and students" (p. 133); they recommend that teachers find ways "to communicate more effectively the bases of their judgments" and "give emphasis to the problem of teaching students the standards they are using" (p. 136). Their advice is as relevant for the elementary and high school years as it is for those at universities.

Up-front, public, open-to-negotiation discussions of the criteria that will be applied when students' efforts, products, and performances are evaluated can be an effective and enlightening way to focus on and communicate our underlying goals and operating standards. In the classroom, this means that when activities and assignments are introduced—*before they've been evaluated, not afterwards*—we explicitly clarify and concretely illustrate for students (a) the qualities that will be looked for and rewarded (i.e., imaginativeness, resourcefulness, accuracy, effectiveness of presentation, etc.); (b) the relative weights given to different aspects (i.e., content/format distinctions); and (c) the characteristics that distinguish a competent execution of the task from a poor one. The relationship of the assignment to the overarching, "big picture" curricular goals also needs to be pointed out.

Student input, commentary, and questioning are crucial at this stage. Criteria need to be presented as available for consideration, examination, elaboration, and even rejection—the value of the exercise derives directly from the criteria being open for discussion, clarification, and refinement (Anthony et al., 1991; Sperling, 1993). Once reviewed, understood, and accepted, these criteria can be put in writing and distributed so that each student has a copy to refer to and work from. Again, much that matters is communicated if these statements are placed where parents also have access to them—such as pasted inside the front cover of the learning log or back-and-forth book, featured as a preface to the research project, placed in a pocket in the front of the portfolio, summarized in a newsletter for parents, or offered for discussion at a parent meeting, and so on. A word of caution is necessary, however: The evaluative criteria we apply reveal more accurately than anything we do or say the values that are actually operating in our classrooms. Therefore, if we plan to use the sharing of criteria as a means of concretely conveying how we interpret and are attempting to realize the big-picture goals and implement the reforms we endorse, then we must make sure our criteria actually embody and (to some degree, at least) actualize those goals. For better or worse, our criteria say a great deal about "what we are about."

Efforts to communicate with the community about what schools are attempting to accomplish need to begin with our students. As Epstein (1995) points out, "Students are often their parents' main source of information about school" (p. 702), and this remains true regardless of grade level. Part of our responsibility as teachers is to equip our students so that they are able to talk informatively to us and to their parents about the work they're doing, the learning they're experiencing, the progress they're making, and "what counts" in their classrooms. When they can do so—and even *young* children can do so—parents are informed about our schools in a way that speaks with a power and impact difficult to top. Fair burden or not, it falls to us to ensure that the education our students describe matches and moves toward the goals and reforms we're espousing.

Seeing Is Believing: Making the Learning Visible

If only parents could see for themselves the evidence of learning and growth that teachers are privileged to observe on a daily basis, at least some of the concern and confusion about what "the schools" are accomplishing would evaporate. Over and over again, the research literature confirms that parents who are involved with and kept informed about their children's schools rate their level of satisfaction with the quality of their children's education much higher than do parents who aren't (Goodlad, 1986; Hoover-Dempsey, Bassler, & Burrow, 1995; Swap, 1993). Further, parents rate teachers who invite their participation far more generously than they rate teachers who don't:

> Parents with children in the classrooms of teachers who build parent involvement into their regular teaching practice were more aware of teachers' efforts, received more ideas from teachers, knew more about their child's instructional program, and rated the teachers higher in interpersonal skills and overall teaching quality. (Epstein, 1986, p. 291)

There's no question that parents want to be kept informed about the goings-on in their children's schools. There's also no denying that far too many parents feel schools do a less than adequate job in this area (Chrispeels, 1991; Epstein, 1990, 1995; Farough, 1995) and that many teachers appear unaware of this dissatisfaction. Following a teacher-initiated survey of parents, Brand (1996) found that "many teachers were surprised to learn . . . that parents felt uninformed about the daily experiences in the classroom" (p. 77). Clearly, for some, a perception *and* a communication gap exists. Equally worrisome is the finding that parental satisfaction with home-school communications diminishes as grade level increases (Epstein, 1990; Farough, 1995).

How, then, do we go about making the walls of our classrooms a little more transparent and permeable? How can we make it possible for parents to gain a richer sense and better picture of the learning their children are experiencing? How can we more effectively share and "show off" the products created by their children, so that parents and family members are helped to see and interpret the learning they represent? And, perhaps most important of all, how do we set things up so that parents feel comfortable, able, and invited to share *their* observations, insights, concerns, and questions about their children's learning with us? How do we inform, include, and consult parents about the way things are changing at school so they become allies, not adversaries? And how do we manage all this and *teach* as well?

As always, the first step is recognizing the real need—and professional obligation—to do so. The second is reassuring ourselves that the goal is attainable, that it need not translate into an overly onerous undertaking, and that it can be approached in ways that enhance, rather than compete with, students' opportunities for learning. Seeking within-school support from teaching and administrator colleagues so that efforts, ideas, and resources can be pooled and coordinated—and problems tackled together—is a wise next move. Before we attempt to add to the repertoire of outreach strategies, it only makes sense to assess those things already being done to see whether they are worth continuing, can be built on, or can be made more effective. With dialogue being the goal, sincere and systematic efforts need to be made to obtain *broad-based* parental input about the sorts of things that would be appreciated, that are already in place, or that have proved worthwhile (or a waste of time) in the past. Such overtures, whether undertaken on an individual classroom or whole-school basis, pay solid dividends, both in building rapport and in finding out the real needs. Regrettably, it appears that schoolwide needs assessments of this sort rarely occur.

On the positive side, more and more school communities are establishing parent advisory or citizens' councils (sometimes of their own accord, sometimes as a consequence of ministry or district directives) with mandates to actively solicit, communicate, and represent parents' views and concerns, as well as to provide input on school policies, problems, and programs (J. B. Artis, personal communication, February 26, 1996; D. Shaw, personal communication, March 1996). When advisory groups are granted a *significant* role in the life of the school, and when the parents and community members serving on them take an active part in their operation, they can work as effective, efficient, and positive agents of support and liaison between home, community, and school (D. Shaw, personal communication, March 1996). If such a parent advisory group is in place, then it should be consulted about ways and means to better inform and involve the parents it represents and should be tapped as a resource for implementing any projects subsequently undertaken. With demands on teachers' time and energies being what they are, a realistic plan to add or reinstitute just one or two strategies is more likely to succeed and be sustained than an overly ambitious plan. Luckily, the best methods of communicating are often the most direct and straightforward. The critical thing is that the effort be genuine and that the effort be made.

If we want parents to appreciate what schools are achieving, attempting, and doing differently, then we have to find ways to let them know what those things are. One of the best ways is to get them into our schools so we can show them firsthand. Many schools take steps to ensure parents feel welcome in their buildings by supplying parent information bulletin boards and lending libraries and by inviting them to join the teachers in the coffee room at recess and lunch. The high school in my neighborhood goes one better by providing parents with their own lounge where they can meet together, leave their belongings while visiting classrooms or working on a school committee, peruse school information, or just have a cup of coffee (D. Shaw, personal communication, March 1996). Having parents visit the classroom, either as helpers or observers, is perhaps the ideal way for them to gain insight into the complexities of school life. Designating and announcing regular times when parents are free to drop in (possibly one morning or afternoon a week or month) and scheduling a mutually convenient time for an observational visit for each parent are practices heartily recommended, regardless of grade level. The simple act of issuing the invitation (rather than leaving it up to individual parents to request one) sends a reassuring signal of openness and professional confidence. When parents, on arrival, are greeted and given a short sheet of suggestions of things they might wish to look for (e.g., "What does your son or daughter select during free choice periods?" "Which activities seem especially to engage your child? Which don't?" "I try to encourage intellectual risk-taking and initiative: Do you see evidence of either in the work the students are doing?" "Is there anything that surprises you about the way things are done in our classroom?" "How does your son or daughter manage spare periods and the transitions from class to class?" etc.), they can be guided to see more subtle dimensions of the program and the learning skills being fostered that otherwise may go unnoticed or be utterly misunderstood (Preece & Cowden, 1993). Informal classroom visits tend to be relatively commonplace in the primary grades but quite unusual in the higher grades—and this is a pity. The notion that parents at this level are not interested in such visits is countered by the experience of Doug Shaw, principal of Oak Bay Secondary School (Victoria, British Columbia); parents at his school are actively encouraged to drop in on classes at any time, and he reports that many do—with positive results for the school atmosphere and the reputation of the school in the community. Parents now routinely come and go in the school with no one, teachers or students, taking undue notice of them—an indicator for Shaw that the open-door policy is a success. Significantly, parents have a variety of reasons to visit because they sit and serve on every school committee, working alongside the teachers to solve problems, enhance programs, and determine priorities. When included in these ways, parents become *in*siders who know about "what goes on in the schools" because they've seen it for themselves. When included in these ways, "they are a part of the process: therefore, they are well-informed and speak with insight and authority" (McCarthy, 1995, p. 142) to other parents. They can be the best ambassadors schools can have.

Useful as they are, in-session school or classroom visits are not a realistic option for many: Some parents aren't free to come; some teachers aren't comfortable being observed. This is where photographs and videos can prove invaluable. When strategically exploited, they offer the next best thing to being there.

Slide shows and video clips featuring classroom vignettes and student activities are invariably the highlight of any parent meeting at which they're shown. When thoughtfully put together (in the upper grades, students can assist with filming), even simple and amateurish visual media presentations can convey an enormous amount of information with an efficiency and impact that is difficult to match. When followed by informal and open discussion and the chance to have questions raised and addressed, such presentations can communicate and accomplish a great deal. Experience has shown the most successful parent-teacher meetings are those that (a) target specific topics *that parents have had input in selecting;* (b) provide concrete examples, demonstrations, and some analysis of the work their children are or will be doing; (c) build in time for parents to talk with each other, pursue questions and concerns, and share reactions and strategies; (d) offer realistic suggestions for ways parents can support their children's learning at home; and (e) are followed up with a request for feedback, further questions, and suggestions for future meetings (Preece & Cowden, 1993). A short series of meetings, interspersed throughout the year and scheduled to accommodate working parents, with each meeting specifically addressing a different subject area or aspect of the curriculum, is strongly recommended. Although schoolwide "Meet-the-Teacher" evenings and open houses most certainly have merit and can offer helpful introductory overviews and orientations, they rarely provide the depth of information many parents want nor the opportunity for them to comfortably ask questions. The time and energy spent on more focused and more frequent meetings is time and effort wisely invested.

Not all parents come out to meetings, however. In this case, creative but easily managed ways of "sending things home" prove their worth. The possibilities here are endless. Often all that's needed is a little imagination and some sturdy packaging. Some of the most effective ways of making parents aware of the nature, focus, scope, and particulars of the curriculum require little more than taking examples of the work being produced by students and "repackaging" them so they can be shared and sent home. Fortunately, this need not require much in the way of additional work on the teacher's part. Often, it simply means attaching an explanatory cover note to things that have already been prepared for use or display in the classroom, sending them home on overnight loans, and keeping them in circulation until all families have had a turn. It's not so much a matter of finding new vehicles as it is figuring out ways to get a little more mileage from those already on hand.

For example, many teachers take photographs of special events, special projects, field trips, and the day-to-day happenings of the classroom. Usually, these are displayed on a bulletin board and, deservedly, become a popular draw for those in a position to see them. Typically, however, once the bulletin board is cleared, the photos are stored or distributed to the children featured in them. If, instead of packing them away, the photos are next placed in an album, with student-created captions added that explain and interpret them, then the album can be sent home on a rotational basis, just as library books are. If, in addition to the students' captions, the teacher adds (a) a cover letter that briefly outlines the goals for the activities pictured and the learning accomplished through them and (b) blank sheets inviting parents and family members to write their comments, compliments, questions, and suggestions, then the photos' potential to mutually inform is more fully exploited. With album in hand, in the privacy of their own homes, parents are in a better position to ask specific questions and learn more about the events captured on film; with album in hand, supported and prompted by the photos, students' talk about school tends to be more detailed and elaborated than is typically the case.

Photo albums—or short videos—used this way can have a great deal of informative value. Their appeal is difficult to resist; an audience is guaranteed. Although albums can be set up to offer a general get-acquainted tour of the classroom, or a "who's who" profile of each of the students in it, a particularly effective tactic is to focus on a single activity or topic and portray it in more depth. For example, an album might be titled "In our classroom, cooperative learning looks like this . . ."; another could feature photos showing students engaging in a variety of problem-solving activities with math-manipulative materials; another might document the portfolio creation process and contain photos of students selecting, sorting, annotating, and sharing their contents. The small plastic-pocket albums are ideal for this purpose; file cards containing explanatory comments fit as easily as the photos into the pockets. When students are involved in deciding what should go into the albums, how best to portray the essentials and complexities of the focus activity, and what the captions and explanatory comments should contain, they are provided with a genuinely significant opportunity to be reflective about particular classroom events for a "real" audience. The inclusion of student perspectives and opinions makes the albums far more attractive and interesting for parents—and increases the likelihood that students will be enthusiastic about showing them off to their families. Teachers' comments, included either in an introductory preface, a summary closing statement, or placed throughout in talk balloons, can succinctly point out the concepts and skills being learned and other things that might not otherwise be appreciated or understood. Although useful for familiarizing parents with almost any aspect of classroom practice, albums that strategically focus on issues and topics about which parents are known to have questions and anxieties ("So, do you actually *teach* spelling?") or that are likely to be new to them ("What exactly *is* a 'life-skills curriculum'?") can prove particularly helpful.

An impressive and appealing "Big Book for Parents," created by two new-to-the-profession teachers, offers another model for sharing information about classrooms. Intended both as an introduction to their classrooms and as a guide through educational jargon, the book offered clear definitions of some of the more opaque terms used to label various school activities—such as Uninterrupted Sustained Silent Writing (USSW), Talent Scouts, Drop Everything and Read (DEAR), Center Time, Author's Chair, Pair-Share, and so on. Each definition was illustrated with photos of students engaged in the activity described. A blank sheet taped to the inside back cover asked readers to list any other terms they felt needed explaining. Their plan was to send the book home (in its own waterproof carry-bag) with a different child each day until all families connected to their classes had a turn to see it. Attractive and genuinely informative, the Big Book struck me as a considerate, clever, and easily concocted means for making classrooms more accessible—and a format that could easily be adapted to make it relevant to any subject or grade level.

Another powerful and positive technique for providing parents, quite literally, with a picture of their child at school is one introduced to me by Colleen Politano and Julie Wilmott of Wishart Elementary in Sooke, British Columbia. Once a year, they inform their students they will take a photo of each one of them when engaged in learning something they (the students, not the teachers) consider to be important or significant. Each student makes the decision about when his or her photo will be taken and what "learning" it will feature. Once developed, the photos are attached to a sheet of paper and the students write (or, if necessary, dictate) an explanation of what it is about the topic of their shot that makes it special for them or interesting or worth capturing on film. The sheets are then copied, and both copies are sent home. The sheet with the real photo is kept by the parents; the copy is returned to school with any comments the parents wish to make written in a specially designated space at the bottom.

For reasons that are obvious, these sheets become treasured momentos; they also provide parents with a "snapshot" of the learning going on at school and insight into what their children value.

Film processing and albums cost money. The realities of school budgets are such that the issue of how to pay for photos and albums of the sort I'm blithely advocating needs to be raised. Realistically, with respect to both money and the time needed to create them, it makes sense to plan for only a couple of albums a year. Gradually, a collection of albums documenting different activities (or new approaches to old ones) will be acquired, and although some will contain photos of "last year's class" or "students from 2 years ago," they will prove no less effective as tools for bringing the classroom to life for parents. The insertion of two or three photos of the current class can easily update an album made several years previously. Often, "old" albums prove the most popular because siblings discover, and delight in taking home, photos of older brothers and sisters. Recognizing their value, some schools consider photos a legitimate budget item and will pick up the costs for processing several rolls of film a term. Home-school groups and parent advisory committees have proved to be good sources of financial support for projects of this sort. Some teachers, promising parents that they will receive photos of their children at school in exchange, include one roll of processing prepaid film on their school supply lists. By taking advantage of special offers, the fact that photos can be successfully photocopied, and by ordering double sets of prints (often marginally more money than a single set), expenses can be cut down. Videotapes are relatively cheap and gloriously portable. Ways to cover the costs can be found; this is not something for which teachers should feel they have to dip into their own pockets.

Many of the displays of student work that grace classroom walls can, with fairly minimal effort, be attractively packaged and made available for overnight home visits or weekend or weeklong loans. For example, a bulletin board display of student writing can easily be recycled as an anthology, prefaced with a description of the specifics and goals of the assignment and supplied with sheets inviting readers' responses and comments. Students' book reviews, research reports, drawings, opinion polls, graphs, maps, and math problems and their solutions—all can be turned into informative class booklets that invite parental attention. The result is that students know their work is granted an audience beyond the classroom, and parents are provided with *concrete* and *contextualized* examples of the work that is being produced by children other than their own. Obviously, samples need to be judiciously but representatively selected, and student permission must always be sought and granted before work is made public. The ideal—not always achievable—is that booklets include a contribution from each student in the class or group.

We need to be alert to the "share potential" of the materials that we and our students create and that surround us in our classrooms. Many would provide parents with powerful and *reassuring* demonstrations of the competencies and skills their children are acquiring, if only they were able to see them. Often, all that's necessary is simply finding ways to send these things home so that they can. Typically, teachers spend hours organizing displays and projects that are seen and appreciated by only those few who enter their classrooms. These represent underexploited and lost communicative opportunities.

This was recently brought home to me by a particularly ingenious presentation of student work that had been created following a second-grade field trip. The class had visited, observed, and interviewed a film crew working on location near their school. On their return, they had recorded their impressions in a series of detailed drawings and written accounts that had been mounted by their teacher, Diane Cowden, on a 20-foot length of black poster paper that had been edged to make it resemble a giant roll of film. Visually stunning, the display dramatically captured the children's fascination with their behind-the-scenes glimpse at movie making. All too commonly, a display of this sort is simply hung in the school hallway, where, at best, it is seen by only a few parents, even if kept and later exhibited at an open house. Imaginative packaging, however, gave this display a much wider audience. After hanging in the hall, the giant "film" was laminated (not essential but recommended, if available), then rolled, film-fashion, and placed in a chunky, oversize poster tube. Once labeled and equipped with a fabric tape handle, the tube was all set to travel between home and school. It's not hard to imagine the delight children felt at the unfurling of such a grand package across their living room carpets! Nor is it hard to imagine how much such a display could convey to parents about their children's developing abilities to write and record. It's only proper to confess that this particular display was hijacked; unfurlings now happen in front of admiring student teachers to whom it's presented as a model to emulate.

Most of the suggestions presented so far share the virtue of providing parents with specific, concrete, readily interpretable examples of what their children and their children's classmates are actually doing and producing in school—and that's the point. None are offered "cold"; each is accompanied with an explanatory, contextualizing commentary, prepared by the teacher, the students, or both. Dialogue is encouraged and made easy by the inclusion of response sheets that invite feedback, reactions, and suggestions—and these sheets are a crucial component. Although there's no denying that albums, booklets, videos, and big books take time to prepare, most of these projects productively involve students in ways that are compatible with the curriculum and valuable as learning opportunities in their own right. All present a proactive, positive picture of school that communicates professionalism and pride in the quality of what is being provided, experienced, and produced by our students. We desperately need such images in circulation.

The emphasis in this chapter so far has been on ways of conveying a richer understanding of the program and the class as a whole. First and foremost, however, parents want specific information about the performance and progress of their own children, and many also want ideas for how they might help at home (Epstein, 1995; Swap, 1993). Comment-based report cards, personal portfolios, back-and-forth books, and student-led conferences have proved to be flexible and increasingly popular tools for helping meet these needs (Anthony et al., 1991).

Back-and-forth books or learning journals can be modified to be effective at *any* grade level. Although these books are organized in various ways with various emphases, the basic idea is that students use the books to record projects and progress, homework assignments, any problems encountered, and reminders or messages that need to be shared with the home. Teachers add comments as they wish or as the need arises. In the elementary grades, the books typically are taken home on Fridays, read and signed or commented in by parents, and returned on Mondays; with older students, this sharing schedule needs to be more flexible. Simple to set up, they keep all parties informed and make contact easy to initiate and maintain (Stevenson & Stigler, 1992).

Annie Davies and her colleagues at Ranchlands Community School in Calgary, Alberta, have implemented a variation with their intermediate students that has particular merit and relevance in the context of this chapter. Taking math as their focus, they use the back-and-forth book idea to help their students review their work and to keep parents closely in touch with the progress their children are making. Every Friday, time is set aside for each student to write a letter to someone at home (usually a parent, but it need not be), explaining specifically what they have been working on in math during the week and creating several examples of the types of questions or problems they've been learning how to solve. If they're having any difficulty, they simply need to attempt to point out where the trouble lies and request assistance. Many take advantage of the opportunity to announce their successes: "We've been doing 5-digit number questions in class. I think they're really easy!" Others take obvious delight in devising math problems and "exercises" for their parents to tackle; one girl created a long list of challenging multiplication questions, followed by a gentle reminder that a calculator was not to be used. Parents are requested to write back to their children, in the books, focusing their comments specifically on math.

The results are impressive. Annie Davies (personal correspondence, December 18, 1993) sums them up as follows:

> Parents are very positive about the weekly letter writing—they know what their child is doing. There are latent benefits, too: e.g., parents who encourage their child to be neater; parents who work with their child to short-circuit any difficulty; kids who desire to work neatly because their parents will see their on-going work; parents are not anxious about their child's progress in math because they can see their work; parents are choosing to extend the work of the classroom on a one to one basis with their child; fathers are involved.

The format has all sorts of obvious advantages, and it can easily be adapted to any subject area and to any age level. Students have an audience for their efforts and a significant reason to review and illustrate the specifics of the work with which they're currently engaged. The requirement that they concretely illustrate and communicate what they are learning to their parents helps consolidate and support that learning. (For those in the higher grades, a peer buddy or someone important to them can be other audience options.) Parents are provided with specific and continuing demonstrations of just what is being taught in school—and a clear idea of what sort of support would be helpful. Everybody gains.

Portfolios can play a similar role in connecting home and school. To be maximally effective and informative for both students and their parents, portfolios should be set up so that their purpose and focus are clear and operating criteria are explicit. Students need to be responsible for selecting the bulk of the samples contained in them and held accountable for explaining why each piece was chosen *and what it reveals about what they are learning.* Brief, dated, student-written annotations that point out the learning in evidence can be attached to each item chosen for inclusion. This is a key and crucial element that, if absent, diminishes the potential of portfolios to help students (and their parents) relate the "products" to the learning they were designed to foster and reflect. When planned so that periodic sharing with parents (either at home or at school) is part of the process and set up so that parents are invited to add their comments to feedback and goal-setting sheets that are included for the purpose, portfolios can operate as a powerful communication link. At the same time, they afford parents tangible evidence of the responsibility increasingly being placed on students to be accountable for, and reflective about, the work they produce at school. Although there is no question that teacher/student ratios and timetable constraints render portfolio implementation more complex at the secondary level, many teachers have successfully negotiated these challenges by having their students create subject-specific portfolios, with contents limited to the scope of their particular course. When thoughtfully set up, portfolios can become powerful evaluative tools that demonstrate *in authentic, individual, and accessible ways* students' understandings and accomplishments.

With student-led conferences (Anthony et al., 1991; Davies, Cameron, Politano, & Gregory, 1992; Little & Allan, 1988), *students'* presentations of their portfolios, or selected work samples, become a central component of reporting conferences with parents. Although the teacher has a vital role in helping students prepare, during the conferences the students (rather than the teacher) are primarily responsible for describing and documenting their progress. Sometimes called three-way or student-involved conferences, versions and variations of this form of reporting have successfully been implemented in classrooms from kindergarten to seventh grade, earning overwhelming support and endorsement from those teachers, students, *and* parents who have experienced them (Anthony et al., 1991; Macdonald, 1989). Parental attendance rates consistently reach 100%. Success and effectiveness can be attributed to many factors. In the first place, the conferences are usually longer than the often hectic 15 or 20 minutes traditionally allotted. Because students share the task and the teacher isn't the sole "reporter," several conferences can occur simultaneously, which means more time for everyone. And this means that family members have time to properly examine the work samples presented and ask specific questions about them—questions they might feel self-conscious or hesitant about raising with the teacher. Because parents are invited as an audience for their children, rather than to talk to the teacher, there is possibly more incentive to attend: They may not want to let their children down. Parents whose first language is not that of the school, or parents for whom a meeting with the teacher might be intimidating, seem more comfortable coming to conferences at which their children are present and can act as interpreters or even buffers. Whatever the reason, these conferences manage to bring into the school parents who have never previously crossed its threshold.

Feedback from parents makes clear that the overwhelming majority find that student-led conferences provide them with informative, engaging, and convincing demonstrations and accountings of their children's performance at school and an in-depth supplement to the teacher's report card. Comments such as the following, written by parents following their conferences, are quite representative of the many hundreds I have now read:

- A well-organized presentation with a terrific format. It provided insight into the everyday occurrences in the classroom. Thanks for the opportunity to view her work firsthand.

- I am impressed with how well prepared Kenny was. I feel it helped him look more closely at his own evaluation, which would not happen in a teacher-parent conference.

- Assuming that Roslyn had worked closely with the teacher(s) to include not only her best work but something representative of all her efforts, then I feel great about the conference. I think it to be wonderful that the kids are given greater responsibility. I also feel that the process may increase personal accountability.

- Alex has shown steady improvement in her work. It has shown areas that require more work at home. I think these conferences are a good idea, and I am going to make a special effort to look at her work more often. Thank you.

Many parents express their gratitude to the teacher for making such a conference possible; others are blunt in their assessment of how much more this style of conference offers them compared with the traditional model. As one parent put it, "I had more time to look over the papers instead of having them flashed before my face and rushed out the door so the next parent could come in." These conferences are able to provide the occasion and opportunity for significant, focused talk about school and a chance to peruse the products of what is being done and what is being learned, firsthand, with their children as guides and interpreters. Obviously, the quality of what students are able to point out to parents depends to a considerable degree on the opportunities provided for them by their teacher to be informed about relevant criteria and standards and to apply that knowledge to their own work.

The attendance rates speak volumes: When the process is inclusionary and the content genuinely informative and personally significant, parents *do* show up and take part. In our search for better ways of talking with each other, student-led conferences offer a powerful model that ranks with the best of these better ways. To date, implementation of and experimentation with these conferences appear confined to the elementary schools. *Direct* application of this model to the secondary school context may not be possible because of different structures and schedules. The lesson learned, however—*that when support and guidelines are provided, students can inform their parents about their progress in school in ways that bring credit to themselves, to their teachers, and to their schools*—is one that does have implications and promise for secondary schools.

Ways and means exist: All sorts of strategies are available to help us initiate, maintain, and *reframe* home-school communications—everything from the tried-and-true, tested-and-trusted, through the neglected-and-rusted, to the novel-

and-new! Those described in this chapter are just a few of many, many possible options (Preece & Cowden, 1993; Swap, 1993). Others that have proved their worth include class and school newsletters that differ from those typically sent out in that they contain student contributions and provide some samples of, and details and discussion about, the work and learning going on in classrooms. On analyzing a large selection of school newsletters, I found many contained little other than greetings and announcements of upcoming sports events, field trips, and fund-raisers—once again, such newsletters are opportunities lost. More to the point, they can contribute to a skewed impression of what schools are about. What we neglect to mention can be as revealing as what we do.

Many schools are successfully experimenting with "Homework Hotlines" and voice mail messages (J. B. Artis, personal communication, February 26, 1996; Bauch, 1990). Teachers regularly record their homework assignments, information about upcoming and/or continuing projects and units, and even helpful suggestions; the information is then available to anyone who dials the school number and punches in the teacher's code. Sometimes on-line help with homework is also available, with teachers taking turns by means of pagers (school supplied) to respond to the requests received. Because homework is an area notorious for spawning frustration and even friction, these lines can offer welcome support and sorely needed information when it is needed most. Message lines have obvious advantages with respect to making contact easy for any parent who has access to a phone—and evidence indicates they're particularly effective for reaching, and reaching out to, seldom-involved families. The obvious advantage for teachers is the comparatively low level of effort and energy required. Although all teachers can appreciate the ease with which one message can be made available to many parents, this feature is especially welcomed by teachers at the junior and senior high levels, who routinely teach well over a hundred students a term and for whom home-school communication can pose daunting logistical challenges. Bauch (1990) reports that the lines are used: "One middle school received as many as 1,800 calls from parents in one week. Schools currently under study are reporting that from one-third to more than one-half of all parents call the school every day to listen to teacher messages" (p. 26). Even those who have not needed to use them report appreciating their existence—in case they do. Benefits include greater parental involvement with homework, but also—and important—parents who make regular use of these lines are found to "feel better about the school" (p. 27).

Inviting parents to attend teachers' professional development sessions is an excellent way to inform them about new practices being advocated, questions being raised about present methods, and the issues that teachers grapple with daily. Space constraints usually make it impractical to issue an open invitation to all parents; reserving a few seats at each session for parents who are specifically invited, however, can generally be easily managed. Invitations should be circulated so it's not always the same few parents who attend. Special evening sessions can be scheduled specifically for parents and for strategically chosen community members. These are important gestures to make: Invitations are almost always appreciated, and guests report gaining a whole new perspective on the topics raised *and* on the value of professional development days, which all too often are cynically regarded by parents as an excuse for a day off. If appropriate, parent participants can be invited to write (but *not* pressured or "expected" to do so) a short description of the session attended for the school newsletter so that other parents may learn of it.

As much as we need to inform parents, we need also to hear from them. Again, some of the simplest methods are the most effective. Suggestion/question boxes can be prominently displayed at parent meetings, open houses, and in school hallways inviting parent input. Tear-off-and-send-back sheets that seek feedback, opinions, and reactions from parents about particular issues and that invite inquiries, questions, and concerns can be attached to newsletters. Responses to questions received can be handled by phone, or they can be written out and printed in the next edition of the school newsletter (anonymity guaranteed where appropriate). However it's done, it's crucial that parents know their feedback has been received and "heard." Even a once-a-term (or year!) phone call asking parents whether they're receiving the information and interaction they need or would like can send a strong signal that parents matter and are taken seriously. The methods are there; what we need to work on is getting into the habit of using more of them more frequently, more systematically, and more strategically.

Easily said. Teachers already have more than enough to do. If schools take seriously the goal of better informing parents, then they need to take seriously helping it happen. Although I am a convinced believer in the power of a single, dedicated teacher to accomplish minor miracles, I also know it's not fair to expect individual teachers to carry the communication burden alone. Systemwide goals warrant systemwide initiatives and tangible support. Without such support, called-for changes will occur only in patches and pockets, and, for most, goals will be little more than empty slogans. Allocating time is one important way of providing that support. Following their cross-cultural comparison of teaching, Stevenson and Stigler (1992) conclude that to make the changes they feel are needed in American schools, "the first thing we would recommend is to decrease the teaching load of American elementary school teachers" (p. 207) to allow more time for planning, preparation, and working with colleagues. Hoover-Dempsey et al. (1995) reach a similar conclusion:

> Thus, the importance of allocating school and teaching time (even if it has to be taken from direct instructional time for students) to parent contact and interaction seems fundamental. Similarly, ready access to communication with parents—for example, through telephones in classrooms, recognized times (during the day or evening) for regular parent-teacher contact—also seems essential. (p. 446)

Even a little school time to plan, consult, and do makes all the difference. Administrative initiative and commitment are essential here.

When administrative support and leadership are present, results can be impressive. Intent on tapping community input and building ownership for school directions, John Artis, Director of Curriculum and Assessment for Dupage High School District in Villa Park, Illinois, invited a large contingent of parents (more than 200) from his district to an "Outcomes Weekend." With the help of an outside consultant, the group examined community conditions and needs; the skills and competencies that employers, business leaders, and futurists were identifying as necessary for success; and current graduation expectations. Following a lively discussion, all helped develop a vision and mission statement for their high schools, along with desired exit outcomes. Many parents made a point of expressing their appreciation at being invited to participate. As a result of this consultation, Dr. Artis reports that his district is presently engaged in extensively altering graduation requirements and in defining key performances that will evaluate the skills the group agreed were desired and important. Plans are in place to present a draft version of these performance outcomes at public hearings to which parents from the feeder schools as well as the high schools will be invited to respond. The process is sound, respectful, accessible, inclusive, and continuing. Through it, parents are informed, involved, and encouraged to work *with* teachers to create schools relevant and responsive to community needs and aspirations.

Teacher education faculties also have a crucial role to play in bridging the gap between home and school. It's not good enough that we simply inform student teachers that communicating with parents will be one of their responsibilities. Rather, beginning teachers need exposure to and actual experience with some of the strategies outlined so far. Much more could be built into their preparation programs on this topic than is typically present (Brand, 1996). For the past several years, in an attempt to partly address the omission in my own courses, I've devised a series of role-playing scenarios designed to help my students "experience" and confront some of the dilemmas and assumptions that can constrain home-school communication. Responses have been positive and confirm the need both novice and experienced teachers feel for tools and support in this area. I now set assignments that require students to develop and fully prepare presentations and/or materials for parents about issues that are current and currently contentious. The results have been extraordinary. As well as creating high-quality "products" of activities and participatory demonstrations for meetings and devising innovative ways of sharing student efforts, these young teachers have made no bones about the fact that these assignments have increased their confidence about undertaking such overtures and their readiness to do so. Some have proudly taken their "parent packages" along to job interviews. Knowing we should do something is a start; knowing how to do it goes a long way to helping it happen; experiencing the benefits almost guarantees sustained efforts. Those of us privileged to work with beginning teachers need to make sure they leave our faculties equipped with a rich repertoire of ideas and practical strategies for reaching out to the parents and communities they will serve. We haven't done this as well as we need to.

Struttin' Our Stuff!:
A Little Community Advocacy Never Hurts

Efforts to inform and educate "the community" about our schools must start with ourselves, include our students, and then reach out in a whole variety of ways to let parents in on the *what*s and *why*s of what we're doing. More is needed, however. The "public," the community-at-large, also needs to be kept informed, because it is the public who pays the bills and the public whose perceptions, misperceptions, and opinions about schools can be manipulated to thwart or short-circuit even the best efforts at reform and renewal (Barlow & Robertson, 1994). Again, systemwide support and systematic efforts are essentials.

There's no shortage of good ideas available. For instance, some school districts are buying time on public service and local television channels to highlight the programs and innovations in their schools. The "Washington State Golden Apple Awards," sponsored and televised annually by PBS Seattle, recognize exemplary teachers and innovative school programs. Film footage of teachers, students, and parent volunteers "in action" make these programs inspiring to watch; they also show people who otherwise wouldn't know about them some of the good things that are happening in our schools. My local community newspaper features a regular column that highlights the happenings, events, contributions, and achievements of our local high school; what distinguishes this lively and engaging column is that it is written by students enrolled in a journalism course at the school. Taking a practical stand against undeserved negative press, one Canadian school district offered any teacher willing to write a letter or article in response to newspaper columns or letters to the editor that were critical or negative or misinformed about schools a half day of paid leave to do so. Many private schools routinely take out large newspaper advertisements to profile the achievements of their teachers and students; we in public education should follow their lead. Other schools advertise the dates and times of their science showcases, art and writing fairs, and young authors' workshops so that interested members of the public can attend. Some schools set up displays of their students' work in local shopping malls and public buildings so that passersby can see for themselves the quality of the students' accomplishments. The list could go on and on—the point is that we need to make sure these things happen; the public won't know what the schools are achieving and striving to achieve unless we tell them and show them. And what they don't know can hurt us.

Ours are contentious, divisive times. Simplistic solutions for complex societal problems are sought and offered, and schools are easy targets. I'm one of the first to proclaim that our schools aren't as good as they could be or as they need to be—but I'm also acutely aware of how much better they are than they used to be and how hard good teachers are working to make them better yet. Opening the lines of communication is only a part of what needs to happen if the reforms and changes that are envisioned and mandated are to become across-the-system realities—but it's a fundamental and foundational part, and it's one to which we can contribute and make a difference. Without communication, the changes we want won't happen. Schools aren't what they used to be and aren't what they're going to be—and we need to get that word out!

References

Anthony, R., Johnson, T., Mickelson, N., & Preece, A. (1991). *Evaluating literacy: A perspective for change*. Portsmouth, NH: Heinemann.

Bauch, J. P. (1990, Spring). Touch 1 for improved parent-teacher contact. *School Safety*, 25-27.

Barlow, M., & Robertson, H. J. (1994). *Class warfare: The assault on Canada's schools*. Toronto, Ontario, Canada: Key Porter.

Brand, S. (1996). Making parent involvement a reality: Helping teachers develop partnerships with parents. *Young Children, 51*(2), 76-81.

Chrispeels, J. (1991). District leadership in parent involvement: Policies and actions in San Diego. *Phi Delta Kappan, 72*(5), 367-371.

Davies, A., Cameron, C., Politano, C., & Gregory, K. (1992). *Together is better*. Winnipeg, Manitoba, Canada: Peguis.

Epstein, J. (1986). Parents' reactions to teacher practices of parent involvement. *Elementary School Journal, 86*(3), 277-294.

Epstein, J. (1990). School and family connections: Theory, research, and implications for integrating sociologies of education and family. In D. Unger & M. Sussman (Eds.), *Families in community settings: Interdisciplinary perspectives*. New York: Haworth.

Epstein, J. (1995). School/family/community partnerships: Caring for the children we share. *Phi Delta Kappan, 76*(9), 701-712.

Farough, D. R. (1995). *The decline of family participation in the intermediate years*. Unpublished master's project, University of Victoria, Victoria, British Columbia, Canada.

Fiske, E. B. (1991). *Smart schools, smart kids: Why do some schools work?* New York: Simon & Schuster.

Fullan, M. G. (with Stiegelbauer, S.). (1991). *The new meaning of educational change*. New York: Teachers College Press.

Goodlad, J. (1986). *A place called school*. New York: McGraw-Hill.

Graham, P. A. (1992). *S.O.S.: Sustain our schools*. New York: Hill & Wang.

Hoover-Dempsey, K. V., Bassler, O. C., & Burrow, R. (1995). Parents' reported involvement in students' homework: Strategies and practices. *Elementary School Journal, 95*(5), 435-450.

Johnston, P. H. (1992). *Constructive evaluation of literate activity*. New York: Longman.

Katz, L. (1993). What can we learn from Reggio Emilia? In C. Edwards, L. Gandini, & G. Foreman (Eds.), *The hundred languages of children*. Norwood, NJ: Ablex.

Kenney, E., & Perry, S. (1994). Talking with parents about performance-based report cards. *Educational Leadership, 52*(2), 24-27.

Little, N., & Allan, J. (1988). *Student-led teacher parent conferences*. Toronto, Ontario, Canada: Lugus.

Macdonald, C. (1989). Reporting to parents: Involving primary children in the process. *Prime Areas, 32*(1), 15-17.

McCarthy, J. (1995). Reggio Emilia: What is the message for early childhood education? *Contemporary Education, 66*(3), 139-142.

Preece, A., & Cowden, D. (1993). *Young writers in the making: Sharing the process with parents*. Portsmouth, NH: Heinemann.

Raths, J., Wojtaszek-Healy, M., & Kubo Della-Piana, C. (1987). Grading problems: A matter of communication. *Journal of Educational Research 80*(3), 133-137.

Sarason, S. (1971). *The culture of the school and the problem of change*. Boston: Allyn & Bacon.

Sperling, D. (1993, February). What's worth an "A"? Setting standards together. *Educational Leadership, 50*.

Stevenson, H. W., & Stigler, J. W. (1992). *The learning gap*. New York: Summit.

Swap, S. W. (1993). *Developing home-school partnerships: From concept to practice*. New York: Teachers College Press.

3

Organizational Learning

The Essential Journey

Laura Lipton
Robert Melamede

Just because we cannot see clearly the end of the road, that is no reason for not setting out on the essential journey. On the contrary, great change dominates the world, and unless we move with change we will become its victims.

John F. Kennedy

Introduction

It is 1960. My younger sister and I squirm and squabble in the back seat of our parents' Chevy Impala as we suffer through the seemingly endless trip to my grandparents' house. Whining queries regarding arrival time are met with my father's sage response, "Enjoy the trip. Get involved with what's passing you by. There's a whole world you're missing!" He called our attention to road signs that marked our progress, to changes in the landscape on our journey from city to country, and to recognizable landmarks, comforting in their familiarity.

Now, almost 40 years later, I share this memory with my coauthor. His work is in molecular immunology, which he views from nonequilibrium thermodynamic principles. My work is with innovative organizations engaged in efforts to be responsive to changing needs and changing times. As we consider my father's advice, we believe it offers an analogy for members of these organizations as they travel together on their essential journey—that it is the journey, not the destination, that offers the potential for growth. Unlike a car trip, however, organizational change is continual and evolving. The journey of organizational change has no final destination; it is the process of becoming that is the ultimate purpose. For schools in a postmodern world, this essential journey, the journey of transformation, is one that mandates our best attention.

Twenty-first-century technologies have created a world of unprecedented economic and social change. Science itself is in transition. Historically, science had taken a classical, or Newtonian, perspective, supporting a view of the universe as linear, mechanistic, and predictable. During the latter part of the 20th century, however, a shift in thinking emerged that views the universe as dynamical, nonlinear, and evolving. Unexpected, and parallel, developments in the theories of classical mechanics and thermodynamics have converged to narrow the gap between "hard" and "soft" sciences and to blur the distinction between simple systems, such as those studied by physics and chemistry, and complex systems, such as those studied in biology and human sciences. Precisely because this gap is narrowing, we may now consider applying new knowledge to situations for which the concepts of classical physics were not only inappropriate but essentially meaningless (Nicolis & Prigogine, 1989).

In this chapter, we offer a perspective on organizations as social systems that are governed by the same principles, specifically those of nonequilibrium physics and evolutionary biology, as physical or natural systems. Just as the 20th century has seen such significant changes in scientific thought, we believe that our schools also must shift from a stable, static view of learning to one that embraces the new concepts in science. Applying this new knowledge has the capacity to catapult our journey into the future.

As we explore preparations for the journey, issues are raised regarding organizations as dynamical, nonlinear systems and the need for responsiveness, adaptability, and comfort with ambiguity to value change—not fear it. We describe learning organizations as self-organizing, collaborative, adaptive, and reflective and offer a process orientation for cultivating these qualities. We suggest methods for identifying landmarks of community and developing cultural guideposts that reduce anxiety and increase latent potentiality as organizations explore the territory of learning.

To apply physical laws to human experiences, the language used to characterize the fundamental concepts must be translated. We intend this chapter to aid in the translation from science to education and to be a catalyst toward organizational learning. As we consider what defines a learning organization, it seems fitting to concern ourselves with how systems learn.

From Being to Becoming

Classically, *learning* is defined as the process by which knowledge is acquired. Knowledge, in turn, is acquired information. Information, at its most fundamental level, is the presence or absence of "something," for example, a plus or minus charge of electricity. The concept of a *bit* in modern computer chips is the presence or absence of an electronic charge taken to represent the zeros and ones of binary language. From this perspective, a system learns simply by acquiring and storing information. This classical view of learning is the essence of the Newtonian model. But in dynamical systems, learning is much more akin to what we might think of as creativity.

The flow of information is, in fact, the essence of modern thermodynamics. Thermodynamically, information is defined as negative entropy, when entropy equals disorder or randomness (Brillouin, 1962). Hence, information is order derived from an incredibly wide range of possibilities and may be described probabilistically. For example, the letters and spaces in this chapter constitute bits of information. If all these letters and spaces were cut up into their individual pieces of paper and thrown from a dice tumbler, the likelihood of their appearing as this chapter is incredibly low. And yet this chapter is before you! When viewed in this manner, it seems that language and any specific application of it appear to be highly improbable.

The complexity of this notion increases when we consider that information is significant only as a function of its context. Meaning is derived contextually and has a reciprocal relationship with the embedded meaning systems within its environment—in this case, the chapter, the current English language system, and the perspectives and understandings of the reader. Thus, learning is a function of the relationship between the learner, the information, and the environment within which it is embedded.

In his book on advanced theoretical physics, *From Being to Becoming*, chemist and Nobel laureate Ilya Prigogine (1980) provides a way of looking at the universe that accounts for seemingly improbable events. On the basis of his studies of far-from-equilibrium systems, he offers a revolutionary view of the world and an intriguing framework regarding learning. According to Prigogine, creativity, or *becoming*, is shown to be an intrinsic manifestation of flowing energy, not simply a strange phenomenon possessed by a few fortunate individuals at rare moments of time. *Being*, in contrast, is a snapshot in time and space. A key premise of Prigogine's work is that although time brings decay and disintegration, it also has an optimistic form, evolution (Briggs & Peat, 1989). Further, Prigogine believes that the unfolding of the universe, although dependent on its past, is not completely predictable by knowing it. For Prigogine, like many systems theorists, chaos is the source of structure and life.

Contrasting views of the icon of 21st-century technology, the computer, offer an illuminating perspective. Although computers themselves are static structures, their evolution reflects the creative processes of humanity. For example, when the computer is programmed, it is limited to operations with a specific set of instructions. That is *being*. The human who develops the algorithms for programming the computer, through his or her creation, has increased the capacity and efficiency of information flow. That is *becoming*. In other words, the characteristics of the advances in computer technology reflect the driving force of the physics of life, whereas a computer itself does not.

Faster chips and wider buses (i.e., 8 to 16 to 32 to 64 bit) lead to greater bandwidths, enabling more information to be transferred per second. Computers have increased their functions from machines that do calculations to multimedia engines of sights and sound. The *being*, or functional capacity, grows larger, but the *becoming* that makes it happen lies in the ever increasing capacity of the programmers for learning and creating.

The perspective set forth in this chapter suggests that healthy systems must embrace learning, or becoming, as a fundamental operand for survival. We propose that this view of learning, as a creative and continual process, should be the essence of our educational system. It is this view of learning, or becoming, that we will refer to in this chapter. What, then, are the characteristics and principles of becoming? A simple example, the Bernard instability, can demonstrate its intrinsic creative power.

The Bénard Instability

Imagine an apparatus, such as a petri dish, that contains a liquid sealed between two glass plates to prevent evaporation. Heat is applied below the container such that the thermal energy will be conducted from the source of heat to the atmosphere above, the sink. (Note: In all open systems, there must be a source, a motivating force, and a capable destination, or sink.) Initially, the liquid flow is fairly smooth. As the heating continues, however, the system becomes increasingly turbulent, with whorls and eddies forming throughout. Suddenly, a pattern emerges. The liquid has spontaneously rearranged to form a regular pattern of hexagons! These hexagonal convection cells transfer the heat from the source to the sink much more rapidly than had the rearrangement not occurred (see Figure 3.1). In essence, a molecular "bucket brigade" has been spontaneously organized by the molecules in the system.

How do we explain this phenomenon? Conventional physics readily explains that molecules of the liquid closer to the heat source will rotate faster, vibrate more intensely, and translate energy into the heat sink above. This explanation, however, does not account for the system's capacity to establish structural conduits to maximize the flow of heat by extracting information from the local environment. In the case of the Bénard instability, when the system reaches a point at which heat dispersal requires large-scale convection currents, the system shifts out of its chaotic state and transforms itself into a lattice pattern. These hexagonal structures exist only while the energy is flowing. They are examples of self-organization out of disequilibrium known as *dissipative structures*. Immediately prior to their formation, at a critical point of energy transfer, the fluctuations of the physical parameters within the system grew exponentially. The system was "confused" until it figured out what to do, and then it took action. Literally, the molecules cooperated and the information content of the system increased. In essence, the system became "smarter."

This dynamic is the essence of becoming. In the Bénard instability, the flow of information is organized through interconnectedness to foster the efficiency of the system. One stream of current scientific thinking is that the spherical shell of the earth's atmosphere, and possibly the entire atmosphere, might be a sea

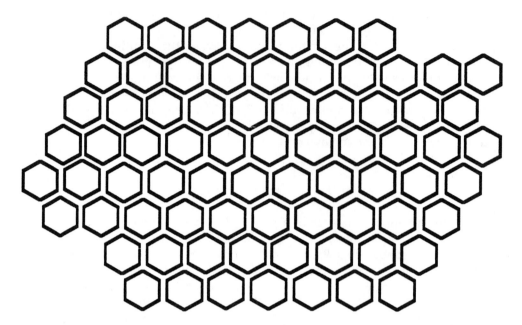

Figure 3.1. The Bénard Instability: Order Self-Organized Out of Disorder

of Bénard cells (Briggs & Peat, 1989). The Bénard instability, and the formation of Bénard cells, is one example that illustrates three critical characteristics of dynamical systems that we will explore in this chapter; self-organization, inter-connectedness, and adaptivity. When we combine these three characteristics with a fourth, reflection, we can make direct application to organizational learning.

Organizational Learning

For the past several years, there has been much writing and research regarding communities of learners (see, e.g., Barth, 1990; Sergiovanni, 1994) and learning organizations (Raitt, 1995; Senge, 1990a, 1990b). Among these authors, however, there is little consensus regarding a definition of organizational learning. A definition that will be useful to our discussion is offered by Huber (1991), who suggests that "an entity learns if, through its processing of information, the range of its potential behaviors is changed" (p. 89). For our purposes, we suggest that the range of potential behaviors is *increased*. Such learning is considered organizational when it incorporates the "combined experiences, perspectives, and capabilities of a variety of organization members" (Raitt, 1995, p. 72).

In the classical, Newtonian sense, the conventional idea of learning is transactional. That is, knowledge can be acquired, refined, exchanged, and modified to fit particular needs or goals. In dynamical systems, learning can be transformational. The elements or components of the system are a part of the information that forms it. As it learns, the system transforms itself into structures that make more efficient use of the available resources, or information, in the immediate environment. As the Bénard instability illustrates, a change in form does not signal the demise of the system; rather, it is an example of a system's responsiveness to the changing nature, or fluctuations, in the information flow. In this case, the simple system being observed self-organized into dissipative structures, more complex configurations structured to meet the changing demands of its local environment.

Dissipative structures are systems capable of maintaining their identity *only* by remaining continually open to the flux and flow of their environment. This concept applied to organizations suggests that learning can occur only if the system is in a state of readiness to learn. Thus, for an organization to be a learning system, its members must recognize that the health and growth of the system require the capacity to be responsive to changing conditions, collaborative in organizing for efficient use of resources, and adaptive by establishing structures that are flexible yet stable. As we shall explore in this chapter, learning in an organization requires a shift from a "fix-it" mentality to the acknowledgment that the only certainty is uncertainty. The willingness to engage in systematic and reflective experimentation is a fundamental requirement for learning.

Self-Organizing Processes: Working Smarter Together

Of all the possible pathways of disorder, nature favors just a few.

James Gleick

The continual move away from equilibrium is a prerequisite for growth in dynamical systems. In other words, to be in a growth state, a system must be in disequilibrium (Prigogine, 1980; Wheatley, 1992). As the phenomenon of the Bénard instability illustrates, when a system in a far-from-equilibrium state gets to a critical point of fluctuation, it will self-organize for the most efficient way of using the information, or energy, in its environment. To increase its capacity to grow, a system has to increase the amount, quality, and type of information it processes.

Requiring a shift in our own thinking as members of organizations, and indeed, of societies, is the notion that disorder can be a source of order. In far-from-equilibrium states, the system does not break down; new systems emerge. Human systems, or organizations, are arranged into structures designed to organize and manage the flow of events, resources, and information. Schools, for example, are organized for teaching and learning. In the main, school districts are structured hierarchically: a district leader in a central office and several school sites of varying grade levels, with one or more administrators, a teaching and support staff, and a student body at each site. Each site is structured around individual classrooms, organized by grade level and/or content area, and so on. Traditionally, most schools are based on the passive, incremental dispersion of knowledge, constrained by perceptions of community expectations, national and state norms, and the diverse needs of both students and teachers. There is a prevalence of isolation and fragmentation operating through fixed roles, rigid rules, and limited resources. As presently conceived, these organizations are "learning disabled" (Marshall, 1995; Senge, 1990a, 1990b).

In contrast, for schools to function as complex, dynamical systems capable of continual learning and growth, they must operate with different premises and structure themselves accordingly. The understanding of the interconnectedness of all aspects of a system would inform decision making. Schools would function to increase the capacity of each member and, thereby, of the system itself. Thus, they could organize and reorganize as needed to creatively interface with the environment and its changing needs and conditions.

Self-organization in human systems is most likely to occur when the group members' idea of what *might be* is more compelling than what *is*. The energy for a phase shift is fueled by the creative tension caused when the collective vision is juxtaposed with the current reality. "Individuals, groups and organizations who learn how to work with [their] creative tension learn how to use the energy it generates to move reality more reliably towards their visions" (Senge, 1990b, p. 9). To do so, however, requires a clear, shared vision, as well as an accurate picture of current conditions. Grassroots movements, local cooperatives, ad hoc committees, and worldwide networks are all examples of self-organizing structures.

Schools that have the capacity to self-organize are hinged on shared leadership. Thinking, planning, and decision making are integrated into all levels of the system. The members of the organization are simultaneously leaders and supporters, sharing roles and responsibilities in a flexible and appropriate manner. Decisions are shared, and so is the responsibility for those decisions as individual members' involvement in the organization shifts from compliance to commitment.

In these schools, the learning space would be shaped for sharing—configured to facilitate conversion for multiple purposes and used to promote connections between members of the school. (See Saban's Chapter 11 in this volume.) Multigrade and intergrade configurations would maximize learning opportunities for everyone in the organization. Cross-function teams, composed of members from various departments, would engage in collaborative learning, problem solving, and envisioning potential futures. Open forums and cross-age collaborations would foster communication, reinforcing the notion that each member of the organization, at all levels, is an integral part and has a unique contribution to the whole.

These schools would be centers of inquiry, in which every member is a learner. The underlying philosophy directing curriculum, instruction, and assessment decisions would be learner and learning centered. Cooperatively structured interactions, authentic learning tasks, and performance-based instruction and assessment would promote learning for all members of the organization—in classroom settings, faculty meetings, community forums, supervisory conferences, and so on. Sensitivity to the internal and external conditions of the system would foster flexible scheduling and role orientations, close and continual involvement with the community, and a team-based approach to data-driven decision making based on cycles of inquiry, experimentation, and reflection.

Strange Attractors and Self-Organization

"In the world of self-organizing structures, . . . useful boundaries develop through openness to the environment" (Wheatley, 1992, p. 92). Dynamical systems maintain themselves within identifiable boundaries; for example, a weather system is contained within its unique conditions (i.e., wind speed, precipitation, etc.). In many instances, these systems are organized around a core, which in quantum physics is called a *strange attractor*. A strange attractor is an entity that attracts turbulence and chaos. Patterns form around this core, or center, defining the boundaries of the system. Thus, although on a micro, or close-up, level, the pattern is not discernible, from enough of a distance, theoretically, one can view the system, its reiterating patterns, and its boundaries. These systems are guided by a set of simple rules that define the system. In a social system, such as a school, a set of common values and shared meaning can provide a cohesive core, or strange attractor, to hold the system within appropriate boundaries while allowing flexibility and dynamic interchange.

In an expansive study of urban high schools conducted during the 1980s, Louis and Miles (1990) discovered that in their more successful schools, "multiple improvement efforts coalesced around a theme or set of themes only after the activity had begun" (p. 206). They found that small centers of activity increased inclusion, motivation, and "the possibility of concerted, more 'tightly coupled' action across the school [while allowing] schools to take advantage of unanticipated opportunities" (pp. 210-211). The successful implementation of the educational innovations evolved as members of the organization, ready and responsive, took actions to support success.

"It seems that with a few simple guidelines, left to develop and change randomly, nature creates the complexity and harmony of form we see everywhere" (Wheatley, 1992, p. 131). In learning organizations, actions, initiatives, and structures self-organize when members of the system have the freedom to be responsive to emerging needs and conditions, as well as a shared understanding of the principles that bound the system. These principles, or strange attractors, can be a set of simple guidelines, such as (a) seek first to understand, (b) seek to be understood, and (c) build toward the common good (Covey, 1989) or (a) know your own values, (b) know our shared values, and (c) act in accordance with our shared vision (R. Garmston & B. Wellman, personal communication, 1993).

"Self-organizing systems demonstrate new relationships between autonomy and control, showing how a large system is able to maintain its overall form and identity only because it tolerates great degrees of individual freedom" (Wheatley, 1992, p. 94). Evoking the differing viewpoints of a diverse organizational community is requisite to its development. It is vital that members of our school systems recognize the importance of each piece to the health of the whole, celebrating diversity and fostering unity.

Collaborative Processes: Unity Through Diversity

Not chaos-like, together crushed and bruised,
But, as the world harmoniously confused:
Where order in variety we see,
And where, though all things differ, all agree.

Alexander Pope

The notion of interconnectedness—that matter is not composed of isolated building blocks but is a complex web of relationships among the various parts of a unified whole—is among the most revolutionary discoveries of modern physics. "Dynamical systems imply a holism in which everything influences everything else—because everything is in some sense constantly interacting with everything else" (Briggs, 1992, p. 17). Thus, although the system's interconnectedness is responsible for its unpredictability, it is also responsible for its resiliency and growth.

This fundamental understanding has great impact for the ways in which schools are organized. It is the vital point that underlies this volume: Process is inseparable from content. We cannot segment organizational functions into isolated compartments. Rather, we must view the various aspects of the organization as a whole, compartmentalizing only to maximize efficiency with the understanding that the compartments are highly interconnected and potentially temporary. For example, the budgetary decisions are not isolated from the instructional choices; the personnel decisions are not isolated from the public relations functions; the transportation system is not isolated from the curriculum department. Each of these areas is connected to the others in myriad and unpredictable ways. Each has a potential impact on the others. Each must embrace a process orientation.

To organize for interdependency and interconnectedness, we suggest three aspects to the collaborative process: developing a common purpose, capacitating dialogue, and building community. It is important to note that these aspects are reciprocal, not sequential. Each resonates with the other to form a powerful triumvirate approach to unity.

Developing a Common Purpose

In the simple system of the Bénard instability, the molecules, "working together," formed a dissipative structure that enhanced the system's capacity for directed energy flow. Complex social systems operate on similar principles. Organizational capacity is enhanced when the diverse elements of the system come together to work toward a common purpose. Current writing in organizational development offers a variety of labels for this concept, such as developing a shared vision, core values, shared meaning, and valued outcomes (Saphier & King, 1985; Schein, 1994; Senge, 1990a, 1990b). According to Schein, values are an expression of fundamental beliefs. Values describe an individual's or an organization's sense of "what ought to be, as distinct from what is" (p. 15). For example, one key premise of this chapter is that the common purpose of schools should be intimately linked to, and reflective of, our growing knowledge of dynamical systems.

In his work on worldwide networking, Weisbord (1992) offers this description of collaborating toward a common purpose on the basis of the value of mutual respect:

> Indeed, we neither avoid nor confront the extremes. Rather, we put our energy into staking out the widest common ground all can stand on without forcing or compromising. Then, from that solid base, we spontaneously invent new forms of action, using processes devised for that purpose. . . . In short, we seek to hear and appreciate differences, not reconcile them. We seek to validate polarities, not reduce the distance between them. We learn, innovate and act from a mutual base of discovered ideals, world views, and future goals. Above all, we stick to business. We make the conference's central task our guiding star. (p. 7)

As described earlier, dynamical systems are composed of chaotic patterns that fluctuate around a central core, or strange attractor, and seem to be organized around a few simple, yet powerful, principles. The parallel for schools is a system organized around a set of core values and guided by a shared vision to which all members are committed. The learning community is bounded by commonality of purpose, shared values, and clearly articulated outcomes. Together, these factors free each member of the organization to create flexible pathways while traveling in a common direction toward agreed-on goals.

The heart of the learning organization beats to the rhythm of its shared vision. Its spirit is sustained by the values that govern its actions. Kim & Mullen (1995) suggest that an organization may want to create a formal declaration of values to liberate the creative spirit necessary for thriving collectively. The following selection of possibilities is adapted from a list they offer as a potential starting point:

As a learning organization,

- we believe that all persons deserve equal respect as human beings, regardless of their role or position in the organization,
- we believe people's potential should be limited only by the extent of their aspirations, not by the artificial barriers of organizational structures nor by the perceptions and judgments of others,
- we value all persons' views as valid and important and honor the life experiences that have shaped them, and
- we operate on the basis of openness and trust, nurturing honest communication and an environment that seeks to explore the multiple truths or meanings that we bring to the community.

For Kim and Mullen (1995), a commitment to the truth might be a strange attractor around which the system organizes its energies:

> When we clearly express our own truth and also our shared truth—our values—we contribute to the constantly-generating field of energy we inhabit. . . . The energy we release with this kind of freedom is infectious.

... When we do not have to censor what we really think and care about, we have more energy to devote to creating something that really matters to us. (p. 107)

The process of collaboration begins when members of an organization gather together with a common purpose and engage with each other in exploring individual truths. The effort to come to some collective, shared truth, respectfully and openly, is a potent endeavor for learning systems. These opportunities for learning are based on capacitating dialogue.

Capacitating Dialogue

Language can be a tool for connecting, creating, and coordinating. "The way people talk together in organizations is rapidly becoming acknowledged as central to the creation and management of knowledge" (Isaacs, 1994, p. 83). For learning organizations, the use of language to explore and develop shared meaning is crucial. This mutual engagement requires opportunities for mixed constituencies; vertical school teams, groups of community members and educational professionals, diverse role teams, students, and teachers, and so on to join together to grapple with key issues, surface individual perceptions and assumptions, and create a shared reality. (See Baker, Costa, & Shalit, Chapter 8, in this volume.)

A learning field is created when people come together, sharing from their hearts and minds with honesty. This is the spirit of dialogue. *Dialogue*, its etymology rooted in the Greek *dia* and *logos,* suggests "meaning flowing through." It is a marked contrast to traditionally mechanistic, fragmented notions of discussion or debate. Dialogue is "sustained collective inquiry into the processes, assumptions, and certainties that structure everyday experience" (Isaacs, 1994, p. 85). When people engage with each other at the level of genuine dialogue, they are deeply connected. They are organized to talk and listen to each other, suspending judgment and seeking common understandings. They are operating together, following shared guidelines, to generate shared meanings. In this way, a powerful field of alignment is created that in itself produces tremendous energy. The potential for inventing and creating new realities is generated through dialogue. "The difference lies in whether we see language as a set of labels that describe a pre-existing reality, or as a medium in which we can articulate new models for living together" (Kofman & Senge, 1994, p. 18).

Fundamental to dialogue is the premise that increasingly conscious environments that promote shifts in shared attention can increase the quality and level of collective inquiry. Physicist David Bohm (1990) likens dialogue to superconductivity. In superconductivity, the very low temperatures of electrons cause them to function more like a coherent whole than individual parts. With little or no resistance, and very high energy, they flow around without collision. These same electrons, at higher temperatures, scatter into random movement, losing momentum and behaving more like separate parts. Similar to superconductivity, dialogue is intended to create "cool" conditions that support high energy and low friction, while allowing for individual difference. Traditional negotiation strategies are also designed to cool down interactions.

However, because conflicting issues are often bypassed or downplayed, rather than confronted, the field may be narrowed. Cool conditions prevail but at the cost of energy and intelligence. "In dialogue, the aim is to create a special environment in which a different kind of relationship among the parts can come into play—one that reveals high energy and high intelligence" (Isaacs, 1994, p. 86). Ultimately, if we follow this analogy, our increasing collective intelligence will allow us to consider potentially volatile, emotionally packed issues without friction.

Establishing forums of this nature in an organizational setting is both a challenge and a paradox. Although people generally come to dialogue with the intention of viewing their problems from new perspectives and with new understandings, dialogue is best served by deliberately not trying to solve problems in any familiar way. Dialogue is designed to explore the potentially unexamined assumptions that inform our thinking, break traditional habits of discourse, share multiple perspectives, and surface any "underlying incoherence of thought and action" (Isaacs, 1994, p. 93) that gives rise to organizational problems. Dialogue provides a balance for structured problem-solving approaches. Through dialogue, an arena is established in which subtle influences on our thinking can be surfaced and altered, thereby opening the field for new and diverse types of collective learning to occur.

The capacity for dialogue develops as group members come together to practice it. On the basis of the work of Bohm and others, William Isaacs (1994), director of the Dialogue Project at Massachusetts Institute of Technology, has identified four evolving stages to dialogue:

1. *Initial conversation/deliberation:* During this phase, members are consciously and unconsciously examining different views—liking some, disagreeing with others.
2. *Suspension, not suppression, of personal views:* During this phase, participants must listen without judgment—beginning to let go of their certainty about others' views, as well as their own.
3. *Collective inquiry:* During this phase, the group is focused on promoting the recognition of inhibiting patterns and the generation of insights.
4. *Metalogue:* "Metalogue" means moving or flowing with one another. The dynamic level of metalogue in many ways captures the essence of this chapter and, perhaps, this volume.

As Isaacs (1994) describes it, metalogue

> reveals a conscious, intimate, and subtle relationship between the structure and content of an exchange and its meaning. . . . Information from the process conveys as much meaning as the content of the words exchanged. The group does not "have" meaning, it is its meaning. Loosening rigid patterns of thoughts frees energy that now permits new levels of intelligence and creativity. (p. 93)

Forums for dialogue are vital to the third function of the collaborative processes: building community. "What nurtures the unfolding community most is serious, active experimentation where people wrestle with crucial strategic and operational issues" (Kofman & Senge, 1994, p. 23). Forums for dialogue offer a field of interaction in which these experiments can be designed and explored.

Building Community

In any community, each member of the organization offers unique attributes, singular contributions, and individual perspectives. Organizational members are each a composite of the ideas, assumptions, experiences, and worldviews that form their very identity. These perspectives, or mental models (Senge, 1990a, 1990b), cannot be shed at will. They constitute the individual. Growth and positive change occur first on an individual level.

Therefore, to engage in community building, each member of the organization must be willing to suspend their preconceptions and to be ready to flow with the possibilities that might emerge through connection building. Nevertheless,

> there is no firm set of formal rules that can tell us when to hold on and when to let go. We learn through experience and reflection and through the experience of others. It is a form of tacit knowing, something that itself emerges through our inner freedom and our creative dialogue with others. (Zohar & Marshall, 1994, p. 136)

Community will emerge only when the attitude of the individual members allows for it.

To enable the probability for community, "static notions of who we are must be checked at the door" (Kofman & Senge, 1994, p. 21). Metaphorically, Zohar and Marshall (1994) suggest that the individual members of the group

> stand ready to become midwives to the unfolding social reality of the situation. . . . [This poised stance relies on trust] in the unfolding potential of the situation and trust in oneself as an individual to "ride" with the situation in a skilled way. (pp. 132-133)

Autopoesis and Building Community

Paradoxically, living systems are in a constant process of both self-renewal and self-preservation. Each structure has a unique identity, a clear boundary, yet it is merged with its environment. The tendency of a system to maintain its structural integrity while rearranging its form to better meet the demands of environmental changes is called *autopoesis* (Capra, 1983; Jantsch, 1980). To facilitate the process of community building, mechanisms to address individual concerns, opportunities for personal meaning making, and forums for developing shared meanings must be available as the individual members coalesce toward community. As the group engages in common experiences and works to develop shared norms, the integrity of the individual identities must be maintained and honored.

An organization of this nature, one that balances autonomy and community, has been described by Costa and Garmston (1994) as holonomous. In a holonomous community, five "poised" attitudes, or states of mind, are continually present: efficacy, flexibility, craftsmanship, consciousness, and interdependence. (For a more elaborate description, see Garmston & Wellman's Chapter 7 in this volume.) These attitudes can be held both by individuals in an organization and by the system itself. The states of mind have the potential to function as strange attractors—the core values and operating guidelines that keep the system within an identified boundary.

We recognize that the evolutionary process—evolving stars, evolving organic forms, evolving consciousness—is fueled by diversity. The pattern of evolution initiates with variation and continues with selection that produces further variation. The evolution of society, or social systems, is most likely a parallel process, requiring diverse and varied lifestyles, cultures, and points of view. This diversity provides a spectrum of social possibilities from which movement toward growth can progress. Each "self" in the system is a point of view. Growth requires that "the evolving system's many diverse possibilities meet. It requires the kind of 'dialogue' that is missing in mechanistic models. . . . Without this [level of interaction] variation can lead to fragmentation" (Zohar & Marshall, 1994, p. 188).

One could say that the purpose of life, and, perhaps, the purpose of organizations, is to generate multiple possibilities for selection to act on. Sharing a common purpose, through genuine dialogue, a learning community is just such an organization—evolving toward increased capacities to adapt to continually changing environmental conditions.

Adaptivity: A Marriage of Symmetry and Chaos

At the boundaries, life flourishes.

James Gleick

Dynamical, or adaptive, systems are highly sensitive to their internal and external conditions. When environmental or internal conditions cause a highly fluctuating response in a dynamical system, multiple possibilities emerge. In nonequilibrium thermodynamics, these moments of possibility are called *bifurcation points*. Given particular conditions and circumstances (i.e., level of heat, timing of an electrical impulse, etc.), certain fluctuations at bifurcation points will amplify through a system, locking the system into a self-organizing pattern or structure. Nature abounds with examples. A tsunami or tidal wave that travels for large distances, essentially intact, and the cyclone structure of a tornado both are spontaneously self-organizing adaptations to environmental conditions.

From a nonequilibrium perspective, chaos is actually a high degree of determinacy, or information. Chaos theory reveals that in complex systems, what may appear to be disorder is actually full of information. The complexity is so great, however, that it cannot be reduced to simple algorithms, or patterns. This nonreducible complexity results in an *appearance* of disorder. Thus, a system can be globally stable but locally changing. For example, a stream flows within its boundaries but is full of turbulence and fluctuation. On a micro, or local level, the inherent order is hidden. Thus, we can predict patterns and ranges of movement in a system but not the details—and not, with certainty, long-range outcomes. For example, we know it is highly probable that a leaf in the stream will find its way downstream, but we cannot know the precise pathway it will take.

Chaos theory gives us a new way to think about predictability and planning on an organizational level. It informs us that in seemingly chaotic—highly fluctuating, random, and unpredictable—circumstances, there is an inherent order. It is for us to forge the understandings and common intent that become guidelines for cohesiveness. To avail itself of the order, or information, in the surrounding environment, a system must be at a stance of readiness to respond to both internal and external fluctuations. This is the nature of adaptivity. It is an interesting counterpoint that to be self-organizing, systems need a high degree of flexibility. "Freedom and order turn out to be partners in generating viable, well-ordered autonomous systems" (Wheatley, 1992, p. 95).

For dynamic growth, systems rely on an incredible partnership between determinism and indeterminism. This duality of chance, or indeterminism, and predictability, or determinism, creates the necessary conditions for a phase shift without a certain knowledge regarding the precision with which it will occur. For example, as in the Bénard instability, it can be predicated that the hexagonal patterns will reproducibly occur; the flow patterns of any particular cell, however, cannot be determined. The paradox, however, is that we can't predefine the optimum "balance between fluctuations, which allow discovery and innovation, and accurate determinism, which allows immediate exploitation" (Nicolis & Prigogine, 1989, p. 127). To undergo a phase change, the system must always be in a state of flux, or becoming. The identity, or integrity, of the system is maintained through the dynamic relationship of the elements that compose it.

A brainstorming session offers an interesting illustration of open system thermodynamic principles at work in a social interaction. The session is organized around a theme, which is determined by a common problem or desired outcome. The singular purpose dictates the direction of discourse—rich with ideas, it is hoped. Ideas bounce off participants with developing excitement as new ideas are examined, refined, embraced, or discarded. When this turbulence of intellectual energy is at its maximum, the bifurcation point emerges, revealing multiple possibilities and directions. Ultimately, this self-organizing process yields a creative and satisfying solution, and order emerges.

> An individual/relational dualism defines the identity of any system and the elements within it. In organizations, individuals are neither completely separate from their part in the system, nor completely immersed in it. The individual/relational balance is maintained by a combination of determinacy and indeterminacy. Determinacy preserves the best of what each brings to the group; indeterminacy comprises our latent potential. Neither state, the individual . . . nor the relational . . . in its extreme will serve the organization's development. It is the balance between the two that allows the most potential for growth. (Zohar & Marshall, 1994, p. 126)

Thus, to foster adaptivity in an organizational community, we must nurture the internal freedom of each member, the freedom to interact, engage, and grow in relationship with others. This concept is substantiated scientifically in Von Foerster's theorem.

Von Foerster's Theorem

Adaptive systems have the ability to maintain themselves through the free exchange of information between the elements, which allows for a type of homeostatic control. This behavior is described in Von Foerster's theorem, which suggests that when the elements of the system are rigidly connected, they have less influence on the system as a whole. Conversely, the less fixed, or more uncertain, the behavior of any elements of a system, the greater influence it will have.

Von Foerster's theorem has powerful implications for social systems because it addresses the correlation between creativity, effectiveness, and organizational procedure. Individuals in an organization, and the organization itself, will exhibit the highest degree of creativity when in the least restrictive organizational environment. Applying this theorem to schools implies that flexibility in the organizational structure, rules, and roles fosters the capacity to function with increased responsiveness to fluctuations in the system, thus greater adaptability. Von Foerster's theorem introduces a concept that is somewhat counterintuitive. Traditional organizational thinking suggests that fixed structures, unambiguous rules and regulations, and clearly defined social roles are required for organizational effectiveness. In vivid contrast, however, Von Foerster's theorem indicates that "pinning down the members of an organization with bureaucratic rules deprives them of any agency or power over the outcome of their actions" (Zohar & Marshall, 1994, p. 129) and promotes alienation and ineffectiveness.

Although there is no quick remedy, it seems apparent that for schools to function in harmony with Von Foerster's theorem, increasing choice over control in all aspects of the organization is indicated. Organizations need to explore the potential for choice making for everyone—staff, students, parents, community members, and so forth. Familiar structures, such as staff meetings, supervisory conferences, and daily announcements, can be restructured for increased flexibility. For example, staff meetings can be interactive opportunities for rallying the collective energies and perspectives of the members of the organization. Reformed in this way, staff meetings are occasions for community building and team learning: sharing successes, problem posing and problem solving, designing experiments, and analyzing data. From a systems perspective, supervisory conferences constitute reciprocal, colearning interactions—open-ended questions designed to promote thinking and reflection regarding instructional decisions, increasing the capacity for informed choice making.

Even the daily announcements, broadcast across an intercom or via an internal computerized network, can communicate a high value for creativity and learning. This important communication link offers multiple opportunities, such as posing a puzzle, riddle, or research question to be answered by students sometime later in the day; sharing an anecdote or announcing an award that celebrates innovation, cooperation, or other dispositions valued by the organization; and providing a forum for members of the school to communicate with each other in a variety of ways. Viewed creatively, the school calendar, the weekly schedule, the instructional day—even a specific period of instruction—all have potential for flexibility.

Evolutionary Planning

Organizational planning offers a good example of the potential for adaptivity. Systems thinkers recognize that a plan is a model of the system and the way in which the planners hope it will function. In many cases, however, so much energy and attention are put into planning that primarily what is accomplished is a plan, with little resource or energy left for implementation. Often, by the time implementation of the plan is to occur, conditions have changed to the degree that the plan itself is out of date! In a well-known study on successful school innovations, Louis and Miles (1990) identified *evolutionary planning* as crucial to sustained change. In their study, the most successful schools were able to adapt their plans as they moved in a desirable direction, taking advantage of unexpected developments and opportunities to continually improve the fit between the innovation and the conditions in the school. In their words,

> The evolutionary perspective rests on the assumption that the environment both inside and outside organizations is often chaotic. No specific plan can last for very long, because it will either become outmoded due to changing external pressures, or because disagreement over priorities arises within the organization. Yet, there is no reason to assume that the best response is to plan passively, relying on incremental decisions. Instead, the organization can cycle back and forth between efforts to gain normative consensus about what it may become, to plan strategies for getting there, and to carry out decentralized incremental experimentation that harnesses the creativity of all members to the change effort. . . . Strategies for achieving the mission are frequently reviewed and refined based on internal scanning for opportunities and successes. Strategy is viewed as a flexible tool. (p. 193)

Evolutionary planning recognizes unpredictability. It fosters calculated risk taking through multifaceted development designed for flexibility and rapid response. To increase these likelihoods, evolutionary planning is collaborative. It builds in "change through exchange" of ideas, approaches, positions, and concerns. Innovation is initiated on a small scale, which includes applications-oriented small starts, pilots of everything, and team development of innovations (Peters, 1987). Benchmarks and feedback loops (see below) are identified to recognize adjustment points and respond accordingly. Decision points are kept as open and flexible as possible.

Just as in directing any production, reciprocity and exchange between the environment and the "players" are paramount to success.

> What is necessary . . . is an incomplete design; a design that has clarity without rigidity; one that can be called "open" as against "shut." . . . A true theater designer will think of his designs as being all the time in motion, in action, in relation to what the actor brings to the scene as it unfolds. The later he makes the decisions, the better. (Brooks, in Zohar & Marshall, 1994, p. 129)

Systems thinking causes humans to explore ways in which individual actions, our own and others, create our collective reality. All members of the system recognize their potent influence on and responsibility to growth and development, for themselves and the organization. As a result, leadership in the learning organization becomes a shared endeavor to cultivate attitudes that embrace ambiguity, celebrate uncertainty, and value risk taking and experimentation.

Reflective Processes: Cultivating Collective Wisdom

Self-reference is what facilitates orderly change in turbulent environments.

Margaret Wheatley

The Nature of Feedback in Dynamical Systems

We have, in this chapter, borrowed from current thinking in several fields of science and put forth the idea that systems must be fluid, or far from equilibrium, to learn. Viewing the organization as a system means that we recognize the interrelatedness of all aspects of the organization—we see the big picture, not a series of individual snapshots. "Dynamical systems are sensitive and non-linear and unpredictable in detail because they are open, either to 'outside' influences or to their own subtle internal fluctuations" (Briggs, 1992, p. 21). They do not operate in isolation but are deeply interconnected. For these systems, the high degree of sensitivity to their initial conditions and to feedback from their internal and external environments can cause radical, unpredictable changes to the system through time.

As we navigate toward our unpredictable future, we are informed most efficiently by our immediate surroundings. In other words, environmental feedback guides our direction and gives us the most salient cues about our progress. The system and its members gather the information necessary to make the next move through a cycle of reflection, experimentation, and action.

Autocatalytic Feedback

An axiom in systems thinking is that every influence is both a cause and an effect. Influence never flows in only one direction. Feedback, from a systems perspective, is any reciprocal flow of influence. "The key to seeing reality systemically is seeing circles of influence rather than straight lines . . . the first step to breaking out of . . . linear

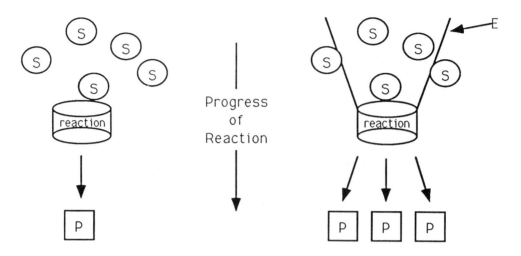

Figure 3.2. Enzymatic Activity

NOTE: The enzyme (E) works as a "funnel" to increase the probability and, therefore, the rate of reaction.

thinking" (Senge, 1990a, p. 75). Feedback occurs in all systems and is intrinsic to life. In living systems, enzymatic allosterism provides an example.

Enzymatic allosterism is a mechanism by which cells control biochemical feedback loops. Enzymes are catalysts that increase the probability of reactions without themselves being consumed (see Figure 3.2). In other words, to increase the reaction rate, an enzyme acts on its reactant, or substrate, and facilitates conversion to a product. Without enzymes, life could not occur because essential reactions would proceed too slowly. For example, in the process of digestion, enzymes break down proteins into amino acids so that they may again be used for protein synthesis. Technically speaking, in a reaction, enzymes reduce the energy of activation, which simply means that they reduce barriers to the progress of the reaction.

The biochemical feedback loop, or allosteric effect, occurs when the activity of an enzyme (E) is modified by feedback from an effector molecule. This regulation of enzymatic activity occurs as a result of the effector molecule binding to the enzyme and altering its structure, creating either positive or negative feedback into the system, increasing or decreasing its effectiveness. When, as in some cases, these effector molecules are the product (P) of the reaction under consideration (see Figure 3.3) and creating positive feedback, the reaction is *autocatalytic*. In these cases, P feeds back and modifies the actual structure of E such that the reaction or conversion rate of the substrate (S) to P is increased, making the reaction more efficient.

Establishing Feedback Spirals

Strictly speaking, the example of allosterism is a feedback *loop*—it is used to maintain homeostasis in the cell. When we apply the concept of autocatalytic

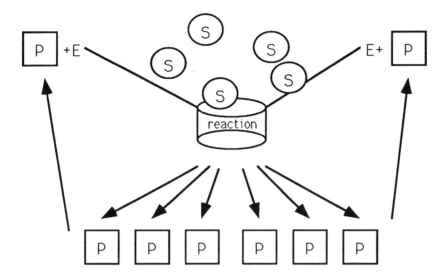

Figure 3.3. Enzymatic Allosterism
NOTE: Product (P) feeds back and modifies the enzyme (E), increasing its effectiveness.

feedback to social systems, we add the dimension of time and change and address the notion of becoming or evolving. Thus, the loop is reconfigured or stretched into a feedback spiral (see Kallick's Chapter 13 in the second book of this trilogy, *Supporting the Spirit of Learning*), as shown in Figure 3.4. In the case of a feedback spiral, the system has experienced a learning process. The initial conditions never return to the same level, and the system has evolved.

Consider an educational parallel. A teacher may be viewed as an enzyme with the role of enhancing learning capacity to convert the student, a substrate, from a state of less knowledge to one with greater knowledge. The feedback *loop* occurs when the teacher, by observing the reaction products, student learning, modifies activities to enhance learning in the moment. The autocatalytic feedback *spiral* occurs when the teacher reflects on the feedback and synthesizes new learning. The integration of this new learning will have an impact on the "reaction rate" in the future. Further, the reaction occurs on at least two levels, continuous improvement in teaching and continuous improvement in learning for both the teacher and the students. Ultimately, and synergistically, there is evolution of the entire system.

Applying Feedback Spirals to Organizational Learning

Incorporating these principles of natural systems, members of social systems, such as schools, can intentionally introduce feedback at critical points designed to cause desired effects. Small, well-focused interventions are able to produce significant and profound change. When members of an organization recognize the holistic nature of systems thinking, they are able to look for areas of high leverage to promote systemic change. The key is to identify the levers that might have the

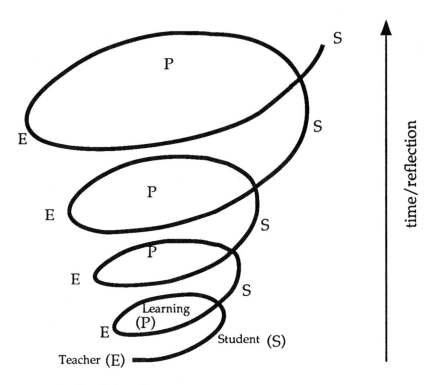

Figure 3.4. Feedback Spiral

NOTE: In this feedback spiral, the elements (students and teachers) evolve, and learning process (P) is enhanced as a result of the increasingly catalytic nature of the interactions (positive feedback).

greatest potential for enduring and positive change. As members and leaders of schools, "we must seek patterns of order beneath the surface chaos and search for structures and patterns of interaction that release and amplify the energies within the system" (Garmston & Wellman, 1995, p. 10).

In schools, feedback spirals guide the growth process through identifying, gathering, analyzing, and evaluating data. This information is then applied by individuals and the system to calibrate direction on the journey toward transformation. Using agreed-on data sources, such as internal monitoring, external observations, and specified products, groups can work collaboratively to identify critical leverage points for data-driven interventions.

Feedback spirals support the cycle of inquiry, experimentation, and reflection. For continual growth and learning in an organization, opportunities and forums for these processes to occur must be built into the norms of the system. In a learning community, these opportunities are built into the natural occurrences of life in the system. The work space becomes a community learning space.

Integrating Reflection Into the Work Space

Regarding learning, educational organizations have a unique problem. Unlike the cast members in a stage production, who engage in hours of individual and collaborative practice before they are required to achieve a flawless performance, educators must perform masterfully *while* they are engaged in learning. Although under the best conditions, learning occurs in a continuous movement between the *practice field* and the *performance field* (Senge, 1990a), in schools it occurs concurrently.

To be learner and learning driven, places of education must carve multiple opportunities for learning, supported by norms of collaboration and experimentation, into the work space. The practice field and the performance field need to be separated to allow for the risks of failing forward. For schools, possibilities for learning and reflection within the work space include the creation of learning laboratories and action research.

Learning Laboratories

Learning laboratories are arenas for collaborative learning that combine relevant school-based issues, such as instructional innovation, curricular integration, and assessment alternatives, with significant interpersonal dynamics, such as honest communication, nonjudgmental listening, and balancing advocacy with inquiry. Learning laboratories focus on case studies or simulations that are as authentic and as real-time based as possible. They are not based on location; they are based on purpose—and the purpose is collective learning. Learning laboratories give participants an opportunity to experience group problem solving, using data-based analysis and synthesis skills, and to practice the requisite communication skills to be effective team learners in an environment designed to be challenging and supportive. Built in is a time for reflecting on the experience, synthesizing learning, and self-prescribing continued learning agendas.

The opportunities for a group to be part of a learning laboratory are multiple. For example, learning labs can be organized for vertical, or mixed, constituent learning teams or grade level groups who want to examine a specific problem or issue. They can be the focus of faculty meetings or the central theme of professional development opportunities when groups want to examine current research juxtaposed with their own theories on practice. Learning laboratories can be created by one learning team for another, can emerge from constraints or issues in the current conditions of the organization, can be scheduled formally, or can arise from collectively expressed needs.

Action Research

Inquiry-oriented learning requires a reconstruction of experience through reflection and integration of new information. When members of an organization use feedback spirals to systematically explore their work and generate new theories from their practice, they are essentially engaged in action research. In schools, this powerful growth process can be individually constructed and classroom based, designed by a learning team that addresses specific issues or questions, or systemically oriented, involving multiple data sources and collectors. Action research offers a powerful opportunity for the collaborative examination and analysis of current reality compared with shared vision and a data-driven exploration of potential paths of inquiry and action.

Assessing Progress

We must take care as we consider possibilities for establishing a present location and plotting progress on the journey toward a desired state. In quantum physics, the mode of measurement determines what we will see. Both matter and light, for example, may appear as particles or waves. If we choose tools that can measure one, we will not learn about the other. In a similar way, assessment and evaluation in our schools become a lens for learning.

Our learners, and our programs, are composed of content knowledge, process skills, and predispositions, or attitudes. If we choose tools that will assess increased capacities in only one area, we may not be able to learn about the others. "The act of measurement becomes an act of participation, signaling value judgments about the use of time, talent, and money" (Garmston & Wellman, 1995, p. 8). Built into any plan for growth must be multiple and diverse measures for gathering information. In this way, assessment will widen, not limit, our perspective.

Bon Voyage

> A ship in harbor is safe,
> but that is not what ships are built for.
>
> *William Shedd*

Essentially, the health of a system may be viewed as its distance from equilibrium. Everything, from cellular health and organismic health to social health and ecological health, may be defined by distance from equilibrium. In other words, when a system is at equilibrium, nothing can happen other than the random fluctuations around the equilibrium point. Equilibrium, therefore, is essentially timeless.

The move from equilibrium requires the input of energy, or information. Without the optimal conditions, or without sufficient flow of motivating force, only linear growth can occur. In contrast, with sufficient force and flow, nonlinear rearrangements occur, and systems make quantum leaps. This is the probable process by which life started and evolves. It seems possible, in fact, that the move from equilibrium is, itself, a strange attractor, and the multitudinous, unpredictable modes and levels by which it occurs are the associated chaos.

Although the paradigm is the same at multiple levels, its manifestation differs for each. This concept has tremendous implications for guiding all forms of development and is foundational to the process of organizational growth. The journey toward transformation is both individual and collective. It begins *inside* the organization, within each member. This essential journey requires a deep understanding of the interrelatedness of each level within the system and a personal commitment to capacity building. This chapter strives to explicate the importance of understanding basic life processes as defined by the physics of dynamical, far-from-equilibrium systems and to integrate these processes into our approaches to personal and organizational development.

Marshall (1995) reminds us that "re-invention is not about changing what is, but about creating what is not" (p. 13). As we launch our unpredictable journey of transformation, aware of the uncertainties, collaboratively poised for the challenges ahead, we must be ready for new ways of being, new ways of behaving, and the emergence of new ideas and ideals. We have few paths, presently, that we can follow. We must literally forge the road while we travel it.

References

Barth, R. (1990). *Improving schools from within*. San Francisco: Jossey-Bass.

Bohm, D. (1990). *On dialogue*. Ojai, CA: David Bohm Seminars.

Briggs, J. (1992). *Fractals: The patterns of chaos*. New York: Simon & Schuster.

Briggs, J., & Peat, D. (1989). *The turbulent mirror*. New York: Harper & Row.

Brillouin, L. (1962). *Science and information theory*. New York: Academic Press.

Capra, F. (1983). *The turning point*. Toronto, Ontario, Canada: Bantam.

Costa, A., & Garmston, B. (1994). *Cognitive coaching: A foundation for renaissance schools*. Norwood, MA: Christopher-Gordon.

Covey, S. (1989). *The seven habits of highly effective people*. New York: Simon & Schuster.

Garmston, R., & Wellman, B. (1995). Adaptive schools in a quantum universe. *Educational Leadership, 52*(7), 6-13.

Huber, G. (1991). Organizational learning: The contributing processes and the literature. *Organization Science, 1*(1), 88-115.

Isaacs, W. (1994). Dialogue: The power of collective thinking. In K. Wardman (Ed.), *Reflections on creating learning organizations* (pp. 83-93). Cambridge, MA: Pegasus.

Jantsch, E. (1980). *The self-organizing universe*. Oxford, UK: Pergamon.

Kim, D., & Mullen, E. (1995). The spirit of the learning organization. In K. Wardman (Ed.), *Reflections on creating learning organizations* (pp. 107-114). Cambridge, MA: Pegasus.

Kofman, F., & Senge, P. (1994). Communities of commitment: The heart of learning organizations. In *The learning organization in action* (pp. 7-26). New York: American Management Association.

Louis, K., & Miles, M. (1990). *Improving the urban high school: What works and why*. New York: Teachers College Press.

Marshall, S. (1995, January). The vision, meaning, and language of educational transformation. *School Administrator*, 8-15.

Nicolis, G., & Prigogine, I. (1989). *Exploring complexity: An introduction*. San Francisco: Freeman.

Peters, T. (1987). *Thriving on chaos: Handbook for a management revolution*. New York: Knopf.

Prigogine, I. (1980). *From being to becoming: Complexity in the physical sciences*. San Francisco: Freeman.

Raitt, E. (1995). Schools as learning organizations. In S. Bacharach & B. Mundell (Eds.), *Images of schools* (pp. 71-107). Thousand Oaks, CA: Corwin.

Saphier, J., & King, M. (1985). Good seeds grow in strong cultures. *Educational Leadership, 42*, 67-73.

Schein, E. (1994). On dialogue, culture, and organizational learning. In *The learning organization in action* (pp. 56-67). New York: American Management Association.

Senge, P. (1990a). *The fifth discipline: The art and practice of the learning organization*. New York: Doubleday.

Senge, P. (1990b, Fall). The leader's new work: Building learning organizations. *Sloan Management Review, 32*(1), 7-23.

Sergiovanni, T. (1994). *Building community in schools*. San Francisco: Jossey-Bass.

Weisbord, M. (1992). *Discovering common ground*. San Francisco: Berrett-Koehler.

Wheatley, M. (1992). *Leadership and the new science*. San Francisco: Berrett-Koehler.

Zohar, D., & Marshall, I. (1994). *The quantum society: Mind, physics and a new social vision*. New York: William Morrow.

4

Designing Learning for a New Work Environment

Key Values and Skills

Michael A. Pennella

Only a few years ago, the work environment reflected a fairly straightforward work formula. People who went to school, became employed and did what they were supposed to do would have a job that enabled them to retire on a pension. Job security and longevity could be assumed if one's knowledge, performance, and attitude were satisfactory.

> Once upon a time, corporations were like ocean liners. Anyone fortunate enough to secure a berth cruised through a career and disembarked at retirement age. A clear agreement chartered the voyage: in return for loyalty, sacrifice, bureaucratic aggravation, and the occasional demanding boss, you received job security for life. In the last decade, ocean liners have started heaving their crews overboard. (Pascale, 1996, p. 62)

Today, those rules have changed. The new work environment no longer routinely responds to the old rules. In today's work environment, a major shift is under way in how workers are perceived. Skills, loyalty, and experience are important but increasingly only to the degree the employer needs them at any given time. This environment creates continuing worker uncertainty and insecurity. This new work environment is considered not an aberration by experts and economic trend watchers but one that will be tomorrow's reality for students. Those who survive and succeed must be armed with new values and skills that enable them to function well in a changed context. A dramatic shift from content-based passive learning to more active, flexible, and team-based processes are increasingly required.

Critical elements supporting this transition are the focus on process thinking represented throughout this trilogy and a focus on the types of values and skills typically associated with independent businesspeople or entrepreneurs. Process thinking and the values and skills implicitly modeled within curriculum and instruction become as important as content itself. A reevaluation of curriculum and its delivery in the light of a new work world is necessary to help students survive and succeed in a different world from that for which the parents and teachers of the 1990s were prepared.

A Journey's End That Began and Ended in Curriculum Design

The perspective that follows is the result of experience in many different work worlds: first, in education as a teacher, curriculum director, and secondary school principal. A second career led to the business world as a company president and later to the role of independent entrepreneur serving as a management consultant to government, education, and business. Having lived the life described in this chapter, I hold a strong sense of cautious but consistent optimism. For the past 6 years, I have been asking, listening, observing, and exchanging ideas with groups in business, education, and government to examine what makes an effective and adaptive worker in a rapidly changing economy. This question has formed the core of a dialogue with a large array of teachers, businesspersons, and curriculum specialists, as well as government experts, on the world of work. The result of this search has led to three conclusions.

1. Because of major shifts in the work environment, a corresponding change in perspective and attitude must occur within all current and future workers. This change must enable workers to feel that they can become active, successful, optimistic participants in, rather than potential victims of, the new work environment and that they can have greater control over their work life.

2. Workers, current and future, will require a reassessment of the values that served previous generations of craftspersons to guide their behavior in the workplace. Employers once placed more value on specific, narrow expertise and solitary work efforts. Passivity and loyalty were exchanged for security. Although these beliefs will not be totally displaced, the "taken for granted" worth of these values will be called into question consistently. Three interacting values appear necessary to help workers function and succeed in this new work environment: the ability to

   • Perceive opportunity

   • Be self-directed, self-monitoring, and self-evaluating

   • Find meaning in the value of one's own work

3. New skills or competencies that support each of the key values above will be built on the types of skills associated with the entrepreneur or enterprising person. "An employed attitude is no longer an option today" (Hakim, 1994, p. 3). These skills may not be associated with traditional evaluations of achievement because they call for the thinking of mavericks or those who see the world in different and creative ways, rather than as others portray it for them. Some of these enterprise competencies are information gathering, learning orientation, visioning or predicting, efficacy, self-awareness, interdependence, service orientation, craftsmanship, courage, and assertiveness.

These competencies require a curricular and instructional design that focuses on creating an environment in which the learners are far more active participants in choosing, planning, teaming, and evaluating success—much as one would treat an entrepreneur, rather than a laborer.

Caveats

The information that follows focuses on what the school—through its teachers, curriculum, and overall program—can foster that will make a difference in the workplace of tomorrow. It does not speak to the role of family, the society, or its culture. It is written from a perspective that the school's mission is to add value to those whom it teaches. Curriculum designers and teachers who are more aware today of the changing workplace, and its different demands can make a major difference in the lives of future adults and in the overall welfare of a productive workplace.

Because the focus of this chapter is on issues related to helping students excel in a new work setting, it would be easy to perceive a lack of balance with other vital purposes of education. I acknowledge this at the outset. The emphasis is intended solely for the purpose of this chapter. Good curriculum design helps students appreciate and participate in all aspects of their lives. The values and skills called for in this chapter will also enhance more than the student's work life, despite the seeming singularity of thought that the words may represent.

This chapter is organized to provide a short background on an economic change that many predict will be as profound as the industrial revolution. An understanding of the factors that drove and continue to drive change is intended to provide a rationale for why curriculum and its delivery must continue to address new values and new skills that may be only beginning to emerge in the literature as the "new basics" of economic survival. This new perspective, however, may not be apparent to curriculum designers, teachers, and school administrators whose work is carried out where rewards and level of security are often not based on entrepreneurial achievements. Following and not making waves often remain the unwritten culture of the school for many adults and certainly for most students. To say that the future is going to demand adults who spend most of their lives drawing outside the lines and "doing their own thing" is not something that schools easily assimilate.

The following information on the new work environment should be read seeking implications for those who would respond to the challenges that this reality offers. It should also be read with the knowledge that many are successfully navigating this changing economic terrain. A spirit of optimism about the future workplace is dependent on the opportunities that lie ahead for an organization properly prepared to think and behave in new, more entrepreneurial ways.

The New Work Environment Develops:
The Lessons of the 1990s

As the economic recovery began in the early 1990s, previous recovery experiences left many displaced workers expecting to be reemployed—they hoped by the same employers, but at least in the same or similar industry at near comparable levels of job responsibilities and salary levels. For many displaced workers, however, these expectations were never realized. Not only were the vast majority of terminated workers not reemployed by their previous employers as the recovery slowly began, but many couldn't find full-time employment in the same industry; some couldn't even find employment in a similar industry. When workers did find jobs, many were not hired full-time or for the same type of job responsibilities or salaries they had previously received. Although the overall economy continued to recover and consumer confidence rose, a quiet but massive turbulence among many displaced workers emerged as they sought to find a method of sustaining their income, careers, and livelihood. After displacement, the vast majority of those recently unemployed undertook traditional pathways for finding positions and jobs similar to the ones they previously held, such as searching and applying for job openings and going through personnel, government, and other agencies to be "placed."

Many displaced workers, however, discovered different expectations and values. Not only was it increasingly difficult to reenter the traditional job market as full-time staff employees, but it was certainly more difficult to acquire positions that took full advantage of their knowledge and experience. Although some individuals found work in a similar capacity, many others accepted positions that were below their expertise, knowledge, or salary expectations.

The belief that a recovering economy would precede the return to the "normal" hierarchical, job-based work setting did not pan out for several reasons. The most popular hypothesis was that corporations were heartless and greedy and that their desire for even greater profits meant that they were not willing to incur salary and benefit expenses at previous levels. Although there may be some underlying truth to this hypothesis, there are several other identifiable reasons. Reengineering and its predecessors, work flow redesign and process redesign, have made companies more efficient and therefore able to provide better service with fewer people. The role of new technologies for processing information and communicating what was once communicated by middle management and the ability to have work completed off-site had a profound effect as well. Further, the realization that the outsourcing of a large company's work to smaller niche vendors produced greater efficiencies had a monumental effect on the establishment of a changed work setting. The purpose of a large corporate workforce had always been to ensure that many types of work could be carried out with minimal transaction costs. As the ability to work beyond the walls of the corporation improved and as external vendor costs became more attractive than internal costs, businesses shed functions and looked outside for these services.

With this change in the economy and the workplace, however, came myriad opportunities for small companies, people willing to work for multiple employers (sometimes their ex-employers), those willing to sell their expertise as independent consultants or temporary workers, and those with an entrepreneurial bent. The organizing principle became less "what job do you go to" and more "what are the types of work that you can do." Those able to sell their talents and ability to carry out valued work benefited more from this new organizing principle in the workplace than from the traditional job. That single shift in thinking launched vast opportunities and, at the same time, set off crises that will endure until the paradigm of one's work value versus one's guaranteed job is fully understood and acted on. It is the type of knowledge that entrepreneurs have always understood. It is not an easy lesson for those clinging to "9 to 5" expectations.

Staying on Board: New Realities on the Inside

While thousands of displaced workers struggled to get a clear picture of what the new work environment was about, millions of workers who remain employed realized that their work environment was also clearly changing.

- Workers were expected to start taking on more and varied responsibility, using an increasing number of outside consultants and temporary help.
- Workers were asked to wear more "hats" and participate in a variety of team and cross-functional configurations. Individuals were increasingly not assigned just one job in the traditional approach but instead asked to work on projects or "jobs," just as consultants do. Each of these projects or jobs required working with a different team, the composition of which varied according to the needs of the project. The individuals' roles also varied somewhat on each project.

After a lifetime of structuring one's responses to function effectively in a more structured, vertical organization, many workers struggled to make a successful, productive transition into this type of fluid environment. Many attempted to build their skills in such areas as "empowerment," "team building," and "cross-functioning," which are now long-term, key aspects of the new work environment.

For many, this change was not an easy one. Charles Heckscher, a Rutgers University sociologist, studied middle managers in 14 units of eight large companies for 5 years. He found that only half the middle managers in these companies were able to make the change in this restructured environment. He also found that they not only were nervous about their jobs and financial futures but also were feeling cut adrift by a fundamental shift in their corporation's values. These middle managers weren't bothered by the downsizing until quite belatedly and, even then, didn't feel the necessity to evaluate or affect decisions independently regarding their future. "It is not easy for people to give up what they believe to be their core values: doing what they are told in exchange for security" (Noble, 1995, p. 21).

Characteristics of the New Work Environment

To determine values and skills that need to be incorporated into curriculum design to help students succeed in the new work environment, the characteristics of the new economy need to be defined. This new economy has certain characteristics that reflect how process will differ from current work patterns. Attributes of this network economy include

- Continual changing relationships among people, machines, and organizations
- Ample opportunity for people and organizations with an enterprise orientation
- Vendors and contingent workers quickly assembled into virtual teams by project
- Talent and value matched to work required, not to jobs

By the mid-1990s, an increasing number of business experts were warning that the workforce must undergo a revolutionary change to effectively respond to this new work environment (Bridges, 1994; Dent, 1995; Drucker, 1995; Hakim, 1994; Rifkin, 1995). Workers would have to rethink their approach to "work" as they knew it previously. For many, this meant focusing less on obtaining a "safe job with an employer" and focusing more on learning how to build values, attitudes, and skills that allow them to survive and succeed through multiple job changes and with far less structure and security.

In his book, *Job Shock: Four New Principles Transforming Our Work and Business,* Dent (1995) states,

> The coming work revolution will force us to rediscover our greatest strength, individual initiative—thus nurturing a spirit of entrepreneurship. . . . We have an entire history and culture of entrepreneurial peoples fostering new technologies. . . . Only individual initiative creates tangible results. . . . When the dust settles, more people will have been forced to move into new jobs and more entrepreneurial opportunities. (p. 37)

The future employee development program is going to be much more like a program for self-employed entrepreneurs than a program for jobholders. Workers won't be dragged into a seminar, the way they often are today. Workers are going to need to know how to do something to get hired for the next project, and getting them to class will be a matter of their push, not someone else's pull. Workers who don't keep up a self-managed program of continuing education will fall behind and will lose out on the opportunities.

Bridges (1994), in *Job Shift: How to Prosper in a Workplace Without Jobs,* states,

Finally, training is going to have to become less outcome and more process oriented in the years ahead, since we don't know what the shape of work will be like in the years ahead, but we do know it will be different. (p. 168)

In a *Fortune* magazine article called "Getting Past Economic Insecurity," Richman (1995) states,

Companies no longer offer people careers. People create their own careers. However it happens, the business of earning a living and planning for the future will require an attitude adjustment of monumental proportions. . . . Career counselors are beginning to offer displaced managers some radical advice: Forget rational notions about hunting for a job. Rather than seeking a specific job title in a specific industry, learn to be flexible enough to take advantage of whatever opportunities come along. . . . The best way to get a good job or remain in one is "to think how to make yourself more valuable." (p. 162)

Preparing Students for a New Work Environment

For purposes of organizing our thinking about the transition from the old to the new work environment, we might envision four sets of competencies around which workforce preparation has been framed. The first of these were the basic skills associated with communication and computation. Recently, the rapid transformation of the workplace by the personal computer has made the use of automation into what is perhaps a new basic skill. The second were competencies associated with understanding one's own and others' culture. The arts, social studies, and foreign language are the most obvious members of this group. The teaching of technology skills that could provide entry to a trade through technical or vocational programs were the third set of competencies emphasized for work preparation. The fourth set has been recently codified through school-to-work initiatives. They include those competencies associated with making career decisions, using labor market information, job application skills, positive and reliable work behavior, maintaining safe working conditions, and the like. In short, they focus primarily on getting and holding a job. Underlying these four sets of competencies are the thinking processes that form the foundation of this trilogy and that remain essential in both the old and new work environments.

These four sets of competencies continue to be important, and no hierarchy needs to exist among them. To see the future as a time of opportunity rather than as a time of scarcity, however, a new perspective and set of competencies are required. The perspective requires a concentrated effort on seeing beyond the traditional ways of doing work, earning wages, and preparing students. The change requires a new way of describing the values and competencies that must be brought from the shadows and into the light of curricular focus. These values and competencies are those traditionally associated with the entrepreneur or enterprising person.

Why do future workers need to be trained with these skills and values? Although many American workers have traditionally chosen working for an employer over being a self-employed entrepreneur, the concept of a steady job is undergoing a major transition. In fact, Handy (1994) predicts that even now,

50% of all workers will function at some time in their career as an "independent who has to find work, not in a traditional job, to produce revenue and create value" (pp. 216-217).

For those who hold, or aspire to hold, positions on payrolls as employees, dramatically different skills will be required than the ones they currently use on their jobs. Workers will be required to consistently add value by being members of a team that supports others as customers (Hakim, 1994, pp. 105-113). In short, whether workers are self-employed or employed by someone else, they will have to behave as if they are selling and providing services in a competitive environment. They will have to acquire more of an enterprising attitude and behave more like an entrepreneur. And for those workers who are employed within companies, they will be expected to take on more varied roles more often to function effectively within the changed environment.

Dent (1995) states,

> We're seeing a permanent re-engineering of the corporate structure and processes. . . . Back line clerical people and experts will either be pulled into front-line teams or become specialized consultants available either inside or outside the company. They will be paid by front-line teams only if they can create value for them. (p. 35)

Workers need to understand how to be entrepreneurs and how to be enterprising on the job or in their own business—to think not of "doing their job" but of "jobs" they perform and the value their work offers to the employer in real dollars and cents. Displaced workers need to understand how to apply entrepreneurial/enterprising skills as employees or as self-employed workers. They have to know how to package and position their skills to make them of value to their employer as temporary or permanent employees or independent contractors or to their customers or clients as a business, how to spot new markets, how to market and sell their services, and how to develop and maintain a productive business relationship as well as nurture new opportunities.

The terms and components of the enterprise competencies described can be renamed, combined, or arguably found within good pre-employment programs. But to argue those semantics or groupings is to miss the point. These values and competencies should spur thinking about what types of activities and classroom modeling are required to best prepare students for a world in which the teachers, professors, and curriculum specialists of the 1990s did not grow up. A radical paradigm shift and new thinking are required. The values and competencies of an enterprise orientation provide a guide or set of filters for the dialogue that shapes those shifts and thinking.

Incorporating Enterprise Values and Competencies Into Curriculum Design

The Value of Perceiving Opportunity

A commercial fisherman recently attributed his outstanding business success to his ability to gather the right information about the fishing process as much as to his ability to actually fish. He spent a large part of his time gathering information rather than fishing. He read every source available about fishing, tried to understand effective application of technology in the fishing process, reviewed trends in fishing, studied the nature of the public's demand for fish, and so on. With correct information, he was able to apply new knowledge as well as create opportunities for himself. The act of fishing almost became secondary to the process of preparing for it. The key to this process is emphasizing the right question, the gathering of sources and data. The use of reflection becomes important versus rapid recall or quick automated response using solutions that worked in the past. The information-gathering competency emphasizes the *use* of the collected information rather than the importance of information as valuable in itself. Success followed a disposition of openness to new learning. The willingness of this fisherman to remain attuned to goals but flexible in the way that technology or other changes would lead him to those goals demonstrated the power of the enterprise skills associated with perceiving opportunity.

This value is associated with the characteristic behaviors of a classic entrepreneur. It will support future workers whether they function as independent consultants who work for several people or as persons working in an organization characterized by increasingly wider spans of responsibility. There are five enterprise competencies linked to the value of perceiving opportunity: (a) information gathering, (b) opportunity identification, (c) flexibility, (d) creativity, and (e) learning orientation.

Information Gathering. The explosion of information and the ability to access that information from one's home will change the way institutions and individuals think about conveying, storing, and using information. The changes will be as dramatic as the changes wrought by the printing press. Those who passed on information through word of mouth could never have envisioned a day when the printed word would be so readily available in libraries. So, too, is it difficult to imagine the day when such access may be available through a device kept in a briefcase. The amount and availability of information, coupled with the speed at which information—specifically, technical knowledge—becomes obsolete, ensure that attaining content will no longer guarantee success.

The implications for teachers and curriculum specialists are to recognize that information gathering is what an enterprising person does now and will need to do even more so in the future as more information and better ways of organizing it become available. The importance of the activity for the students lies not so much in the ability to gather content from disparate sources but in the ability to identify relevant information, as well as generate and synthesize it to solve problems or reap opportunity. The key to this process is being able to ask the right questions and to view sources and data from various perspectives.

Opportunity Identification. Curriculum can help build students' ability to evaluate an event or situation with available opportunities. Students should be able to formulate and answer three types of critical questions about events or situations. These events may be in the form of day-to-day problems, history, the arts, and literature, among others. This process will help students think through any situation for its potential for opportunity as well as help condition students with the belief that opportunity exists in most every situation.

Question #1: What opportunity exists here, and for whom?

Question #2: What is beneficial about this opportunity, and for whom?

Question #3: How could this event be changed to become an opportunity, and for whom?

The intent of opportunity identification is to create a countering orientation to the paradigm of problem solving. Problem solving, although a higher-order thinking skill, often involves the manifestation of the known. It is a response. The person who perceives as an entrepreneur sees that which is not there, actually changing the definition of or orientation to the problem into one of opportunity. He or she asks, "What is or might be great about this?" This thinking seeks to counter a sense of victimization or helplessness that will defeat the self-starter in the face of adversity.

Flexibility. To be able to mix and match information in different ways, students need to be ready to look at gathered information and each situation for its potential for opportunity from a variety of perspectives. Flexibility is more than just being able to change with the times. Flexibility is about looking at a situation and information from someone else's viewpoint as well as one's own, the ability to step into a situation from another vantage point, much as the entrepreneur studies and then predicts potential market impact. Flexibility is about *not* looking into single solutions or a single orientation to problem solving or acting.

Creativity. Once the right information has been gathered and various opportunities have been identified, students learn how to use their creative powers to blend information in different and unique ways to come up with potentially new solutions to an event or situation. Creative thinking is nothing more than twisting the dials on an old idea (Hofstadter, 1985). There are really no new ideas, only basic knowledge that one sees in different ways and combines to create answers. Curriculum design that fosters inquiry and the combination of the disparate is a remarkably powerful tool to help students think creatively and think about their creativity. Students must recognize that the process of creativity is not only designing a great work of art but also taking information that they have gathered and mixing it and matching it in different ways to come up with a viable solution. This process is what enterprising people currently use and will have to apply with yet greater proficiency in the future to enable them to discern opportunities.

Learning Orientation. Students have to be better prepared to question themselves as to what they did learn from every experience and what can be learned. Good process helps students to question themselves as to where their assumptions might be leading them in a limited direction. Using this approach, students build the ability to tap into major sources of information, to identify what sources are of most importance to them, to better synthesize information so it can be useful, and to be better able to identify opportunities.

Curriculum design needs to include an orientation that learning is more important than the drive to achieve a certain grade. Students need to know that what they actually learn about process is of greater value then the grade they receive. Good practice strives to take students beyond the "what (grade) did you get" mentality.

This understanding comes about through an awareness that from learning comes the generation of hypotheses. Students' ability to create better hypotheses is affected by the amount and quality of information they gather. It is here that content becomes fuel for thinking. Curriculum content does not become secondary to the curriculum process; content feeds the process.

In the new work environment, it is more important than ever for enterprising people to make accurate predictions and hypotheses to achieve perceived opportunities. If more and better information is available to people, they can make better hypotheses. Students living within the new work environment have an increased ability to effectively gather and evaluate information to make effective hypotheses for themselves. This process isn't something radically new. The work of Jerome Bruner and those who have applied his work to the teaching of reading and social sciences gives insight into how the teaching of hypothesis testing can be applied in the classroom for genuine links to the *real world*. The creation of better hypotheses in a less structured environment supports creativity and flexibility, whereas the ability to generate hypotheses is built on information gathering.

In a downsized, restructured work environment, many more workers will have to "lead their own way"; they will have to apply these skills so they can work effectively with an increasing number of other workers who are required to do the same. They will be called on to do more than follow orders. Workers must be able to create opportunity for themselves and for the organizations with which they are associated.

The Value of Self-Direction

Today's curriculum increasingly appears to reflect an understanding that text and time cannot unduly dictate how learning is organized for individual students. A sense of student choice based on participative generation of learning goals and activities is being added to new series of curricular materials. The ability to set learning goals and to have some inclination to be flexible in the obtaining of these goals was once outside the reach of students. This top-down approach was also a technique used in the old work environment. The goals and direction were set by the boss. Traditionally, workers were given fixed job parameters and limited decision-making power and were told to do the job in front of them. In the new work environment, this process is changing. Workers are given increased responsibilities, including individual and team-based goal-setting responsibility and greater latitude to achieve these goals.

Is it appropriate to use traditional curricular goal-setting techniques with students who soon will have to function in this new work environment? Is it effective, and for that matter, fair, to continue using traditional techniques of setting curricular goals and direction for students who, in a few brief years, will be expected to alter the very nature of how they have been trained to function in responsibility and goal setting? The fostering of choice in activities, sequence, time, and materials represents a significant curricular and organizational challenge but one that must be considered in the light of both a changed work environment and new technological opportunities to provide choice and greater opportunities for self-direction.

In a new economy, two key enterprise competencies associated with self-direction are the ability to (a) vision or predict and (b) have a sense of efficacy, to influence one's own direction.

Visioning and Predicting. The ability to remain in the present and pay attention to the future is a competency that effective entrepreneurs display. From this ability flows their sense of direction on the basis of how they see the world and their place in the world. The ability to possess, understand, and articulate what one wants in the light of a sense of purpose is the cornerstone of self-direction. Senge (1990) calls for organizations that foster continuous learning based on shared organizational and individual vision but laments that "most adults have little sense of real vision. . . . When asked what they want, many adults will say what they want to get rid of. . . . They are the by-product of a lifetime of fitting in, of coping, of problem solving" (p. 147).

Vision is born from a sense of purpose, one's core values, what one believes in. The examination of one's actions in light of a set of values is where one's reliance on principles emerges as the essence of inner guidance or true self-direction. It remains the role of the very human teacher to enhance this competency. It is not an easy role, however, and may easily be abdicated among competing demands.

The second characteristic of self-direction and vision is the ability to look into the future and set one's own path. Downhill skiers learn that progress as skiers comes only when they lift their heads from staring at their skis in fear. The only way to improve is to look down the mountain toward one's destination. Helping students to be able to predict the consequences of action or to describe what the successful completion of a project will entail moves the students toward the development of *mental pictures* or visions of desirable ends. It is the dialogue of the learning setting that fosters the power of individual vision, facilitates its unity with group and individual purpose, and reaffirms the importance of picturing the future as a means to attain self-direction.

Sense of Efficacy. In the previous work environment, workers didn't have the same need to shape their own direction. There were often traditional boundaries and ways of moving ahead. Today, those methods are less explicit. In the new workplace, workers have a need for a sense of efficacy, to see acceptance of their own ability to influence their own direction. In the new environment, workers are expected to set and achieve their own goals as individuals and teams. Because workers will have increased responsibility, more of them are expected to display intentions that help achieve organizational goals. Workers are measured not only by their employer, client, or customer but also by themselves to goals set and achieved.

The implications for curriculum are made manifest by this approach. Learning goals should not be driven by only the teacher but also by enabling the learners to become active participants. Technology enables students to leap forward in this process by allowing them to select activities and learning routes that are more individually driven. Students can move forward at their own pace and can set learning goals that will be determined largely by technology's ability to allow students to access information individually. A day will arrive when teachers will become monitors of the information-acquiring process. Students should be encouraged to set goals and direction and then be monitored for their progress toward obtaining these goals and direction.

Individuals attribute the source of either their own or others' success to a variety of factors. Some people ascribe success to luck, others to heritage, and some to wealth. The future demands instructional practice that attributes success to *effort* rather than to a sense that things happened because that person "got lucky" in the workplace or because of background or because of someone they know of particular importance. In the new economy, in which people are forced to rely on their own "value added" contributions, a person's efforts will be the main factor that drives a sense of direction.

The Value of Meaning

People have always needed to find meaning in the value of their work. In the past, people have often found that meaning through feedback from others. Although people often valued their own work, many were just as likely to value it because others found meaning in it. In the new work environment, people will be functioning more independently from coworkers or contractors than ever before. Many people will work for or with several employers during their careers. Many will work from remote sites connected by technology rather than by shared office space. In this environment, there is much less likelihood that people will find continual support for their sense of meaning.

Subsequently, people will first have to look to themselves to find the meaning of the value of their work before they look to the workplace for this meaning. Recent studies indicate that many recently displaced workers who had often looked to their employer for much of the meaning of the value of their work were particularly disheartened and took longer to recover from the shock of their displacement. If workers don't have a sense of opportunity and don't have a sense of self-direction, it will be nearly impossible to have a sense of meaning in the value of their work. For some workers, even perceiving opportunity and being self-directed won't guarantee that they will have a strong sense of meaning.

The need to design curriculum and processes that build students' abilities to develop their own criteria for meaning and success is critically important. Six enterprise competencies are associated with creating a sense of meaning in the workplace: self-awareness and interdependence, service orientation, craftsmanship, and courage and assertiveness.

Self-Awareness and Interdependence. Workers' ability to be aware of their own behavior and their ability to monitor its effect on other people are critical. Covey (1990) maintains that workers must first be able to be self-aware of their behavior before they can move from a state of dependence to independence and, eventually, in an ideal setting, to interdependence.

> Independence is an achievement. Interdependence is a choice only independent people can make. Unless we are willing to achieve real independence, it's foolish to try to develop human relations skills. . . . The most important ingredient we put into any relationship is not what we say or do, but what we are. (pp. 186-187)

The new economy is a place in which virtual teams form, in which people operate under a wider span of control, and in which the team is a vital component—and therefore, interdependence is critical. The team not only must be aware of and monitor itself but also must take into consideration how it reacts to and works with other groups in the organization.

In the concept of holonomy, workers realize that they must function simultaneously as individuals and as members of a group to find a greater sense of meaning. The workers are individuals maintaining their self-awareness and also members of the group. The workers have to see themselves as getting meaning individually and interdependently from their teams and contributing to that meaning within their organization.

In the 1960s film *The Graduate,* the uncle predicts the future by whispering into Dustin Hoffman's ear the word *plastics.* If the 1960s were plastics, it could be said that the 1970s were oil, the 1980s were money, and the 1990s are an information economy dependent on relationships of teams, individuals, and organizations all connected interdependently and serving each other. *Relationships* is the watchword of the future.

Curriculum design could enable students to work on various projects in a variety of team configurations as well as individually. Curriculum could also afford students the opportunity to participate on virtual teams, that is, team members known to each other only through school partnerships and/or on-line opportunities. Students could also experience some curricula that relate to work-world tasks and challenges, interacting with representatives of local or national partner industries.

Service Orientation. Service orientation is critical as an implicit value to find meaning in the workplace. Robert Greenleaf, quoted in Senge (1992), wrote about the importance of leaders serving those who led. Greenleaf says that leaders exist for those who follow:

> Leader as teacher does not mean leader as authoritarian expert whose job it is to teach people the "correct" view of reality. Rather, it is about helping everyone in the organization, oneself included, to gain more insightful views of current reality. This is in line with a popular merging view of leaders as coaches, guides, or facilitators. (Senge, 1992, p. 86)

Meaning is found in the ability to make a contribution to an organization or to others. The real gains are in the deposits, not the withdrawals. Club and team structures that are the informal curriculum of both middle and secondary schools provide the opportunity to experience performing as serving leaders. Teachers and administrators have the opportunity to build governance and interpersonal behavior based on the model of the serving leader. Such actions change the culture that envelops the curriculum, the instruction, and the schools themselves. Such actions move toward behaviors that support the values and competencies of the entrepreneurial perspective.

Craftsmanship. Craftsmanship and the pride associated with it constitute the foundation of quality. Without quality, any venture is destined to failure. The enterprising person internalizes a sense of quality because meaning is found in the work and the work is first judged by the craftsperson. In the work world, work will increasingly have to meet the standards of individual workers, team members, clients, and supervisors. The curriculum promotes craftsmanship when students generate criteria for quality work as individuals, as team members, and as workers seeking to satisfy clients or supervisors (teachers). The participation in the generation of criteria and in self-assessing work supports the competency of craftsmanship. The awareness of working at times to meet one's own criteria generates meaning and a sense of productive self-worth.

By creating experiences through which students serve multiple clients and audiences, the opportunity to judge the meaning of work is encountered. By recognizing that preset criteria for success is possible, the students begin to join craftsmanship with the other enterprise competencies and begin to move past the passive stance of waiting to be told what to do and waiting for a grade based only on the feedback of the teacher.

Things happen when people write curriculum and deal with meaning. Curriculum designers and teachers often don't just write curriculum, they craft it. This feeling helps define a sense of meaning. Students build this valuable enterprise skill by participating in the process as well.

Courage and Assertiveness. The ability to take intelligent risks is perhaps the way entrepreneurs are most often perceived. All risks are not the same, and the ability to take on different risks is dramatically influenced by the individuals' particular circumstances. Imagine for a moment a rope stretched at 5 feet from the ground. Only a few people might take the risk of attempting to jump over the barrier formed by the rope. Now imagine one end of the rope held at the 5-foot level and the other end rolled out along the ground. Anyone could select a point along the slanted rope to jump over. So, too, do many opportunities need to be presented in which students have the experience of finding differing levels of challenge to test themselves and take intelligent risks. The selection of the challenge, ideally coupled with a vision of success based on criteria, is the foundation for meaning with work when associated with active choice and self-driven risk.

Finally, the ability to capitalize on opportunities and to succeed at the risk taking involves a clear understanding of the difference between aggression, submission, and assertiveness. Methods for interacting assertively require positive sanctions and require explicit teaching and continuing reinforcement. These interactions require greater risk taking by both students and adults because they foster greater questioning of the status quo and can be perceived as threatening. Only by focusing on the paradigm of teaching the entrepreneur, rather than the laborer, does the importance of these institutional risks become clearer. Student assertiveness abilities must include the ability to call for equitable treatment, to demand to be treated with dignity, and to negotiate with others to reach common objectives. The ability to employ the tactics of assertiveness communication and to take risks composes the basis for the enterprise competency of courage and assertiveness that will be essential to life in a changed work environment.

Summary

The values of opportunity, self-direction, and meaning, along with the enterprise competencies, provide a basis for dialogue. Based on the recognition that the workplace has changed, they are presented as a framework for thinking about how enterprising behaviors can be fostered in teaching and supported in the culture of the school. They likely require neither special programs nor courses but rather require attention to a more encompassing view of how curriculum and instruction are designed and delivered. Developing these values necessitates a reexamination of the implicit beliefs and associated activities that influence learning from kindergarten through graduate school.

References

Bridges, W. (1994). *Job shift: How to prosper in a workplace without jobs.* Reading, MA: Addison-Wesley.

Covey, S. R. (1990). *The seven habits of highly effective people.* New York: Simon & Schuster.

Dent, H. (1995). *Job shock: Four new principles transforming our work and business.* New York: St. Martin's.

Drucker, P. (1995, January 29). The network society. *Wall Street Journal,* p. A14.

Hakim, C. (1994). *We are all self-employed.* San Francisco: Berrett-Koehler.

Handy, C. (1994). *The age of paradox.* Boston: Harvard University Press.

Hofstadter, D. (1985). *Metamagical themes: Questing for the essence of mind and pattern.* New York: Basic Books.

Noble, B. P. (1995, January 29). If loyalty is out, then what's in? *New York Times,* p. 21.

Pascale, R. (1996, April-May). The false security of "employability." *Fast Company, 2*(1), 62-63.

Richman, L. F. (1995, April 17). Getting past economic insecurity. *Fortune, 131,* 161-168.

Rifkin, J. (1995). *The end of work: The decline of the global labor force and the dawn of the post-market era.* New York: G. P. Putnam.

Senge, P. M. (1990). *The fifth discipline.* New York: Doubleday.

Senge, P. M. (1992). The leader's new work: Building learning organizations. In J. Renesch (Ed.), *New traditions in business: Spirit and leadership in the 21st century.* San Francisco: Berrett-Koehler.

5

Staff Development

A Process Approach

Fred H. Wood

Staff development is a key process in current efforts to improve educational practice in our schools. It is a process by which professional educators identify what they believe ought to be improved in their schools and then plan and implement learning experiences for teachers and administrators to make those changes a reality. For nearly two decades, this process view of professional development has driven the design and delivery of in-service education.

Since the early 1980s, one of the more popular processes for staff development has been the RPTIM model (Wood, 1989; Wood, Thompson, & Russell, 1981) for school improvement through professional growth and learning. This school-based process has five stages that include readiness, planning, training, implementation, and maintenance. As school faculty members experience and complete each step of this process for designing and delivering their plans for school-based improvement, they learn and use many of the skills and operations identified in the first book of this trilogy, *Envisioning Process As Content.*

The remainder of this chapter will describe the stages of the RPTIM model for school-based staff development. This description will include a summary of the major tasks that occur within each stage and the skills and operations that are learned and used by educators to complete those tasks.

The RPTIM Staff Development Process

Preconditions

The RPTIM process is based on a set of assumptions and the district's commitment of human and fiscal resources. Successful implementation of this approach to staff development requires that these preconditions be in place before a school moves into this process.

The first step in initiating this process is to examine the assumption on which it is based. Clearly, the district and school leadership team must understand the rationale for the tasks and activities within the five stages. Not only should they understand these assumptions, but the leadership team also needs to support them. This means that administrators must take time to examine, discuss, clarify, and, finally, indicate whether they support the following research-based beliefs:

- The school, not the district, is the primary focus of improved practice and staff development.
- Significant changes in educational practices take considerable time and are the result of staff development that is planned and conducted during several years.
- A school culture supportive of improved practices and professional growth is essential to successful staff development.
- All educators should be involved in staff development throughout their careers.
- The principal is key in any staff development effort to improve professional practice.
- Selection of improvement goals that guide staff development should involve those who have a stake in the future of students in the school.
- Those who are changing their professional behavior must make an individual and collective commitment to and feel ownership for the new program and practices before they will want to participate in in-service activities.
- Staff development should enable school personnel to improve professional practices in ways that increase student learning.
- Knowledge about adult learners should serve as a basis for planning and implementing staff development.
- Change in professional practice is difficult and requires systematic support to implement and sustain it through time.
- School districts have the primary responsibility for providing the resources and staff development necessary to implement new programs and instructional practices.
- Staff development should support instructional and program improvement and should be closely linked to instructional supervision, teacher evaluation, and curriculum implementation.
- Staff development, site-based management, and site-based budgeting are all important components of school-based improvements. (Wood & Thompson, 1993)

Another step in establishing a supportive environment for successful implementation of a staff development process is the allocation of adequate resources by the district. This includes identification of funds, personnel, and time required to complete the process within individual schools. Resource allocation also includes ensuring that trained facilitators are available to guide a school faculty through the five stages of staff development (Wood, 1989).

Most of the tasks and activities in the RPTIM stages are completed by a school planning team. The membership of this team consists of representatives from the school, district, and community who have a stake in the future of the students served by a particular school. Typically, the team includes 15 to 18 people, representing teachers, the principal, central office administrator(s), parents, and community and business leaders. This team has the responsibility for developing the school improvement goals and programs, designing in-service programs, and transferring the new programs and improved professional behaviors into practice. They are also responsible for involving others from their stakeholder groups so that the plans they develop and implement include the best thinking and have the support of those they represent (Wood, Killian, McQuarrie, & Thompson, 1993).

Once the school planning team has been selected and resources allocated, the conditions necessary for moving into the RPTIM process are now in place. Now, the school faculty, with the support of their planning group, can begin the process of improvement through staff development.

Readiness

The first stage in this process of school-based staff development is readiness. Several important tasks are completed during this stage, including (a) establishing a supportive climate for change and improvement, (b) developing awareness of the school and educational practices, (c) creating new expectations and commitments for improved practice, (d) selecting new programs and practices, and (e) obtaining support for specific improvements in the school (Wood, 1989; Wood et al., 1993).

Team Building: Establishing a Supportive Climate

Before the planning team begins its work to select improvement goals and programs for the school, it is essential to develop a climate supportive of open communication and collaborative decision making among its membership and within the faculty of the school. For a faculty and the planning team to work effectively in making decisions, "they need to develop the skills, understandings, and relationships necessary to make decisions about school improvement goals and programs" (Wood et al., 1993, p. 4). As people make important decisions about their school, they need to know each other, become aware of the similarities and differences in what they and others value, and use effective communication skills.

The early meetings of the planning team members are spent in small groups sharing information about themselves, identifying what they value in their working relationships with colleagues with whom they work, and setting criteria for evaluating whether they are functioning as an effective group. They also spend time developing and/or practicing some basic skills in listening, two-way communication, self-evaluating, and improving the effectiveness of their group.

In addition to the team-building activities, the group also learns or relearns and practices some basic problem-solving skills. Typically, these include the use of brainstorming to generate alternatives and consensus-seeking strategies. This combination of building understanding of the similarities and differences within the group—what individuals value and why and the knowledge and strengths of the group members—and developing the skills to solve problems builds a planning team that is empowered to make important decisions about improving a school through staff development (Institute for Development of Educational Activities, 1995).

Developing Awareness

In addition to these understandings and skills, early in the readiness stage the planning team needs to become aware of the strengths and weaknesses of the school. Some districts using the process provide the team a data profile on the school. The profiles may include information about such things as student achievement and attendance, parental and student views of the school, descriptions of current programs and practices and their impact, and data related to district goals for improvement. The planning team members discuss, analyze, and clarify this information early in the process.

They also spend time learning about the most promising new programs and practices in education. Awareness of the possibilities for improved practice is accomplished through the team members' involvement in sharing information from professional readings, study groups, presentations by consultants, and workshops. It is important to recognize that the improvement goals and programs selected for a school are limited by what the planning team knows; one cannot choose to do something one does not know about. Thus, awareness of good practice in the school and current ideas in education is an essential starting point for decisions about improvement.

Creating Expectations

Once the planning team has completed its initial team-building and awareness activities, the team begins to create a vision of how the school would operate in 5 or 10 years. This vision includes an idealized view of the organization and operation of the school, curriculum, instruction and learning, involvement of parents and community, and so forth (Chance, 1992). It is developed as the team reads, discusses, analyzes, brainstorms, and reaches agreement about what team members want related to specific areas or aspects of the school program, such as how kids learn and how parents and community resources can be used to support learning.

The final product of vision building is a description of the way the school "should be" in the future. This ideal view of the school is used as a basis for deciding which specific changes and improvements the team wishes to make in the school during the next 5 years. In most cases, it will not be possible to achieve the entire vision in 4 or 5 years. This requires that the planning team make some choices about which of all the possible improvements they will make during the next 5 years.

Selecting Goals and Programs

Given the need for choice, the next activity for the planning team is to select specific goals, programs, and practices the school will implement. To accomplish this, the planning team determines what already exists in the school and discovers other programs and practices related to the vision that exist in other schools and/or are described in the professional literature (Wood, 1989; Wood, Freeland, & Szabo, 1985).

To gather this information, the team members organize into three study groups. Some members of the team work with the faculty to determine what things in the school are consistent with their ideal school and what are inappropriate practices that need to be eliminated.

A second study group identifies schools that are already using programs that might be adopted by the school. This group's members work with the rest of the planning team to determine plans for the site visits to these schools, including the what, who, how, why, and when questions to pursue during the visit. Once the plan for site visits to schools and programs are set, the visits are conducted and the team members observe, interview, analyze, and systematically collect the information requested by the entire team (Wood & McQuarrie, 1984).

A third group reviews the literature related to areas of interest to the planning team. Here information is identified about best practice and research related to programs that might be used to implement the school's vision.

Information obtained by each of the three study groups is then shared with the entire team. On the basis of these data, the planning team selects specific goals, programs, and practices for implementing part of its vision.

Obtaining Support

When these decisions are made, the team designs procedures to present their recommendations to the faculty and to gain approval and commitment to the improvements that eventually will serve as the basis for school-based in-service education. Throughout the readiness stage, there is a concerted effort to inform, get feedback from, and develop ownership by the total school faculty for the final decisions made by the planning team.

During, or before, the initial team-building activities for the school planning team, the school faculty members go through the same small-group team-building and awareness activities. This creates feedback groups that meet with representatives after each planning session. These meetings with the faculty are used to share what is being considered and decided by the planning team, to make sure the team is aware of faculty reaction to the proposal, and to tap the opinions and expertise of the entire school. These sessions also allow the planning group members to identify where they can get strong, broad-based support for specific improvement goals, programs, and practices that they are considering. With this involvement and feedback, the chances are much higher that the goals and programs the planning team proposes will have the support of the stakeholders at the completion of the readiness stage.

At the End of Readiness

By completion of the readiness stage, the planning group has developed a vision for the school and a set of three or four improvement goals and programs for which the faculty has given a clear indication of support. As a result of this process, the faculty is generally positive about the changes that are projected for the school and sees improvement goals as the goals for the future in-service activities (Wood et al., 1993).

Skills and Operations

During readiness, the planning team and, to some extent, the faculty have learned or relearned and practiced the skills of listening, brainstorming, questioning, analyzing, consensus seeking, organizing, data gathering, clarifying, observing, and setting priorities. They have also experienced the operations of decision making, investigating, problem solving, communicating, collaborating, imagining, creating, and inventing. According to Costa and Liebmann in the first book of this trilogy, *Envisioning Process As Content: Toward a Renaissance Curriculum,* these are all important components of an effective process. They are also important tools that can and should be used by teachers and administrators to be effective in all aspects of their professional and personal lives.

Planning

The second stage in the RPTIM staff development process is planning. In this stage, a systematic plan is designed for in-service and implementation to achieve the goals and specific improvements identified in readiness. The five tasks in planning are (a) defining the specifics of what will happen in the school when improvements are in place, (b) conducting a needs assessment, (c) determining resources available for training and follow-up activities, (d) developing a written 5-year plan for making the desired changes, and (e) obtaining faculty and district approval of the school's written plan. As with the previous stage, the planning team serves as a representative group that writes the plan while working closely with school faculty (Wood, 1989; Wood et al., 1981).

Defining the Desired Outcomes

The first task in planning is to determine what faculty, students, and others will be doing when the improvement programs or practices are actually in place (Charters & Jones, 1974). This requires that the actual planning team or a subgroup of that team analyze each of the proposed improvements to identify the specific behaviors, activities, and strategies that teachers, administrators, and students will be using when implementation is complete. This list of

outcomes describes more completely the ideal practice; it is the basis for conducting a needs assessment.

Conducting a Needs Assessment

Once the outcomes analysis is completed, the planning team conducts a needs
assessment to determine what teachers and administrators need to learn before
they can implement the desired improvements in practice within the school. A
needs assessment identifies the difference between knowledge, skills, and attitudes
required when a new program is in place and the current conditions in the school;
it is the gap between "what exists" and "what should exist" (Wood, 1989).

The planning team identifies and then carries out the procedures for collect-
ing data to determine learning needs. This includes such things as direct
observations in the school or classroom, interviews with those who will eventually implement the new practices, and questionnaires that provide faculty
perceptions concerning the extent to which desired outcomes are currently
practiced (Wood et al., 1993). These needs assessment data provide the planning
team with a diagnosis of the specific objectives that ought to be addressed
during in-service (Wood et al., 1981).

Determining Available Resources

Before developing the long-range plan for helping faculty learn and implement the objectives identified through the needs assessment, the planning team
must identify what resources are available to support the plan. Here is where
those developing the plan need to determine the extent of their budget, availability of trainers, access to assistance from central office personnel, and time
allocated to training and follow-up activities after in-service.

Clearly, the availability and extent of these resources will influence decisions about what can be accomplished and how long it will take to achieve their
school improvement goals. Any realistic plan for in-service training and implementation of what is learned during training must take into account the level
of resources to support that plan.

Developing the 5-Year Plan

Armed with the needs assessment data and information about availability
of resources, the planning team develops a written plan for in-service training
and implementation of improved practice and programs. An essential step in
developing an effective plan is to identify and use the expertise available in the
central office. Here is where the central office curriculum generalists, subject
matter specialists, and staff developers are asked to assist the school planning
team in the areas in which improvements are proposed. For example, the central
office staff might help the planning team locate specific in-service programs and
trainers to achieve a thinking skills goal or locate information related to parental
involvement to support learning in the home (Wood et al., 1993).

Usually, the entire planning team takes responsibility for the overall development of the plan and keeps the faculty informed of tentative decisions about

plans through the faculty feedback groups established in readiness. The writing of the plan, however, is typically assigned to a smaller group of two to four team members. If expertise in systematic planning is needed to guide this task group through the development of the written plan, the team seeks that help and may add experts from inside or outside the district to the task group.

The written plan identifies a detailed agenda of training and implementation activities for the first year and a general outline of the following 4 years (Wood, 1989; Wood et al., 1993). The task group working with the planning team finalizes the goals and programs for school improvement, identifies the specific in-service activities that will be conducted to achieve these goals, determines follow-up strategies to transfer learnings from in-service into practice, develops a timeline for in-service and implementation, and decides the expected outcomes for each of the 5 years of the plan. This task group will also work with central office and/or consultants to determine how the school will monitor progress toward achieving the improvement plan and the impact of implementation on the students, school faculty, and others involved with the changes in practice. Finally, the planning team analyzes the plan and then allocates the available resources and builds a budget (Wood et al., 1993).

While decisions are made about different aspects of the plan, members of the planning team schedule meetings with small groups of faculty to share what is being considered and to seek reactions and suggestions. These periodic meetings with faculty during the 6 to 8 weeks of planning enable the team members to inform their colleagues about what they believe ought to happen during the next 5 years and to obtain faculty reactions and ideas about how to improve or strengthen the plan. They also help the planners determine the level of commitment they can expect to the written plan they develop and what changes they might make to ensure support of the plan when it is submitted to the faculty for approval.

Gaining Formal Approval

The final task in the planning stage is to obtain formal approval of the school's written 5-year plan from the faculty and the central office. Once the proposed plan is completed, the planning team develops a strategy for gaining both approval for and commitment to the plan. Of course, if the planning team has informed the faculty about what it has been considering and used the reactions and suggestions from the small feedback group, it already has developed some of this support. Nevertheless, it is important for planning team members to plan a set of activities to acquaint the school faculty with the team's final written plan and obtain formal commitment from a critical mass of faculty members that they will support and pursue that plan. The strategy for faculty approval may include sharing the written plan with the entire faculty, meetings with feedback groups, a faculty orientation, and/or a formal vote on the plan (Wood & McQuarrie, 1984).

District approval and support may be developed by (a) involving central office administrators and board members as members of the planning team, (b) making sure district and administrator organizations are involved in the planning and approval process, (c) briefing key central office administrators about tentative decisions, (d) seeking reactions to tentative plans from central office and other district groups, and (e) involving district curriculum and staff development specialists as resources during readiness and planning (Wood et al., 1993).

At the End of the Planning

By the end of the planning stage, the school has an approved plan for staff development that will enable the faculty to achieve its improvement goals. This plan has the formal support and the commitment of the teachers, principal, central office, and board of education.

Skills and Operations

As with each of the stages, planning involves the planning team and school faculty in learning and using some important skills and operations. These skills and operations, although applied to developing a blueprint for improvement and in-service education, have broad application in the professional lives of educators. Throughout this stage, the planning team and school faculty are using the skills of analyzing, observing, data gathering, consensus seeking, priority setting, judging, listening, and two-way communicating. They are also involved in decision making, investigating, problem solving, communicating, collaborating, creating, and self-evaluating. These all are important operations within the process of planning, whether to develop a staff development plan, to prepare for teaching students, to supervise and evaluate instruction, or to write a more effective curriculum.

Training

In training, the third stage, in-service learning programs are selected, planned, scheduled, and implemented (Wood, 1989). Here is where the teaching and learning of new instructional skills and professional practices identified and planned for in the previous two stages take place.

There are four tasks in this stage. They include (a) selecting and designing effective in-service programs, (b) selecting experienced trainers, (c) scheduling the in-service activities, and (d) ensuring participation of the principal in training. Responsibility for these tasks may be assigned to the school's planning team or a new group of faculty who become responsible for in-service education and follow-up implementation (Wood et al., 1993). The group responsible for in-service in the school is often referred to as the professional development team (PDT).

Selecting Programs

Selection of in-service programs that are consistent with what we know about adult learning is essential to successful training. Prior to choosing programs, the PDT for a school establishes priority criteria for in-service. These criteria should be based on what is known about adult learning (Thompson & Wood, 1982; Wood & Thompson, 1980).

Typically, effective in-service programs include the use of small group or team learning, provide the learners some choices and opportunity for control over their learning experiences, include experimental activities in which the learners have opportunities for directed and independent practice, are delivered by a peer trainer, and conclude with the development of a personal or group action plan for implementing what was learned (Joyce & Showers, 1982; Wood et al., 1993). In addition to these characteristics of effective in-service, another criterion used to select specific programs ought to be sufficient evidence that it will facilitate the achievement of the desired changes in practice.

In-service programs are selected on the basis of these criteria. If one of these characteristics of in-service programs is absent from a packaged program that is selected, then the program is modified to include that item. In cases in which a school develops its own in-service program or hires a consultant to plan and deliver a program, the PDT ensures that these characteristics of effective in-service learning are addressed. The PDT members monitor training practices and ensure control quality for their faculty.

Selecting Trainers

Either during or shortly after the programs are selected and/or developed, the PDT must identify the trainers who have the expertise to facilitate the in-service learning. Expertise implies knowledge of both the professional content and skills to be learned and ability to use effective training practices that are consistent with the research on adult learning. Often, the PDT will seek assistance from central office curriculum administrators and district staff development staff in identification of appropriate in-service leaders. Although the district personnel help, the final decisions rest with the school.

Because of the high cost of trainers and the desire to develop teacher leadership within the school, the school's PDT may decide to train teachers and administrators to become local in-service trainers. As the result, the PDT may arrange with those conducting the initial training to develop an add-on program to train the local trainers as they facilitate in-district training for the school faculty.

Scheduling In-Service

Once the training programs and trainers have been selected or trained, the training activities are scheduled by the PDT. Prior to finalizing a schedule, the PDT develops a comprehensive catalog of all the in-service options available to teachers within the district and through other sources in the geographic area related to their school improvement-staff development plan. This might include such things as training programs delivered at their school; workshops delivered at the district level; state, regional, and national workshops and conferences; and university courses. On the basis of the available training, the school develops a schedule of in-service options for the faculty. This schedule may include training during district in-service days, learning and sharing during faculty meetings, after-school volunteer sessions, use of orientation preschool meetings, summer programs, and other times that may be available for in-service learning.

Ensuring Participation of Administrators

One of the keys to success of any training session is for administrators to participate with their teachers (Sly, 1992). This involvement by principals is important because it shows their commitment to the training and changes that will result from that in-service. It also prepares the principals to support teachers after the training when they are implementing their new learnings back on the job.

At the End of Training

After the training stage is finished, faculty members have learned what they need to implement the new practices and programs defined in the school staff development plan. In-service instruction is completed, and now it is time to transfer what has been learned into daily practice.

Skills and Operations

Throughout the planning, scheduling, and conducting of in-service learning programs, the PDT members use the skills of comparing, considering alternatives, analyzing, organizing, evaluating, judging, data gathering, and sequencing. They also are involved in the operations of decision making, operationalizing, problem solving, communicating, transferring, creating, and designing. These same skills and operations are used by teachers when they plan and conduct instruction for their students.

Implementation

The fourth stage of the RPTIM process is implementation. During this stage, teachers and administrators adapt what they have learned in the controlled setting of in-service programs and make it part of their work behaviors. This is where learnings are transferred into practice. Transfer of in-service learning is not automatic; it is something that must be planned for and facilitated.

Three tasks are important in implementation: (a) providing assistance and coaching when the new learnings are being practiced and refined, (b) providing recognition and rewards to those implementing what they have learned, and (c) making sure those trying to improve current practice have the resources they need. The principal, along with the PDT, plays a key role in facilitating these tasks (Goins, 1991; Sly, 1992; Wood & Kleine, 1988).

Providing Follow-Up Assistance

The first task is to provide teachers and administrators assistance as they attempt to integrate their new skills and knowledge into day-to-day practice. Some of the more common ways to provide follow-up support include direct observations of attempts to use newly acquired skills and understandings by the trainers, peers, principal, and supervisors. Follow-up meetings with the trainers and sharing sessions at which in-service participants can communicate successes and solve problems are also helpful. Without this support and feedback after in-service learning, it is quite likely that what has been gained from training will be lost, and faculty will return to the more comfortable practices of the past (Joyce & Showers, 1982).

During these follow-up sessions, teachers plan and try out what they have learned. They, then, have an opportunity to analyze their activities with the help of a supervisor-coach or a peer. Once they have identified what they are doing well and where they need to modify what they are doing, the teachers redesign their professional behavior and go through additional trial, analysis, and revision sessions. They do this until they have become comfortable and automatic in using the new professional practices.

Providing Recognition and Reward

Making changes in professional practice is difficult and time-consuming. It is important to ensure that those who are making an effort to improve how they do their job be recognized and rewarded (Sly, 1992; Thompson, 1982). This requires that the principal and the PDT make a concerted effort to gather information about what faculty members are doing to change current practice and then recognize those people for their efforts and successes.

Faculty members can be recognized in a number of ways. For example, the principal might ask faculty members to share what they are doing with a new program, have others observe a successful teacher, use faculty meetings as a time to share successes, write thank-you notes for a job well done, and/or invite people from outside the school to observe what a faculty member is doing (Wood et al., 1993). Recognition and reward might also take the form of additional responsibility (Herzberg, 1987), for example, asking a teacher to become a trainer or to coach peers.

Providing Resources

Finally, it is important that the principal ensure that those using the new practices and programs have access to the resources they need to implement what they are learning in training. This includes adequate books and printed materials, audiovisual material, time for coaching, and access to consultants and curriculum experts. Although these resources are identified during planning, they need to be available and distributed when they are needed, when faculty are practicing and refining their learning during implementation.

At the End of Implementation

When the implementation stage is complete, the new program and practices are in place and part of the school's vision is realized. The professional practices that were learned in in-service are now being used in a manner consistent with the written school plan.

Skills and Operations

As principals and others engage faculty in coaching and other follow-up activities, all those involved in these experiences use the skills of observing, analyzing, comparing, questioning, listening, data gathering, evaluating, judging, and empathizing. They are also involved in the operations of decision making, inquiring, problem solving, communicating, collaborating, transferring, and self-evaluating. The degree to which these skills and operations are used effectively determines the extent to which the desired practices from training are actually integrated into the daily operations of the school and classroom.

Maintenance

The final stage of the RPTIM staff development process is maintenance. This stage begins when the desired practices and programs have been learned and operationalized in the school. The focus here is to ensure that improved practice remains in place through time. This stage is also when teachers and administrators continue to refine and extend the use of the innovations that have been put into place. These are the two tasks of this stage in the RPTIM process (Wood et al., 1993).

Ensuring Use

Because there is a tendency in education for schools to return to previous, more comfortable ways of operating, the first task in maintenance is to monitor practice to ensure that new practices and programs that have been installed in the school are still being used. Here is where principals, teachers, and others provide those who have implemented new professional behaviors with feedback about continued use and the quality of use of what they had put in place to realize their vision. Through the use of systematic observations, surveys, teacher self-evaluations, and examination of materials and documents, the faculty members are provided data, both as individuals and as a group, which they analyze to determine the extent to which desired practices are being implemented in their school.

Refining and Extending

In the maintenance stage, educators who have implemented improvements refocus on refining and extending successful changes in practice. Once faculty members become familiar with their new behaviors and begin to see positive results for students, they begin to seek ways they can make more extensive use of those practices and extend their applications to different areas of the curriculum or school (Hord, Rutherford, Huling-Austin, & Hall, 1987).

As faculty members move to this point, the school planning team or the PDT brings them together to discuss their interests and ideas. These faculty groups then begin to develop their own plans for working together or individually to expand and extend effective practices. Organizing to plan and implement may occur through such things as establishing study groups, working with existing teaching teams or grade-level groups, developing action research projects, promoting peer observations, and establishing discussion and support groups (Wood et al., 1993).

To facilitate monitoring and extending activities requires active support. The support includes supervision focused on maintaining effective practice, availability of coaches who can facilitate sharing of information and practices with faculty, and time for people to engage in monitoring and extending effective practice. The focus is on faculty members sharing, planning, and learning from the experiences they have had as they carry out their professional responsibilities.

At the End of Maintenance

When the maintenance stage is complete, the school has implemented and is in the process of monitoring and extending part of the ideal it established with its vision during readiness. It is now time to return to the original vision and begin the process of selecting new goals, programs, and practices that will become the basis for additional planning, in-service learning, and implementation (Wood et al., 1993).

Skills and Operations

In this final stage, teachers and administrators in a school become involved in activities that require them to compare and contrast, consider alternatives, observe and analyze, listen, gather and interpret data, and evaluate and judge. As with the previous stages, they are also involved in the operations of decision making, inquiring, problem solving, communicating, collaborating, creating, and self-evaluating.

Some Closing Thoughts About the RPTIM Process

Interactive Stages

This school-based staff development process has been described as if it is highly sequenced and there is a logical, systematic connection from stage to stage. It is important to understand, however, that the stages in the process are highly interactive. For example, it is quite possible that as the planning team moves through the planning stage, it will discover and make modifications in the improvement goals and/or programs selected in readiness. During implementation, a school faculty may identify and make changes that are needed in the in-service training activities or discover a need for modifications in the written plan. Once in maintenance, it is quite common for the faculty and planning team or PDT to discover new needs and additional opportunities for improvement in the school.

Experiences in any stage after readiness may result in the planning team revisiting and revising the school's improvement goals, plans, and in-service programs. In addition, each spring the planning team examines its plan and develops the details of training, implementation, and maintenance for the next year. Thus, each year, the team and faculty determine and commit to a new set of in-service learning activities, to implementation strategies, and to efforts to monitor and extend new practices in their attempt to operationalize the school's vision.

Process for Today and Tomorrow

Another important point about this process is that as faculty and others become involved, they are learning and using important skills and operations that have broad applications in a wide range of professional activities for teachers and administrators. Educators who are able to make decisions, investigate and solve problems, communicate effectively, work collaboratively, transfer knowledge and skills, develop a research-based vision and pursue it, create new ways of teaching and leading, and self-evaluate are equipped for the uncertainties of schooling in the 21st century. Although educators are planning and implementing staff development for improvement in the schools of today, their involvement in the process described here is giving them the skills and operations they will need to function effectively as teachers and administrators in the future.

When Process Is Content

While writing this chapter, I had an additional insight—that the RPTIM process can be used to prepare educators to teach students to use other important processes. As schools and our society grow to understand the importance of process over knowing specific content, more and more of our staff development will focus on preparing educators to teach in ways that develop students' ability to *do*, rather than to memorize. For example, more and more of the leaders in the public and private sectors are recognizing that problem solving, collaboration, and communication are keys to success in the decade ahead.

We are already seeing major staff development efforts in the school districts such as Adrian, Michigan, to prepare teachers to teach students these processes. Of course, this means they are using a staff development process to teach other processes. Maybe, as Art Costa has said, process will become the content of our staff development.

References

Chance, E. W. (1992). *Visionary leadership in schools: Successful strategies for developing and implementing an educational vision.* Springfield, IL: Charles C Thomas.

Charters, W. W., & Jones, J. E. (1974). *On neglect of the independent variable in program evaluation.* Eugene: University of Oregon, Center for Educational Policy and Management.

Goins, D. T. (1991). *Teacher and principal involvements in managing school-based improvement.* Unpublished doctoral dissertation, University of Oklahoma, Norman.

Herzberg, F. (1987, September-October). One more time: How do you motivate employees? *Harvard Business Review, 65*(5), 109-120.

Hord, S. M., Rutherford, W. L., Huling-Austin, L., & Hall, G. E. (1987). *Taking charge of change.* Alexandria, VA: Association for Supervision and Curriculum Development.

Institute for Development of Educational Activities. (1995). *School improvement process: Site facilitator preparation, Workshop I.* Dayton, OH: Author.

Joyce, B., & Showers, B. (1982, October). The coaching of teaching. *Educational Leadership, 40*(1), 4-10.

Sly, G. E. (1992). *A survey of effective staff development practices in schools implementing school-based improvement programs.* Unpublished doctoral dissertation, University of Oklahoma, Norman.

Thompson, S. R. (1982). *A survey and analysis of Pennsylvania public school personnel perceptions of staff development practices and beliefs with a view to identifying some critical problems or needs.* Unpublished doctoral dissertation, Pennsylvania State University, University Park.

Thompson, S. R., & Wood, F. H. (1982, October). Staff development guidelines reaffirmed: A response to Fonzi. *Educational Leadership, 40*(1), 34-35.

Wood, F. H. (1989). Organizing and managing school-based staff development. In S. D. Caldwell (Ed.), *NSDC staff development handbook.* Athens, OH: National Staff Development Council.

Wood, F. H., Freeland, R., & Szabo, J. (1985, March). School improvement is more than school improvement. *Educational Leadership, 42*(6), 63-67.

Wood, F. H., Killian, J., McQuarrie, F. O., & Thompson, S. R. (1993). *How to organize a school-based staff development program.* Alexandria, VA: Association for Supervision and Curriculum Development.

Wood, F. H., & Kleine, P. F. (1988, Fall). Rural staff development research: A small step forward. *Journal of Staff Development, 9*(4), 2-7.

Wood, F. H., & McQuarrie, F. O. (1984, December). The missing link: A process to select and implement the recommendations. *Journal of Staff Development, 5*(2), 57-64.

Wood, F. H., & Thompson, S. R. (1980, February). Guidelines for better staff development. *Educational Research, 35*(5), 374-378.

Wood, F. H., & Thompson, S. R. (1993, Fall). Assumptions about staff development based on research and best practice. *Journal of Staff Development, 14*(4), 52-57.

Wood, F. H., Thompson, S. R., & Russell, F. (1981). Designing effective staff development programs. In B. Dillon-Peterson (Ed.), *Staff development/organization development* (pp. 59-91). Alexandria, VA: Association for Supervision and Curriculum Development.

6

Preparing New Teachers

Process as Curriculum

Gloria Appelt Slick

The Call for Process Education

Whether in the college or the public school classroom, learning is the business at hand. How learning takes place and how to teach others the many ways to evoke/promote learning are the main foci of preservice teacher education programs. As the profession explores and engages in the processes of restructuring education in the United States, we find ourselves questioning how we go about preparing someone to be successful at helping someone else learn. Our traditional teaching methodologies are challenged by technology with its glitzy graphics and its accessibility to the phenomenal explosion of information, by social changes in the structure of the family unit and value systems, and by diverse populations and people needs. Education in the past has consisted of linear bytes of information that built a knowledge base that gave individuals, it was hoped, the ability to function successfully in society. Instruction today, however, is moving toward a more process-oriented curriculum, in large part because of the volume and complexity of information available to us. This chapter will explore the reasons that teacher preparation programs are turning to process as curriculum. The transition will be considered in light of the most recent reform ideologies and movements.

Process as curriculum in teacher education is emerging from a closer philosophical and experiential relationship between institutions of higher learning and public schools. Instead of a linear accumulation of knowledge and theory in isolation of application, a process-as-curriculum teacher education program provides teacher education students with a focus on the integration of theory and practice while dealing with relevant issues in the profession. The issues are centered on a problem-based curriculum that requires teacher education students to apply appropriate processes to resolve the real-world situations that arise in teaching. A cooperative relationship between public schools and colleges of education makes it possible for students to experience situations that challenge them and require them to engage in creative problem-solving. Higher-order thinking skills and decision-making processes are nurtured through the experiences provided them during their preservice training. The purpose of the two institutions working together is to create a mutually beneficial method for guiding the learning experiences of preservice teachers.

In addition, this chapter will explore the rationale, need, and avenues possible for achieving a process-as-content curriculum in teacher education. It can be easily argued that on-the-job training must be a part of any teacher preparation program, but the real questions are when should this type of training begin, and how should it be implemented? I believe that the solidification of theories and skills presented in teacher preparation programs occurs only when there are opportunities for their application. Articulating, experiencing, and applying the knowledge base through carefully selected processes lead to the progressive development of professional competencies and successful teaching, the essentials of a total teacher education program. A process-as-content curriculum provides opportunities for preservice teachers to be analyzers, problem solvers, consensus builders, decision makers, compromisers, arbiters, and creators of ideas, as well as information gatherers. Future teachers need to learn processes for becoming lifelong learners: to explore, reflect about, massage, and assimilate information and experiences as full participants of the learning continuum in a teacher preparation program.

The Case for Process as Curriculum

Historically, teacher education programs have emphasized how to teach without considering carefully whether the methods being taught were internalized by students. Student teaching has been the timeworn hallmark determining whether preservice teachers could actually apply all that they had learned in their education classes. In the past, learning processes typically focused on empirical data assimilation evidenced by the achievement of linear components of knowledge acquisition. Methodologies that brought about sequential concept assimilation seemed to be the key to successful teaching. The students' learning styles and particularly their level of interactive participation, as well as the processes contributing to the learning event, were not often considered. Today, there is general awareness that all these factors are critical to learning. According to Rogers and Freiberg (1994), significant learning combines the logical and the intuitive, the intellect and the feelings, the concept and the experience, and the idea and the meaning. They further state that when we learn that way, we are whole. Traditionally, educators have thought of learning as an orderly type of cognitive, left-brain activity. According to Rogers and Freiberg, the left brain functions in a linear fashion, assimilating learning experiences step by step in a straight line, emphasizing the parts—the details that make up the whole. Learning theorists and practitioners today view learning as occurring when both sides of the brain cofunction in the assimilation of unfamiliar cognitive stimuli, thereby positing that optimum learning occurs when both logical and emotive faculties are engaged in the learning experience.

The question then becomes, how do we effectively engage both determining functions of the brain for the best possible learning experiences for our students? Learning how to learn throughout a lifetime; knowing how to behave when answers to complex problems are ambiguous, dichotomous, and paradoxical; and generating, organizing, and applying an abundance of technological information are just a sample of the types of educational goals we need to establish (Costa, 1993). Because of the numerous variables involved, our goal must be total immersion of the whole person into learning experiences that provide relevant interaction with important concepts.

It further seems a given that the best way to accomplish this is by providing students with a curriculum that is process focused and problem based. Given the voluminous quantity of information available via technology, it is ludicrous to believe that we can absorb all available information within any reasonable amount of time. Therein lies the dilemma of education in the information age. There's too much information to comprehend, therefore our focus should be on processes—processes to retrieve information, processes for analyzing information, processes for assimilating information, processes for reflecting about information and experiences, processes for using information, processes for creating new information out of current information, processes for discovery of new information, processes for using information to solve problems, processes for working together cooperatively, processes for managing information and people, processes for communicating, processes for establishing belief and value systems, processes for managing change (a given in today's information explosion), and processes for establishing respect and understanding of others, including their differences and their similarities.

Planning for Process as Curriculum in Teacher Education

For process learning to be successfully implemented in public schools, teacher preparation programs and the professors and practitioners involved in doing the preparing will also have to shift to a new paradigm of curriculum and instructional processes. Preparing teachers apart from real school contexts has always been a problem for teacher education (Lieberman, 1992). A curriculum that is process focused as opposed to content focused must be modeled by those persons guiding preservice teachers in their preparatory programs on the college campus as well as in the field. College professors, of necessity, will need to incorporate the process-as-content focus into their classroom teaching and field-based operations. A clear understanding of the processes to be taught and the methodology for teaching them must be in place. Further, there must be a faculty commitment to an emphasis on process curriculum. This move from a content-centered curriculum to a process-centered curriculum will necessitate a close, collaborative relationship between universities and public schools.

Planning for Collaboration

The business of transforming the relationship between institutions of higher learning and public schools to one of mutual benefit and respect will be no small task. There seems to be a general consensus by all parties concerned that this is the direction in teacher preparation that needs to be taken. Both institutions, however, are guided by long-standing traditions of operation that heretofore have been for the most part mutually exclusive. This is somewhat ironic in that the preparation of preservice teachers is inextricably linked to the public schools. Historically, however, the connection between the two has been minimal and generally occurred most often, and for the longest period of time, during a preservice teacher's student teaching. Such a connection has not required any major compromise or paradigm shift by either institution.

To shift, however, to the process-as-content model for teacher preparation by either institution would mean considerable changes and collaboration by both institutions. Among the most tenacious issues of organizational culture needing change are the low values placed on teacher education in the university and on professional development activities in the school—and the concomitant lack of rewards for teacher learning in both places (Darling-Hammond, 1994). She states further,

> Since teacher learning is the primary mission of the Professional Development School, its disdain by these organizations (which both reflects and reinforces the fundamental problems of the profession), threaten the long-term viability of the PDS concept—and the prospects of teaching becoming a profession. (p. 22)

Professional development schools aim to provide new models of teacher education and development by serving as exemplars of practice, builders of knowledge, and vehicles for communicating professional understandings among teacher educators, novices, and veteran teachers. Fullan (1995), in his introduction to the recent ASCD teacher education yearbook, states that there is overwhelming evidence that schools and school districts are conservative rather than innovative as systems and that schools are frequently not particularly healthy organizations for the growth and development of their members.

There are, however, configurations of university and public school collaborations that are much more healthy than the token participation of professors of education who make infrequent visits to supervise students during student teaching and practitioners' occasional contributions to classroom discussions on the college campus. Theory-in-practice—the building of conceptual knowledge through engagement in practice—is being carried on both at existing sites and in the development and explication of new models of schooling—by university researchers and school people working in and with schools at the school site.

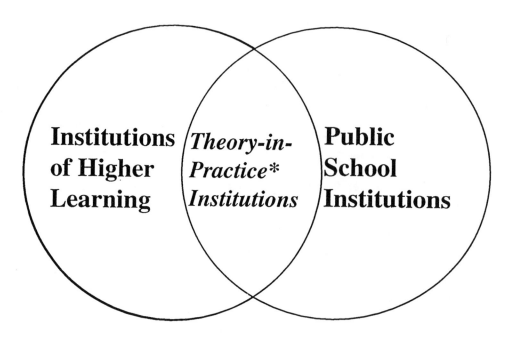

Figure 6.1. A Model of Collaboration

NOTE: *To my knowledge, this term was first used as a hyphenated concept by A. Lieberman in "Commentary: Pushing Up From Below: Changing Schools and Universities," *Teachers College Record, 93*(4), Summer 1992, p. 718.

Such endeavors, of necessity, redefine the role of professors and practitioners alike in teacher education. The scholars involved in these new forms appear to be tackling an expanded view of their work and are increasingly broadening the view of scholarly activity through new research methodologies, new forms of collaborative work, and new structures to support them.

Collaborations between institutions of higher learning and public school institutions require a new structure and conceptual model for both institutions. Figure 6.1 illustrates the simultaneous, continuing autonomy of each institution's structure, while at the same time, it indicates the existence of a new collaborative institution whose focus is on the blending of both parent organizations. Among the factors that distinguish the cultures of public schools and universities are the uses of time, differences in norms and work styles, and traditions regarding status. The development of the new collaborative institution requires risk-taking and risk-making efforts, as well as a great deal of creative thought, by both institutions. In addition, both parent institutions must be willing, committed participants. Needless to say, this commitment brings to the table resources contributed by both in the form of people, finances, and time. New and daring configurations of the use of people, time, and material resources will be required to meet the challenges of teaching in the 21st century. The classroom may not look anything as it does today, but it is certain that technology will connect it to the worldwide community.

Whether the collaborations between the institutions are called professional development schools or something else, certain guiding principles that others have learned from experience must occur if the collaboration is to be successful. In his article "Can School-University Partnerships Lead to the Simultaneous Renewal of Schools and Teacher Education?" Teitel (1994) provides six steps that potential collaborative partners must follow.

1. The partners must decide to collaborate.
2. They must decide who will be involved—how many (from each institution), and what is their position in the organization they represent.
3. They must identify and select their partners.
4. They must define and negotiate the extent of the collaboration.
5. They must build interorganizational structures.
6. They must assess and reassess if the partnership is meeting their needs. (pp. 248-249)

Both institutions must operate from a common philosophical base that energizes their commitment to changes in teacher preparation. All participants—reformers and school people alike—are confronting the complexities of the culture of the school and the process of change. New understandings of practice are changing the roles of reformers as much as their ideas are changing the schools. Professors from institutions of higher learning can no longer just be disseminators of information based on theoretical research. Practitioners can no longer just be frontline problem solvers devoid of a theoretical research base. Both groups of players must take on new roles that join them on a common team with a common purpose: the preparation of teachers for the 21st century—the age of information explosion!

Theory-in-Practice Institutions

The creation of a new institution and/or a new paradigm for effective teacher preparation is a necessity if teacher educators are going to be able to provide the type and quality of professionals that are needed for schools in the 21st century. This new model of teacher preparation will mean that the two institutions intricately involved with each other will need to give birth (through compromise, consensus building, renewal, and innovation) to a teacher preparatory process that has never existed before. It is an opportunity for both institutions to envision the best of all possible worlds existing for the good of all parties concerned. Successful collaborations have the potential of positively addressing the educational and welfare needs of our nation's young people. According to Goodlad (1990),

Settings for internships and residencies must be examples of the best educational practices that schools and universities are able to develop together, and the internships obviously must be conducted collaboratively. These are "teaching schools," paralleling the teaching hospitals essential to medical education. It is the responsibility of universities to work with school districts in ensuring that these teaching schools are in economically disadvantaged as well as advantaged areas and that future teachers get teaching experience in both. (p. 61)

In this quote from *Teachers for Our Nation's Schools*, Goodlad (1990) brings up the issue of school culture by charging teacher educators with the responsibility of providing aspiring teachers with experiences in both the advantaged and disadvantaged classroom settings. An issue that emerges repeatedly in dealing with preservice teachers during their student teaching internship is professional culture shock. The surfacing of this issue begs for the need to immerse novice teachers into the culture of teaching while simultaneously nurturing their cognitive constructs related to the profession. This can best be done not only by making astute field placements of preservice teachers throughout their teacher preparation program but also by including problem-solving, decision-making, participatory discussions among them that involve not only faculty input but practitioners' input as well. In his postulates outlining conditions for effective teacher education, Goodlad states, "Programs for the education of educators must engage future teachers in the problems and dilemmas arising out of the inevitable conflicts and incongruities between what works or is accepted in practice and the research and theory supporting other options" (p. 62). Such discussions not only familiarize education students with the theories and research concerning actual practice but also are realistically couched in actual experiences in which the preservice teachers are participating. The students are therefore "living" the "practice-in-theory" model of teacher preparation.

Teacher Preparation Programs Based on the Process-as-Content Model: What Do They Look Like?

Preparing preservice teachers to function effectively in learner-centered public schools that incorporate process as content means that institutions of higher learning must consider what these schools are like and how they can best prepare new teachers for such schools. Several models of school reform and/or restructuring appear to focus on learner-centered instruction, a core feature of a process-as-content learning environment.

One of the models of teacher preparation, the professional development school (mentioned previously), realistically assumes that the best teacher preparation models that could exist are those that join the forces of the public schools and universities. Efforts to restructure teacher education by redesigning curriculum and establishing professional development schools are already under way in the Holmes Group institutions and many others (Darling-Hammond, 1993).

In professional development schools, public school and university faculty members interact in a conscious effort to merge theory and practice, knowledge and skill development. This new learner-centered emphasis in teacher education is enhanced by collaborative research and development efforts conducted by universities and public schools. These efforts generate and disseminate knowledge that is useful to teachers and constructed with teachers. Teachers have opportunities to engage in peer coaching, team planning and teaching, and collaborative research that enable them to construct new means for inquiring into their practice. Peer coaching and/or mentoring become key issues for the development of novice teachers.

Costa and Garmston (1994) espouse a special type of coaching between a novice and a veteran teacher referred to as *cognitive coaching*. Cognitive coaching is a nonjudgmental process, built around a planning conference, observation, and a reflective conference. The goals of cognitive coaching are threefold: (a) establishing and maintaining trust (between the novice and the veteran teacher), (b) facilitating mutual learning, and (c) enhancing growth toward holonomy— individuals acting autonomously while simultaneously acting interdependently with the group.

Coaching by peers is just one of many processes that should exist in a professional development school. It promotes important communication between the novice teacher and the veteran teacher. Coaching embodies some of the principles of constructivist pedagogy. Much like constructivist teaching, coaching is people based, desires to enhance individual creativity, stimulates collaborative efforts, and emphasizes learning how to learn. Both teacher education programs and public school classrooms must embrace a constructivist philosophy for successful collaboratives to occur. In so doing, they launch the expansive possibilities of sophisticated cognitive construct development. This metacognitive explosion occurs when the creative and unshackled minds of people in a state of holonomy are released. Paradigm shifts in education must occur. The mimetic approach to learning must be abandoned, and teachers must implement practices that encourage students to think and rethink, demonstrate, and reflect (Brooks & Brooks, 1993).

Classrooms and instruction using the constructivist philosophy provide hands-on experimentation on learner-generated questions, investigations, hypotheses, and models. Teacher preparation instruction, whether on the college campus or within a public school, provides instructional settings that invite student participation. This participation focuses on curriculum that is student centered, problem based, and relevant to the cognitive skills and processes necessary to become proficient, effective teachers. Problem-based instruction serves as the vehicle for learners to integrate, reflect on, and transfer the unique knowledge, structure, and modes of inquiry of several disciplines (Costa, 1993).

The advent of technological advances catapults teacher preparation into a new paradigm as well. Information technology in the classroom does much more than boost enthusiasm or expand information sources. Its use fundamentally alters the roles of teachers and students (Peha, 1995). Because of the plethora of information available through technological connections, teachers may find themselves more frequently in the position of saying "I don't know" in answering students' questions but should also be able to reply, "But I know how to find out." The access to information is exciting because it is the first step in access to expertise, to investigations, and to knowledge construction (O'Neil, 1995). Access to these data should be seen as a first step, rather than as a means to an end. It is also important to know that real-world situations and authentic phenomena contain all the disciplines (of information and processes) swirled around within them (O'Neil, 1995). Learning from this perspective becomes a self-regulated process of resolving relevant inner cognitive conflicts that often become apparent through concrete experience, collaborative discourse, and reflection (Brooks & Brooks, 1993). Teacher preparation must be based on these premises and embody the five overarching principles of constructivist pedagogy if future teachers are to be prepared for meeting the challenge of teaching the children of the 21st century.

Brooks and Brooks (1993) outline the five overarching principles of constructivist pedagogy as (a) posing problems of emerging relevance to learners, (b) structuring learning around "big ideas" or primary concepts, (c) seeking and valuing students' point of view, (d) adapting curriculum to address students' suppositions, and (e) assessing student learning in the context of the teaching (as it occurs). The beauty of teacher preparation programs that are based on the theory-in-practice model is that novice teachers will actually have the opportunity to practice what is being preached as well as what is being demonstrated, modeled, facilitated, and guided through a variety of processes.

Models of Process-as-Curriculum Programs in Teacher Preparation

In both models presented here, the assumption is that they represent a collaborative commitment for teacher preparation by universities and public schools. The models described are based on this premise. They both envision cooperative efforts by both institutions. Each necessitates a change in roles of the university and public school personnel.

University Professional Laboratory Experience Model

In this model, the majority of the training for preservice teachers occurs on the college campus. Careful articulation of continuing field experiences, however, occurs along with the university instruction. This model envisions a new type of college classroom environment. The classroom consists of one large room that is arranged into sections providing different work activities. Although there are virtually no physical barriers between these sections of activity, distinct functions are occurring in each. In one section of the room, group collaborative problem solving is guided by a team of instructors composed of a university professor and public school practitioner. In another section, role playing of a problem-solving situation is occurring, once again facilitated by a team of instructors. In still another section of the room that is enclosed to provide a soundproof environment, preservice and veteran teachers are engaged in demonstration teaching with classes of children. Within this section of the room, audio and video equipment records the lessons being taught by both professionals. Around the periphery of the teaching area are small conference rooms with one-way glass, allowing other preservice teachers and their mentors to view the teaching and to critique the instructional processes. In another conference room, a preservice teacher and mentor teacher(s) are watching the videotape of a lesson the novice teacher taught earlier. A professional development plan is generated between these professional learning partners that assists the novice teacher in developing more sophisticated and smoothly presented teaching processes.

Another room is filled with computers used for information gathering and networking purposes while preservice teachers conduct research relative to the classroom experiences they have had in their problem-solving groups, role playing, and actual teaching in the laboratory. In still another section of the large room, two instructors (professor and public schoolteacher) are team teaching using a direct instructional model while incorporating Power Point technology for information imparting. Adjacent to this section is an area of worktables and instructional materials resources. Preservice teachers in this section are busy both individually and in groups preparing peer lessons generated on topics of their choosing that are related to cognitive concepts important to the knowledge base of the teacher preparation program. In a larger section of the big room, a group of 30 to 50 preservice teachers are gathered to hear a presentation by a noted authority in the profession. Exhibits of the novice teachers' projects, displays, and written work are evidenced throughout the entire large room. There is an overwhelming atmosphere of mutual learning and respect among all those present. By interviewing some of the students in this teacher education program, we learn that they are assessed authentically, they develop a portfolio of their expertise throughout their instructional program, and they progress through the experiences and processes of becoming effective teachers at their own pace. Throughout the room are teams of both practitioners and professors engaged in all the instructional processes offered in the room.

A second component of this model takes us into the public school classroom, where once again professors and practitioners are modeling teaching strategies in the public school classrooms. Novice teachers observe, participate, and reflect on their experiences throughout their teacher preparation program. Groups of preservice teachers observe, tape, and write critiques on the demonstration lessons provided them by the professors and practitioners. As groups, the preservice teachers meet to discuss their perceptions of the lessons they have just seen demonstrated. Subsequently, the preservice teachers are taped while teaching lessons to a whole class of students, with both self-critiques and feedback critiques provided by professors, practitioners, and peers.

Communication is a key factor in this collaborative teacher preparation model. It involves mutual respect and understanding that the preservice teacher is evolving and the master teachers—professors and practitioners—are there to guide, facilitate, nurture, and provide feedback concerning the progress of the preservice teacher.

Site-based Professional Laboratory Experience Model

In this teacher preparation model, a cadre of master teachers, professors, and practitioners is identified as the mentor resource group located at a specific public school campus. The expertise of this entire mentor group is available to a corresponding group of preservice teachers assigned to that same campus. A large laboratory room at each campus serves to facilitate direct instruction, simulated problem solving, and discussion seminars, all of which are based on relevant topics and situations existing at the school site that the preservice teachers are encountering. In the laboratory room also are areas sectioned off from the other areas that can be used for role playing, videotaping, and use of and demonstration of instructional technology that augments the instructional processes in the classroom. Preservice teachers are videotaped while they teach lessons on the campus. In the laboratory room, they are able to view these tapes and receive immediate feedback from the mentor resource team as to their success with the lessons. The laboratory setting also houses several small conference rooms in which individual conferences are held with students. Groups of children from the classes on the campus may be brought into the laboratory room from time to time to assist preservice teachers with a transition of working with small groups into the full responsibility of teaching an entire classroom of children. Within the professional laboratory experience room, practitioners, professors, and preservice teachers have access to computers that will allow them to develop instructional packages and to network professionally.

The obvious benefit of this model is that the preservice teachers are receiving all their training in a field setting. Therefore, all the knowledge base, experiences, and processes being explored throughout the preparation program are viewed in the actual workplace. Also, the emphasis is placed distinctly on effective teaching processes. Content specialization and management strategies are taught within the context of the actual setting of the teaching situation. The professional laboratory experience room serves as both a college classroom and a field-based experiential classroom. It is the blend of the best of both institutional worlds. Such an arrangement, however, requires a great deal of commitment to restructure schedules, to the donation of time and talents, and to financial contributions to the total effort. Careful consideration also must be given to the value of professional endeavors that require professors and practitioners to contribute a large portion of their expertise in the field experience arena as related to preservice teacher preparation.

The Mentor Master's Program

Teacher practitioners who decide to obtain their master's degrees in this prototype of professional teacher preparation should commit to preparing themselves to be certified teacher mentors along with the receipt of their master's degrees. Consequently, these "master" teachers would then be professionally prepared to nurture and guide the professional development of preservice teachers. They would be able to help at any point in the field experiences training process. The profession desperately needs well-trained mentors for aspiring neophyte teachers to emulate and work with as they proceed through their training programs. To date, the number of preservice teachers needing positive mentoring relationships far exceeds the number of well-trained mentors. If every master's level teacher education program included an add-on certification in mentoring, soon a large cadre of teachers would be available to assist new teachers into the profession. To be successful mentors, people must have the ability to work with and teach another adult. They must also be able to give constructive feedback, be able to identify a novice's strengths and weaknesses, and be able to help the novice plan a process for growing and improving his or her expertise as a teacher.

In discussing these three possible models and/or solutions to providing process-as-curriculum, problem-based, and constructivist professional experiences, I have identified some of the critical holes in successful teacher preparation programs. One of the most significant holes is the lack of successful, effective collaborations between institutions of higher learning and public schools. The other major hole is the lack of training that public schoolteachers have to be effective mentors. These represent two tremendous mountains to climb, and like most ascents, it will take a lot of perseverance, attempts, and skill to reach the top.

The exhilaration of ascending to the top, however, cannot be matched, and it makes all the effort, strategizing, risk taking, and mistakes worthwhile when, at last, we achieve our goal. Darling-Hammond (1994) gives us some guiding principles to follow in our attempts to work together collaboratively, whether we call these attempts professional development schools, professional laboratory experience schools, mentor programs, or master teacher programs. Whatever we call them, the *process* ultimately is what matters. She identifies the following characteristics of successful collaboration:

- Mutual self-interest and common goals of the participants
- Mutual trust and respect—this is built through time by experiencing common successes prior to the development of a PDS
- Shared decision making—requires successful use of consensus building and communication across organizational and cultural barriers
- Clear focus—needs a strong consensus regarding the outcome, a vision
- Manageable agenda—everyone needs to understand his or her part and to have a sense of the enormity of the venture, thereby realizing that invention and adapting will occur along the way
- Fiscal support—clear expectations and commitment of operational expenses must be made by both institutions
- Long-term commitment—the changes may occur slowly, so celebrations of accomplishment along the way should be made to give courage and impetus for carrying on
- Dynamic nature—experiencing the process of creating a PDS is highly developmental; even carefully developed plans should be expected to change from time to time
- Information sharing and communication—communication within and across institutional boundaries (pp. 209-217)

Concluding Remarks

It seems that we are at significant crossroads in our profession. We obviously need to pool resources in people, time, and materials to meet the challenges we will face in teacher preparation to competently and effectively address the educational needs of children in the future. What must happen will require risk taking and risk making, as well as envisioning a new system of operation. It will take some brave souls moving forward with what they believe is possible and necessary to preserve public school education. The alternatives are to perpetuate the systems as they currently exist. We can allow public school education to fail as a process because we default on meeting the challenges being brought about by the age of technology—the information age. Or, we can plan for the future of the profession, act for the future of the profession, and be the masters of our own ship. Colleges of education cannot do it by themselves; public schools cannot do it by themselves; we must proceed together through compromise, consensus, and creativity to establish a new era, a new system based on collaborative efforts. Our efforts together in teacher preparation must be process focused to continue the necessary renewal of preservice teacher education that meets the challenges of the ever changing world about us.

This process-as-content teacher preparation curriculum means that teacher preparation programs of the future

- Are student centered
- Are problem based
- Develop leadership potential and skills in preservice teachers
- Are interactive, with continuing participatory involvement of students
- Provide a theory-in-practice format that integrates field experiences throughout the preparation program
- Are technology rich for instructional and networking purposes
- Are focused on the *how* (processes) to teach as opposed to the *what* (content) to teach
- Are built and generated on information and skills experienced in real and/or simulated situations
- Enable preservice teachers to be lifelong learners by developing an appreciation for and positive attitudes toward learning
- Assess students authentically by providing them avenues for demonstrating their knowledge base and teaching capabilities while continuously gathering exhibits of their work (These documents of their exemplary work should demonstrate their progressive, professional development throughout the program.)
- Provide numerous opportunities to develop and practice the healthy professional habit of reflection

These characteristics of process-as-content teacher preparation programs can be accomplished through

- Nontraditional university and public school collaboratives
- Laboratory experiences settings
- Professors and practitioners serving as mentors, role models, resource persons, guides, facilitators, advocates of students, and careful, constructive evaluators of students

- Use of instructional processes being implemented by professors and practitioners alike that involve students as active participants in higher-order thinking processes, problem-based issues, and group decision-making processes
- Reflective processes concerning classroom experiences through interactive dialogue with professors, practitioners, and peers
- Student immersion into teaching processes in real as well as simulated and/or role-playing situations
- Personal reflective processing of experiences in daily journals, anecdotal records, and the construction of personal professional development plans

The teacher preparation programs that implement the above-mentioned principles will be those that make it possible for public education to survive and flourish in the future. These schools will originate from innovative ideas that have been articulated by people who have the vision, knowledge, and experience to conceive and express them, which, if they are to have impact, must be transformed by these people into activity that engages people deeply enough to commit them to take risks. Glickman, Lunsford, and Szuminski (1995) refer to the public school and university collaboration as a *co-reform* approach to change in education. For a substantive co-reform revolution to occur, both institutions need to develop a moral framework for decisions about symbiotic programs. Glickman, Lunsford, and Szuminski state that co-reformers need to develop

- A covenant of learning based on the democratic goal of education (i.e., mission, vision, and principles of learning) that serves as the core values of education at both the public school and the teacher education institution
- A democratic charter for decision making that ensures the equal representation of both parties in developing the covenant and subsequent implementation decisions
- A critical study process that includes a data collection process (i.e., action research) to assess the effects of programmatic changes on public school students, future teachers, and current teachers (pp. 18-19)

Who among us will have the courage to meet the challenge? With care and intelligence through the systemic process of change, hard work, and sincere consideration of all those involved, I believe it is possible to make the visions into realities.

References

Brooks, J. G, & Brooks, M. G. (1993). *In search of understanding: The case for constructivist classrooms.* Alexandria, VA: Association for Supervision and Curriculum Development.

Costa, A. L. (1993). How world-class standards will change us. *Educational Leadership, 50*(5), 50-51.

Costa, A. L., & Garmston, R. J. (1994). *Cognitive coaching: A foundation for renaissance schools.* Norwood, MA: Christopher-Gordon.

Darling-Hammond, L. (1993, June). Reframing the school reform agenda: Developing capacity for school transformation. *Phi Delta Kappan, 74*(10), 753-761.

Darling-Hammond, L. (Ed.). (1994). *Professional development schools: Schools for developing a profession.* New York: Teachers College Press.

Fullan, M. (1995). Contexts for leadership and change [Introduction]. In M. J. O'Hair & S. J. Odell (Eds.), *Educating teachers for leadership and change* (Teacher Education Yearbook, Vol. 3). Thousand Oaks, CA: Corwin.

Glickman, C. D., Lunsford, B. F., & Szuminski, K. A. (1995). Co-reform as an approach to change in education: The origin of revolution. In M. J. O'Hair & S. J. Odell (Eds.), *Educating teachers for leadership and change* (Teacher Education Yearbook, Vol. 3). Thousand Oaks, CA: Corwin.

Goodlad, J. I. (1990). *Teachers for our nation's schools.* San Francisco: Jossey-Bass.

Lieberman, A. (1992, Summer). Commentary: Pushing up from below: Changing schools and universities. *Teachers College Record, 93*(4), 717-724.

O'Neil, J. (1995, October). How technology is transforming schools on technology and schools: A conversation with Chris Dede. *Educational Leadership, 53*(2), 6-12.

Peha, J. M. (1995, October). How K-12 teachers are using computer networks. *Educational Leadership, 53*(2), 18-25.

Rogers, C. R., & Freiberg, H. J. (1994). *Freedom to learn* (3rd ed.). New York: Macmillan College.

Teitel, L. (1994, September-October). Can school-university partnerships lead to the simultaneous renewal of schools and teacher education? *Journal of Teacher Education, 45*(4), 245-252.

7

Developing Adaptive Schools in a Quantum Universe

Robert J. Garmston
Bruce M. Wellman

Our purpose in this chapter is to extend the dialogue relating information from the new sciences to the processes of organizational development and school improvement. We do this with humility, because the information base is relatively new to nonscientists and admittedly incomplete for ourselves, and with caution, recognizing that simplification of the topic is necessary but dangerous in so brief a chapter. Two dangers occur with a simple treatment: First, concepts might be trivialized, and second, applications of new science principles might be made to sound too certain and concrete—because in truth, the new findings are disturbing, even to the scientists discovering them, and how to apply them in human organizations is still far from obvious. We hope to avoid these two concerns in what follows as we examine discoveries from the new sciences, explore how these principles might be used to rethink approaches to school improvement, and suggest some practical tools and tips for school refinement leading to improved and continuous learning for all stakeholders.

The headwaters of our work lie in the new sciences: quantum mechanics, chaos theory, complexity theory, fractal geometry, and the new biology. It also flows from a constructivist perspective of learning and leadership, democratic values, and our personal experiences in a variety of educational roles—teacher, curriculum consultant, principal, superintendent, professor, and our current work as educational consultants with schools, school districts, and educational agencies throughout North America.

As we struggle to understand and improve the organizations we call schools, the new sciences reveal to us that chaos and order are part of the same system, existing simultaneously. It is increasingly clear that we live not in a world of *either/or* but in the dawning of a world of *both/and*. The appearance of order or chaos is determined by subtle changes in conditions within and around the system. We learn that schools are dynamical systems—systems that are continually influenced by many variables, just as wind, temperature, and moisture affect a weather system and affect each other, making weather forecasts and the course of school improvement unpredictable in their details but not in their patterns.

Briggs (1992) describes this new world as follows:

> It appears that in dynamical systems chaos and order are different masks the system wears: in some circumstances the system shows one face; in different circumstances it shows another. These systems can appear to be complex; their simplicity and complexity lurk inside each other. (p. 20)

We believe that information from the new sciences can clarify the challenge to educational leaders. The new challenge is not about working harder—there is hardly a profession in which people pour out as much energy and work—but it is about working in new ways within principles suggested to us by the new sciences.

What Is an Adaptive School and What Is a Quantum Universe?

The Adaptive School

Our first essential metaphor comes from the field of evolutionary biology. As biologists and paleontologists observe present-day animal species and examine their evolutionary history, they are redefining the meaning of success as a species. In the national parks of South Africa, more than 40 species of wildebeests roam the grasslands. This ability to develop new and subtly different species was long seen as a sign of evolutionary success. Wildebeests are specialists, grazing in dry, open spaces and willing to migrate long distances in search of their preferred niche. Because of these eating habits, they, like other specialists, are more sensitive to environmental changes and under greater evolutionary pressure than are generalists. Wildebeests are adapted through specialization to specific conditions within tightly defined boundaries.

Paleontologist Elizabeth Vrba was one of the first to notice and question this notion of success as she studied the fossil record and speculated about the driving forces beneath these changes. She also noted another significant species in the parklands of Africa, the impala. In Kruger National Park in South Africa, more than 72% of all antelope present are impalas. Impalas thrive in a wide variety of vegetation and can make themselves at home in many different settings ranging from open savanna to woodlands. Because of this flexibility, impalas are highly adaptive and are able to adjust as conditions around them change (Shell, 1993).

All around us, we see organizations struggling to attain the impala's degree of adaptability as the climate around them continues to shift. As an example, the Eastman Kodak company is aggressively embracing the electronic era as it shifts its core business from film-based images to digitally created and manipulated pictures (Bounds, 1994).

The best counterexample of adaptivity may be the U.S. postal system, which may not be sure what its core business is. Year by year, the private express package firms and the newer electronic carriers erode its volume. The postal system, like the wildebeest, is adapted to a defined niche and has not yet figured a way to migrate to new feeding grounds.

The traditional North American high school also serves as a striking form of an adapted, not adaptive, organism. Designed in another time for the purposes of that time, typical high schools often show a remarkable lack of flexibility, with staff members clinging to tightly defined niches within increasingly fragile specialties.

The basic design of the "modern" high school dates to 1892, when an august body called the Committee of Ten met to develop uniform entrance requirements for colleges. Their goal was to create a smoother transition from high school to college for the elite students of the day. It is important to note that in 1890, only 360,000 students, ages 14 to 17, attended high school in the United States. That was around 6.7% of the total age group. And of that number of students, only a small percentage was college bound (DeBoer, 1991).

The basic course structures the Committee of Ten recommended are still in place today. In a rapidly changing world, we cling to the comfort of tradition and do not effectively question the roots of our institutions and norms. The students we serve and our expectations for them are substantially different from the structures that contain them.

To be adaptive, organizations need to continually ask themselves two vital questions: (a) Who are we? and (b) What is our purpose? Schools create adaptivity by

- Basing decisions on these two questions and filtering their questions and responses through agreed-on core values, such as a respect for human differences and respect and caring for others
- Shifting decision-making authority to the people most influenced by the decision
- Restructuring the day and year to increase the time teachers have to interact collegially with one another
- Setting outcomes and standards that signal a passion for excellence and habitual attention to qualities that are based on real-world needs
- Supporting faculties in collaborative setting and working toward self-defined goals

If adaptivity is the central operating principle for successful organizations and for successful schools, then we must search for sources of energy to vitalize and invigorate these processes.

⌄ A World of Energy—Not Things

Our century-old school designs draw on even older models of how the world works. The architects of the 17th-century scientific revolution, René Descartes and Isaac Newton, pictured the universe as a giant machine and informed this vision with the then modern metaphor of the world as a giant clock governed by simple and direct cause-and-effect relationships. Science was shaped by this sensibility, which in turn shaped the structure and function of social institutions and our view of human interactions. In this framework, the world is a collection of discrete entities or substances. Basic materials then are composed of tiny bits of isolated matter, and this matter is separate from the sources of energy with which it interacts (Devall & Sessions, 1985).

In that model, still pictured in most textbooks, electrons orbit a nucleus composed of protons and neutrons. The number of protons in the atoms of an element determine the element's chemical composition. All atoms are extremely small. And the constituent parts are smaller still. To see the nucleus with your naked eye, the atom would have to be the size of the dome of St. Peter's Cathedral in Rome. Typical textbook pictures of atoms show the inner parts as little colored BBs, leading to a belief in solidity and "thingness."

This view of the "nature of things" remained intact for almost 300 years. Then, in the early part of this century, a revolution in the field of physics began reshaping human thought in ways that still ripple through all science and is causing a radical rethinking of our most basic assumptions about how the world works.

The formal name for the 20th-century revolution in physics is *quantum theory*. This new approach to atomic theory was developed in the 1920s by an international group of physicists that included Niels Bohr from Denmark, Louis de Broglie from France, Erwin Schrödinger and Wolfgang Pauli from Austria, Werner Heisenberg from Germany, and Paul Dirac from England. Exploration of the quantum world focuses on the identification, behavior, and interactions of subatomic particles.

Quantum theory moves beyond the planetary model of the atom. In the quantum world, "thingness" gives way to a conception of a world composed of energy—a world in which subatomic particles appear as waves of probability. These probabilities are not probabilities of things but rather probabilities of interconnections. This view of the natural world shows us a universe composed of webs of relationships created from and connected by energy in motion. The term *quantum mechanics*, the formal name for this way of studying the world, means bundles of energy (quantum) in motion (mechanics) (Capra, 1991).

This is a world governed by paradoxes. In the quantum world, elementary matter loses its "thingness" by displaying two identities. Matter can appear as particles, localized points in space, or it can appear as waves, energy spread over an area of fixed volume. The total identity of matter is known as a wave packet. It contains the potential for both forms, particles and waves. This wave packet contains two complementary aspects of one existence. These two aspects cannot, however, be studied at the same time. This essential paradox was first noted by physicist Werner Heisenberg and is known as Heisenberg's uncertainty principle.

Physicists can measure the position of basic particles, or they can study the pattern of movement and momentum by concentrating on the properties of the wave. They are unable to do both at the same time. Quantum matter is influenced by the very act of observation. If the investigator chooses to study wave properties, matter appears in wave forms. The act of observations joins in the greater process, removing the ideal of a pure objective science. To observe and measure is to make a choice. In such choice making, the observer joins in the system being observed. Each act of observation is also an act of influence.

The paradoxes of the subatomic world are modeled today in human social systems. School improvement has a dual nature, a focus on content and a focus on process simultaneously. One cannot be considered without the other. Our need to measure, record, and report may actually inhibit deep reforms. The act of measurement becomes an act of participation, signaling values about the use of time, talent, and money.

In quantum schools, leaders pay attention to the flow and interchange of energy. Energy, not things, becomes the avenue to attainment. Marshaling, focusing, and developing energy, information, and relationships become the role of leaders (Wheatley, 1992). We expand on this idea with a set of four leadership roles later in this chapter.

Tapping Energy Fields in a Quantum Universe: A New Symmetry of School Improvement Processes

To use emerging understandings of the quantum world for school improvement, educators must be willing to move beyond information provided them by the five senses and consciously work with that which is not so easily discernible but powerfully present in the ceaselessly flowing quantum soup of the universe (Chopra, 1989). Modern precedent for this orientation began early in the 20th century when systems were devised for converting sounds into electromagnetic waves and transferring these directly through space, without connecting wires, to a receiving set. It wasn't long before radio was taken for granted. Later, we learned to transmit images via television. Today, we rarely question this miracle. More recently, faxes, cordless phones, and information highways are becoming coins of the realm as systems of instantaneous, flexible communications almost anywhere in the world.

Before modern times, precedent for this orientation existed in the ways we naturally used energy *fields*. These phenomena have been used by humans even before the dawn of consciousness. Gravity, magnetism, and static electricity are examples. We know of their presence because we have evidence of their results. We can experience their effects but not hear them. We can feel them but not see them. We can use them but not put them in our pocket or hand or even accurately diagram them.

In the future, we may take for granted that *human* energy fields exist and that educators can deliberately tend, harvest, and use these to support schools and the people within them to be continuously adaptive. Costa and Garmston (1994) report evidence of five such fields they term *states of mind*. These five states are efficacy, flexibility, craftsmanship, consciousness, and interdependence (see

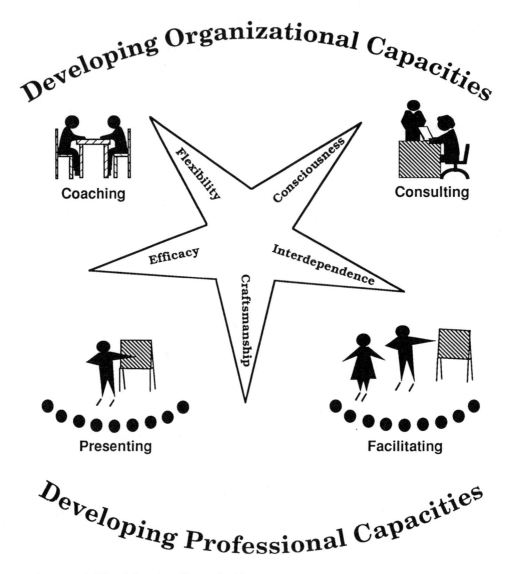

Figure 7.1. The Adaptive Organization

Figure 7.1). The first four are related to independence. In a quantum universe, each unit is independent and autonomous—a complete system unto itself. But also characteristic of a quantum universe is that no one or no thing is ever completely alone, truly an island, or fully separated from the larger systems encompassing it. The state of mind of interdependence is the connecting element between the individual and the unit, between the school and the district, and between the district and the community.

These states of mind are the catalysts, gyroscopes, and energy sources fueling self-renewal and high performance. For an individual, they represent the continuing tensions and resources for acting holonomously, that is, independently and interdependently. For an organization, they form an invisible energy field in which all parties are affected as surely as a strong magnetic field affects a compass. Taken together, they are a force directing persons toward increasingly authentic, congruent, and ethical behavior, the touchstones of self-improvement and renewal. The culture of the workplace will either encourage the development of these states of mind or suppress them.

Efficacy. To be efficacious is to believe one can achieve and to be willing to exert the necessary effort. Efficacious people have an almost unassailable belief in the likelihood of their own success (Garfield, 1986), work harder then those who are not efficacious, persevere through failures and disappointments, and experience less stress (Laborde, 1984). They control performance anxiety and recognize what is not known by the self and productively seek to learn it. They regard events as opportunities for learning. Fullan (1982) regards efficacy as a vital factor for successful implementation of change. Rosenholtz (1989) found that teacher efficacy influenced student learning. Poole and Okeafor (1989) found that the dual factors of teacher efficacy and interdependence significantly predicted the implementation of new curriculum guides.

Flexibility. Peak performers have and exercise multiple perspectives (Garfield, 1986). They are able to view events and circumstances egocentrically through their own eyes, allocentrically though the eyes of others, macrocentrically from an objective third-party position, historically from a futures orientation, in detail, and in broad strokes. They are open and tolerant of differences. They are creative. They have the capacity to change their minds as they receive additional data. This state of mind is prerequisite to the more advanced forms of classroom management, curriculum, and lesson planning.

Craftsmanship. The drive for elaboration, clarity, refinement, and precision is borne by the state of mind of craftsmanship. High-performing individuals and groups strive for mastery and improvement. They persevere to resolve disequilibrium between present and desired states. They create, hold, calibrate, and refine standards of excellence (Costa & Garmston, 1994). They seek elegance. They strive for precision in language and thought. They know they can continually perfect their work and are willing to pursue continuous learning.

Consciousness. Self-reflective consciousness is a recent development in human evolution. It is a state of mind of catalytic properties because it is the state of mind prerequisite to self-control and self-direction. Consciousness means that one is aware that certain events are happening (thoughts, feelings, intentions, behaviors, etc.) and can direct their course (Csikszentmihalyi, 1993). Awareness of others' styles, values, and behaviors; alertness to patterns in group interaction; the ability to hold and monitor one's progress within a plan; and moment-to-moment metacognition all flow from this source. Although everything one thinks, feels, smells, sees, and remembers is a candidate for entering consciousness, the nervous system has definite limits on how much information it can process at any given time. Therefore, an important capacity of consciousness is the ability to selectively attend to stimuli.

Interdependence. Interdependence is achieved by adults who have attained the highest developmental level of meaning making (Kegan & Lahey, 1984). Persons enjoying this state of mind regard conflict and divergent views as opportunities to learn, they are autonomous and self-authoring without self-sealing logic, and they are more likely to be altruistic. They see the potential within groups, can set aside their own needs, know that they and their work benefit from collaboration, and are willing to change relationships to achieve those results.

Engaging and Focusing Five States of Mind in Schools

One fated day in 1961, Edward Lorenz, a meteorologist at the Massachusetts Institute of Technology, went out for a cup of coffee. That simple event changed forever our understanding of the use of energy and data in dynamical systems. As we noted earlier, a dynamical system is one being continuously affected by a variety of influences, each of which, in turn, affects the other. Weather, which is influenced by wind speeds, humidity, temperature, and air pressure, is a classic example of a dynamical system. So are schools. Lorenz was working on a simple three-variable model in forecasting weather. Discovering that he needed to extend his forecast, he set a second run. Because computers were quite slow in those days, he rounded off one number by 0.02%. He went out for coffee. When he returned, he found a set of numbers that looked nothing like his original forecast.

At that moment, two fresh understandings of the world were born. First, minor changes in initial conditions will produce major changes in dynamical systems. Lorenz's minute rounding of a number produced a significantly different pattern for the weather ahead. Second, more data will not permit more accurate predictions in such systems. Because each event affects another, which in turn affects another, more information complicates forecasts to a point of uncertainty, rather than understanding, of what is to be.

Lorenz's work led to the butterfly metaphor popularized in the movie *Jurassic Park.* Because the wind generating from the wings of a butterfly affect tiny air currents around it, and because tiny inputs into dynamical systems create major changes, a butterfly stirring the air in Peking can influence a storm system over New York City some time later. Or, in a parallel metaphor, a pebble, under the right conditions, can stimulate an avalanche.

The butterfly principle is at work when fractional changes in degrees of temperature on the ocean surface turn tropical storms into hurricanes. It is working when in a middle school, a small group of teachers decide to intervene with the norm of negative and put-down humor in the hallways by modeling positive comments to each other and students. They achieved major changes in this aspect of school culture within 3 months.

Schools, like weather systems, are nonlinear systems that change radically through the folding and refolding of feedback into themselves. Because tiny inputs reverberate into big changes, we can work for transformational results by deliberately influencing the right inputs. Both the energy fields and events stimulated by the five states of mind are so webbed in the interactions between people in an organization—adult to child, child to adult, person to system—that the slightest twitch anywhere becomes amplified into unexpected convulsions somewhere else in the system. The web of values, visions, and culture, when plucked, reverberates throughout an entire gossamer network.

States of mind can by learned, mediated, and brought to bear fruit in an organization dedicated to tending them and harvesting them as resources. This is important because not only are they the self-referencing resources of high-performing individuals, but also, in an organization, they create the interacting energy fields in which all parties are collectively affected—as surely as a strong magnetic field affects a compass (Berman & McLaughlin, 1977; Poole & Okeafor, 1989).

Out of Chaos Into Complexity: How Adaptive Organizations Operate in a Quantum Universe

A major tenet in the scientific study of chaotic and complex systems is that components that initially seem unrelated—components with no direct connections—interact and influence one another (Gleick, 1987). As the energy in the system feeds back into itself, it is slightly amplified during each return loop, achieving results seemingly out of proportion to the degree of initial input. The feedback loop set up by a microphone placed too closely to a loudspeaker is an unpleasant example of this phenomenon.

In other systems, almost magical-like outcomes occur when the system's energy reaches threshold levels. In the quantum world, subatomic particles jump from one energy state to much higher or lower states without passing through intervening levels. This so-called quantum leap is a measurable and much studied event.

In human organizations, we must learn to embrace complexity, seeking patterns of order beneath the surface chaos, and continually search for structures and patterns of interaction that positively release and amplify the energies within the system. To do so, school organizations must attend simultaneously to twin goals: a focus on developing organizational capacities for adaptivity and a parallel goal of developing the professional capacities of all employees (see Figure 7.1). We regard the subtopics related to each of these goals as a continuing curriculum outline for school leadership teams. These are the areas about which leaders in adaptive schools need to be continually getting smarter. To navigate within the first goal, we offer the map shown in Figure 7.2 as a guide to the processes of developing organizational capacities.

Processes for Developing Organizational Capacities for Adaptivity

Initiating and Managing Adaptivity

Continuous renewal in complex human systems requires ongoing dialogue within the organization and between the organization and its surrounding

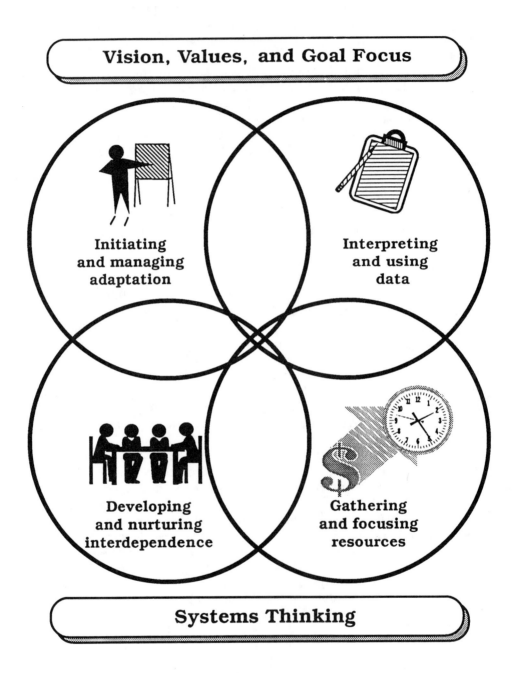

Figure 7.2. Developing Organizational Capacities

environment. The essence of adaptivity is the ability to change form while staying true to core identity. This presumes that the organization's identity is deeply understood and that there is clarity and consensus regarding core purposes. It is often easy to confuse task with purpose and role with identity. The willingness to struggle and continually define and refine "who we are" is one of the hallmarks of the adaptive organization. Another hallmark of such an organization is shared knowledge and skills in managing change and the psychological transitions that come with change (Bridges, 1980). In a world in which change is a norm, not an exception, such knowledge and skills must be in the portfolios of all leaders.

Developing and Supporting Vision, Values, and Goal Focus

An organization's identity is shaped by many interacting factors. The context within which a school operates has much to do with shaping the mission, vision, values, goals, and norms of the work culture. The school's responses to the questions "Why are we here?" "What should we do?" and "How should we do it?" are evidence of the organization's commitment to its role and to itself. Congruence between vision, values, and goals releases and focuses the deeper energies within the hearts and minds of all engaged in the enterprise.

Developing and Nurturing Interdependence.

As discussed earlier, interdependence is a state of mind representing both an organizational core value and an energy field that shapes the actions of those within it. The degree of interdependence is a central capacity that must be continually nurtured within the system. This is the capacity to draw strength from one another, to seek clarity and shared effort in the often difficult work of modern classrooms, schools, and districts.

Developing and Applying Systems Thinking

In chaotic and complex systems, cause and effect are often separated from one another by both time and distance (Senge, 1990). Today's difficulties are rooted in solutions to yesterday's problems. For example, changing demographic patterns in a community accumulate through time until we notice that once successful teaching strategies no longer motivate the students now served by the school. When we apply systems thinking, we look for patterns of interaction within the system and subsystems, seeking key and often nonlinear relationships between seemingly unrelated elements. In this way, new images of the territory emerge, making possible more creative responses within a greater sense of the whole.

Generating, Interpreting, and Applying Data

Data in and of themselves have no meaning. Meaning develops when skilled leaders support individuals and groups in generating, interpreting, validating, and owning the data. When this is not done, objective and even high-quality data are often rejected. This helps explain the often low impact of standardized test scores as a means of motivating school and classroom renewal efforts. Facilitative leaders also need to support the application of data to real problems and real solutions. By establishing such linkages, the data develop deeper importance and become a resource, not a burden to be forgotten or sidestepped.

Gathering and Focusing Resources

Focusing resources is a key organizational capacity. When purpose, core values, and goals are clear and widely shared within the organization, deciding where and how to target resources becomes easier. The greatest underused resource within most schools and districts is the resource of adult learning, planning, and reflecting time. In adaptive schools, time for adult interactions is a critical statement of values and a practical recognition of the importance of this vital energy source.

The processes of developing the organizational capacities described above, however, are not sufficient. The parallel goal of developing professional capacities must be addressed at the same time. We offer the following six areas for consideration as the territory to be explored within this map (see Figure 7.3).

Processes of Developing Professional Capacities

Fostering Collegial Interaction

This is a necessary professional role and one that does not develop without mindfulness, training, and commitment to self and to others. True colleagues develop teaching materials together, plan together, seek each other's help, observe each other teach, and reflect together about their students and their teaching (Little, 1982; Rosenholtz, 1989). Coaching skills are a vital component in the collegial relationship. In too many settings, collegiality is confused with conviviality. Here we move beyond staff room conversations to real dialogue about learning and teaching.

Engaging the Cognitive Processes of Instruction

Teaching is among the most cognitively complex of all the professions. A teacher's decision-making and metacognitive processes before, during, and after teaching may be the most important component in his or her professional portfolio of skills and awareness (see Costa & Garmston, Book II in this trilogy). These are the essential planning, in-flight monitoring, and reflecting tools that support high-performance teaching and continuous professional renewal.

Developing Knowledge of the Structure of the Discipline(s)

Content knowledge is insufficient to ensure high-quality instruction in the academic disciplines for which each teacher is responsible. Professional capacities are informed by knowledge of the deeper structure of the discipline with awareness of the organizing principles, cognitive skills, methods of inquiry, and required habits of mind for work in the disciplines. Teachers' manuals and

Figure 7.3. Developing Professional Capacities

in-service sessions on teaching strategies typically do not open up this territory. The critical arenas for exploration here are these: (a) What do experts currently believe is the most valid content in a particular field? (b) How do they inquire into this field? and (c) What is the path from novice to expert thinking and action in this field?

Enhancing Self-Knowledge, Values, Standards, and Beliefs

True professional capacities are rooted in the essential knowledges of self. As we search for clarity about the essence of our professional identity, we uncover our values and beliefs about living, learning, and how to be successful. Related to these areas of understanding are the issue of standards for performance and standards for products. These standards apply to our own work and to the expectations we hold for others. Self-knowledge here is not enough; we need to constantly filter for congruence between our inner structures and our outer actions and communications (Dilts, 1990).

Increasing Repertoire of Teaching Skills

Like the queen on a chessboard, the teacher with the most moves has the most options and the greatest degree of influence. There is always another way to do things. As a profession, we must move beyond the folk wisdom that governs discussions about teaching and learning and reach out to the knowledge bases to constantly expand our repertoire (Saphier & Gower, 1987). This area of the map interacts dynamically with the other elements. Academic disciplines have content-specific teaching repertoires. For example, skilled elementary teachers know which math manipulative material to use to introduce equivalent fractions, and experienced middle school language arts teachers know which short stories engage their learners as they explore literary elements such as character, plot, and setting. The nature of the learners also has a major influence on appropriate pedagogical choices and options.

Expanding Knowledge About Students and How They Learn

The students in our schools bring their own unique characteristics to the learning process and to the culture of the school and classroom. Who they are to us as individuals and who we are to them matters first and foremost at the human level. In any group of learners, we face a variety of learning style differences, requiring multiple approaches to both content and process (Gardner, 1983). Within a typical classroom, we also encounter a remarkable range in developmental levels, often spanning a 4- to 6-year spread in cognitive age within a grade-level cohort (Goodlad & Anderson, 1987). Added to this are the significant variations in cultural beliefs, perceptual style, values, and approaches to learning embedded in our changing student population and their families.

Developing Four Leadership Roles

In the adaptive school, leadership is shared in pursuit of the goal of developing organizational and professional capacities for adaptability. At the deepest level, leadership is about directing and adding a positive charge to the many energies within the organization. We offer definitions illustrating the major functions of four major leadership roles and distinctions between the roles (see Figure 7.1).

In an adaptive school, all the players wear all the hats. Whether they are managing themselves, managing students, or leading other adults, knowledge and skill in each of the hats is a prerequisite to fully functioning, interdependent teams. Leadership is a shared function—in meetings, in staff development activities, in action research, in networking different levels of the organization, and, indeed, in classrooms as well. Recognizing hats and knowing when and how to change hats is shared knowledge within the organization because when roles and work relationships are clear, decisions about appropriate behavior are easy. In an adaptive organization, clarifying and aligning the twin goals, developing the four hats, and harvesting the five states of mind become the organizing processes of the system and live at three levels: the district, the school, and the classroom.

Facilitating

To facilitate means to make easier. A facilitator is one who conducts a meeting in which the purpose is shared decision making, planning, or problem solving. The facilitator directs the processes to be used in the meeting, using nonjudgmental, facilitative behaviors. The facilitator choreographs the energy within the group, maintaining a focus on one content at a time and one process at a time, clarity about task and procedures, and positive relationships. The facilitator's goal is to support the achievement of a maximum amount of work being accomplished in a minimum amount of time with a maximum amount of group member satisfaction. The facilitator should never be the person of positional power.

Presenting

Presenters teach groups. This role is most closely associated with staff development work but is also often a portion of team meeting agendas. The goals in a presentation are to develop knowledge, skills, and attitudes that will be applied in persons' work. How content is presented often determines whether the content will be internalized by individuals and groups and whether it is acted on. To present is to teach and requires clarity about outcomes, interactive teaching strategies, and ways to assess the effectiveness of the learning (Garmston & Wellman, 1992).

Coaching

Coaches mediate the development of invisible skills—cognitive operations and states of mind—particularly the states of mind of consciousness and interdependence. In its original derivation, the term *coach* referred to a form of conveyance. To coach is to carry valued individuals from where they are to where they want to be. In coaching, a developmental stance is taken regarding the perceptions, mental processes, and decisions of high-performing individuals and groups. Coaches remain nonjudgmental, employ skills of reflective questioning and inquiry, and help others direct the consciousness to the most useful stimuli. By focusing on the inner thought processes, perceptions, and decision-making processes of the persons being coached, skillful coaches mediate the five states of mind, developing resources for present and future actions (see Costa & Garmston, Chapter 9 in this volume).

Consulting

Consultants bring expertise to the relationship and an intention that their expertise be used by the other party. Consultants can be information specialists or advocates for content or process. As information specialists, the consultants deliver technical knowledge to other persons or groups. In this aspect of the consulting relationship, information is provided without recommendation. As content advocates, however, the consultants, on the basis of their broader knowledge, will encourage the other party to use a certain instructional strategy, adopt a particular curriculum, or purchase a specific brand of computers. As process advocates, the consultants attempt to influence the client's methodology, for example, recommending an open meeting rather than a closed one to increase trust in the system. To be effective, consultants must have trust, commonly defined goals in the work relationship, and the client's outcomes clearly in mind (Block, 1981).

The adaptive school's four leadership roles, twin goals, and five states of mind are the *strange attractors* within the system described by the science of chaos (Gleick, 1987). In chaotic, or dynamical, systems, small inputs can lead to dramatically large consequences. Persistent attention to the development of consciousness accelerates learning and results in more effective behavior. Just as sustained teacher talk, observed by students in the hallways of a middle school, can change the way students talk with one another, values such as the five states of mind become fractally represented within the behaviors manifested in the school. The most chaotic system never goes beyond certain boundaries identified by its strange attractors.

A World Governed by Relationships

To live in a quantum world, to weave here and there with ease and grace, we will need to change what we do. We will need to become savvy about how to build relationships and how to nurture growing, evolving things. All of us will need better skills in listening, communicating, and facilitating groups because these are the talents that build strong relationships.

Wheatley, 1992, p. 38

An organization's power to get things done comes from its energy source. Relationships produce that energy. Relationships can be either negatively or positively charged. In a recent study at the Claremont Graduate School, members of an educational community were asked what contributed most to the system's success. The answer, whether from teachers, community members, or district office personnel, was the same—it was the positive relationships people experienced.

Recently, after a year of working with members of a district's exit outcome steering committee, we asked, "What have you learned?" The most frequent response was about relationships. Two themes emerged: (a) They valued time spent in learning processes of communications, consensus strategies, and meeting techniques before they began their task of recommending exit outcomes to the governing board; and (b) they reported discovering that they could like and respect people with whom they disagreed. This was a committee of parents, teachers, businesspersons, and administrators holding widely divergent philosophies.

Increasingly, self-renewing schools are collaborative places in which adults care about one another, share common goals and values, and have the skills and knowledge to plan together, problem solve together, and fight passionately but gracefully for ideas to improve instruction. Wheatley (1992) notes a general movement in all organizations toward participation. This is not a fad that will pass this way and be gone. This tendency for participation is rooted, "perhaps, subconsciously, in our changing conception of the organizing principles of the universe" (p. 143).

References

Berman, P., & McLaughlin, M. W. (1977). *Factors affecting implementation and continuation* (Federal programs supporting educational change, Vol. 7). Santa Monica, CA: RAND.

Block, P. (1981). *Flawless consulting: A guide to getting your expertise used.* Austin, TX: Learning Concepts.

Bounds, W. (1994, March 29). Kodak to ask computer firms for alliances. *Wall Street Journal.*

Bridges, W. (1980). *Transitions: Making sense of life's changes.* New York: Addison-Wesley.

Briggs, J. (1992). *Fractals: The patterns of chaos.* New York: Touchstone.

Capra, F. (1991). *The Tao of physics.* Boston: Shambhala.

Chopra, D. (1989). *Quantum healing: Exploring the frontiers of mind/body medicine.* New York: Bantam.

Costa, A., & Garmston, R. (1994). *Cognitive coaching: A foundation for renaissance schools.* Norwood, MA: Christopher-Gordon.

Csikszentmihalyi, M. (1993). *The evolving self: A psychology for the third millennium.* New York: HarperCollins.

DeBoer, G. E. (1991). *A history of ideas in science education.* New York: Teachers College Press.

Devall, W., & Sessions, G. (1985). *Living as if nature mattered.* Layton, UT: Peregrine Smith.

Dilts, R. (1990). *Changing belief systems with NLP.* Cupertino, CA: Meta.

Fullan, M. (1982). *The meaning of educational change.* New York: Teachers College Press.

Gardner, H. (1983). *Frames of mind.* New York: Basic Books.

Garfield, C. (1986). *Peak performers: The new heroes of American business.* New York: William Morrow.

Garmston, R., & Wellman, B. (1992). *How to make presentations that teach and transform.* Alexandria, VA: Association for Supervision and Curriculum Development.

Gleick, J. (1987). *Chaos: The making of a new science.* New York: Penguin.

Goodlad, J., & Anderson, R. (1987). *The ungraded elementary school.* New York: Teachers College Press.

Kegan, R., & Lahey, L. (1984). Adult leadership and adult development: A constructivist view. In B. Kellerman (Ed.), *Handbook on socialization theory and research.* Chicago: Rand McNally.

Laborde, G. (1984). *Influencing with integrity.* Palo Alto, CA: Syntony.

Little, J. W. (1982). Norms of collegiality and experimentation: Workplace conditions of school success. *American Educational Research Journal, 19,* 325-340.

Poole, M. G., & Okeafor, K. R. (1989, Winter). The effects of teacher efficacy and interactions among educators on curriculum implementation. *Journal of Curriculum and Supervision, 4,* 146-161.

Rosenholtz, S. (1989). *Teacher's workplace: The social organization of schools.* New York: Longman.

Saphier, J., & Gower, R. (1987). *The skillful teacher: Building your teaching skills.* Carlisle, MA: Research for Better Teaching.

Senge, P. (1990). *The fifth discipline.* New York: Doubleday/Currency.

Shell, E. R. (1993, May). Waves of creation. *Discover Magazine, 14,* 54-61.

Wheatley, M. J. (1992). *Leadership and the new science: Learning about organizations from an orderly universe.* San Francisco: Berrett-Koehler.

8

The Norms of Collaboration

Attaining Communicative Competence

William Baker
Arthur L. Costa
Stanley Shalit

Thought is largely a collective phenomenon.

Of all the attributes of effective thinkers, universally and cross-culturally the capacity for communicative competency is paramount (Bowers, 1987). It is the most needed and probably least taught skill in schools and homes. Communicative competency is basic to the resolution of any problem or disagreement. Because people have not learned this discipline, they resort to self-centered or ethnocentric means to resolve problems—separation, divorce, or abusiveness in settling domestic disputes; filibustering in politics and meetings; and terrorism, street violence, hate crimes, wars between nations, and ethnic cleansing.

This chapter will demonstrate how the Norms of Collaboration serve as the webbing to link discourse in meetings and group interaction. At first, we will

AUTHORS' NOTE: The evolution of this chapter and the Norms of Collaboration are the results of long deliberation and refinement through time by the chapter coauthors and the Co-Director, Robert Garmston, and the Senior Associates of the Institute for Intelligent Behavior: John Dyer, Laura Lipton, Peg Luidens, Marilyn Tabor, Bruce Wellman, and Diane Zimmerman. For their assistance and dedication, we are deeply appreciative.

focus on two forms of discourse: dialogical and dialectical. Later, we will discuss other forms of discourse.

Our purpose is to support educators, parents, and community leaders in understanding the dynamics of different forms of discourse and to encourage them to nurture communicative competency as a means of redesigning, restructuring, and renegotiating the culture of our schools, communities, and society. We begin by contrasting two important forms of discourse: dialogical and dialectical.

What Is Dialogical Discourse?

Dia comes from the Greek and means through, between, or across two points. *Logos* means "the word." Thus, *dialogue* means a verbal interchange and a sharing of ideas, especially when the exchange is open and frank. The goal of dialogical discourse is to seek knowledge, mutual understanding, harmony, and a meeting of minds. Dialogical discourse involves an extended exchange between different points of view, cognitive domains, or frames of reference. Whenever we consider concepts or issues deeply, we explore their connections to other ideas and issues from different points of view. A dialogue can be among any number of people, not just two. Even one person can have a sense of dialogue within him- or herself. Dialogue connotes a stream of meaning flowing among, through, and between us.

What Is Dialectical Discourse?

Dialectical discourse intends to test the strengths and weaknesses of opposing points of view. Court trials, negotiations, debates, and arguments are dialectical in form and intention. They pit idea against idea, reasoning against counterreasoning, to get at the truth of a matter.

Dialectic is the art and practice of examining opinions or ideas logically through talk—often by the method of question and answer to determine their validity. As in the word *dialogue, dia* comes from the Greek for through, between, or across two points. *Legein* means to choose, to talk, or to choose between two points. The terms *dialectical* and *dialogical* have come to mean something quite different. The goal of dialectical discourse is to win, convince, or persuade. Hegel believed that for every thesis, there was an opposing point of view or antithesis leading to an understanding of and reconciliation of opposites. This concept of the dialectic gives rise to debates, negotiations, court trials, and compromises; the intent is that one side wins, and the other loses (Paul, 1991).

Other Forms of Discourse

Dialogical and dialectical discourse are only two forms of group interaction or communication. Other forms of discourse have different structures and intentions. The most well known forms of discourse for group interaction are lecture, discussion, deliberation, conversation, and therapy. All these forms of discourse can readily be observed in meetings. Sometimes, all these forms of discourse occur in a single meeting. In a meeting in which all forms are occurring, chaos or harmony can be observed. Chaos occurs when self-centered behavior dominates and members are not conscious of the effects of the modes of discourse on themselves or others. Harmony occurs when the Norms of Collaboration are consciously or unconsciously used to weld the discourse together, resulting in all members at the meeting feeling a strong sense of satisfaction and accomplishment.

Each form of discourse has a different structure. Each has a different intent, and each can be used successfully or unsuccessfully. We describe the most common forms of discourse below so that the reader can consider these in relation to dialogical and dialectical discourse.

- *Lecture:* Lecture is characterized by an emphasis on individuals in a meeting presenting data, information, positions, conclusions, issues, and recommendations. The intent is to inform or convince others of the validity and reasonableness of what is being presented.
- *Discussion:* Discussion in meetings emphasizes the introduction of a wide variety of individual perspectives. During discussion, individuals offer data, information, and rationales for positions and frequently try to convince others to take on their position. The intent is to talk about something in a constructive and amicable manner. When discussion goes awry, the root of the word predominates. *Cussion* comes from the Latin *cussio,* which means to shake violently. It is the source for our words *concussion*—shaking—and *percussion*—beating or striking. Members talk past one another and little understanding occurs.
- *Deliberation:* Deliberative discourse occurs when members of the group identify and analyze data, information, positions, ideas, and issues together. An important aspect of deliberation is dialectical discourse. Frequently, deliberative discourse results in decisions. The intent is to reach a deeper understanding of the content and the group members' attitude toward that content to decide on a group course of action.
- *Conversation:* Conversational discourse takes place in meetings when members relate personally to each other. The intent is on building or maintaining relationships rather than on attending to the topic. The conversation can be far-ranging with seemingly little focus.
- *Therapy:* Sometimes referred to as sensitivity training or encounter groups, therapeutic discourse is characterized by an emphasis on drawing out, feeding back, and analyzing individuals' affective states during meetings. The intent is to relate individuals' affective states to what is occurring during the meeting. Individuals decide publicly or privately on a private course of action.

Contrasting Dialogical and Dialectical
as Opposite Ends of a Continuum

Although the reader may choose to consider dialogical and dialectical discourse as in opposition to each other, we invite the reader to consider that dialogical and dialectical are at opposite ends of a continuum of discourse (Table 8.1). We invite the reader to place the other forms of discourse along such a

Table 8.1 Elements of Dialogical and Dialectical Discourse

In Dialogical Discourse	*In Dialectical Discourse*
Different views are presented as a way of discovering a new view.	Different views are presented and defended in search of the best view to support a decision.
There is a free and creative exploration of complex and subtle issues.	An issue is analyzed and dissected from many points of view.
Finding common ground is the goal.	Winning is usually the goal (one's view prevails) but must take second priority to coherence and truth.
One suspends personal views to understand the others' views. There is evidence of deep listening and empathizing.	There is a ping-ponging back and forth of ideas and positions between individuals.
There is playfulness with ideas.	Decisions are made.
Two or more sides collaborate toward common understanding.	Two sides oppose each other and attempt to prove each other wrong or their own position right.
One listens to the other side(s) to understand, find meaning, and find agreement.	One listens to the other side to find flaws and to counter the arguments.
Participants enlarge and possibly change their points of view.	Participants affirm their own point of view.
The positions and issues become more complex.	The positions and issues become more simplified.
Assumptions are revealed, examined, and reevaluated.	Assumptions are defended as truth.
Introspection of one's own position is invited.	Critique of the other position is produced.
It is acceptable to change one's position.	It is a sign of weakness and defeat to change one's position.
The skills of synthesis and flexibility are stressed.	The skills of analysis and persistence are stressed.
There is the possibility of reaching a better solution than either of the original solutions.	One's own position is defended as the best solution and excludes other solutions.
Participants strive for multiplicity in perspective.	Participants strive for singularity in perspective.

SOURCE: Adapted from Isaacs (1993).

continuum. Where they fall on a continuum often relates to whether the form of discourse is being used successfully. Only in the most formal group meetings, however, can such a continuum be observed. Examples are when parliamentary rules are in place, when a therapist controls a session, or when a facilitator insists on people using a particular mode of discourse at any time. When people of good will get together, one can observe that the Norms of Collaboration weld the meeting together by producing the webbing for participants to move seamlessly from one mode of discourse to another.

Table 8.1 shows that both forms of discourse are useful, but it is in the dynamics of shifting from one mode of discourse to another that groups grow, make new leaps, come to terms, or arrive at consensus. By using what we call the Norms of Collaboration (Figure 8.1), an individual member of the group can facilitate the shifting from one form of discourse to another. The key Norms of Collaboration are as follows:

- *Pausing:* Granting time before responding to or asking a question allows time for more complex thinking, enhances dialogue and discussion, and produces better decision making.
- *Paraphrasing:* Rephrasing lets others know that a group member is listening, that the member understands or is trying to understand, and that the member cares.
- *Probing:* Probing increases the clarity and precision of the group's thinking by clarifying understandings, terminology, and interpretations.
- *Putting ideas on and pulling ideas off the table:* Groups are productive when members share their thoughts, dreams, mistakes, and opinions. There are times, however, when continuing to advocate a position might block the group's functioning. Knowing when to pull ideas off the table may be as important as getting them on the table.
- *Paying attention to self and others:* Meaningful dialogue is facilitated when group members are conscious of themselves and of others. Members are aware of what they are saying, how it is said, and how others are responding. Paying attention to learning styles, modalities, and beliefs when planning for, facilitating, and participating in a group meeting enhances group members' understanding of each other as they dialogue, discuss, and make decisions. Managing emotions is a critical part of paying attention to self and others. Being sensitive to one's own and others' emotions and discovering underlying causes that produce those emotions enhance group work and decision making.
- *Presuming positive intentionality:* People operate on internal maps of their own reality and, therefore, we assume that they act with positive intentions. This assumption promotes and facilitates meaningful dialogue. Using positive presuppositions assumes and encourages positive actions.
- *Providing data:* Productive groups act on information rather than hearsay, rumor, or speculation. Data and feedback serve as the energy sources for group action and learning. Seeking, generating, and gathering data from group members, as well as from a variety of other sources, enhance decision making.
- *Pursuing a balance between advocacy and inquiry:* Advocating a position and inquiring into another's position assist the group to continue to learn.

During a meeting in which a group is engrossed in a dialogical discourse, exploring ideas, one member of the group can shift the discussion into a dialectical discourse by using one or more of the Norms of Collaboration, such

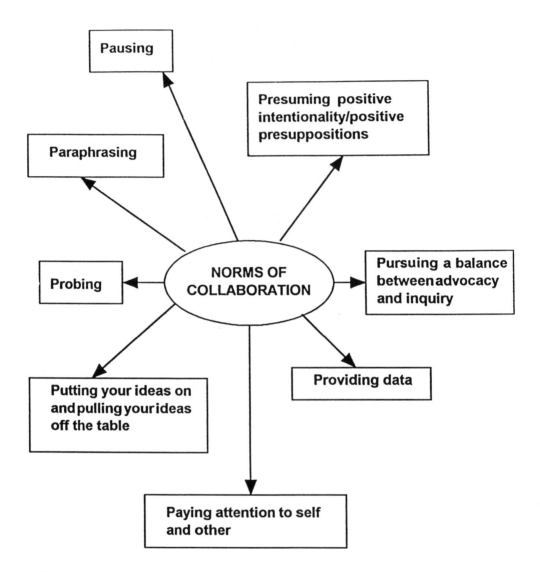

Figure 8.1. Norms of Collaboration

as a combination of a paraphrase and probe to analyze and decide which ideas to accept or reject. On the other hand, a facilitative participant might use the Norm of Collaboration of paraphrasing to synthesize what has been going on in a dialectical discourse to invite understanding, integrating, and harmonizing the group's thinking and to encourage generation of new and divergent solutions and directions.

Focusing on the Norms of Collaboration
Enhances the States of Mind of Individuals and the Group

Using the Norms of Collaboration increases **consciousness.** Applying the Norms of Collaboration causes us to think about what is being said, how it should be said, and what reaction it evokes. We monitor how well we understand what is being said and what we are doing to further the discourse. We monitor our own feelings, choose words and terminology to fit our audience, and select among alternative choices of words and pathways. We suppress and hold in abeyance our own feelings, emotions, judgments, impulses, and desires to allow others to express theirs. The skillful participant in a meeting, one with high communicative competence, demonstrates an awareness of what is occurring by employing the Norms of Collaboration regardless of the form of discourse being used.

The Norms of Collaboration enhance **craftsmanship.** They build skillfulness in the behaviors of listening: questioning, attending, clarifying, paraphrasing, and pausing. They demand precise language and clarification of terms, beliefs, and values. They encourage decision-making based on data rather than impulse. The norms facilitate an increase in the group's communicative competence by encouraging members to spend the necessary time to gain deeper understanding.

The Norms of Collaboration produce **flexibility.** They require allocentric and empathic listening to understand the other person's point of view. They also demand drawing on and developing alternative forms of expression and response patterns. The norms demand that participants pay attention to the varying beliefs, values, and styles of other members of the group. In doing so, members select from a broad repertoire of language to respond to the differences expressed within the group.

The Norms of Collaboration evoke increased feelings of **efficacy.** Using the norms causes us to feel in control; they cause us to self-evaluate, self-monitor, and self-analyze our own listening and communicative competencies. They produce a feeling of mastery within us because we realize that we have powerful ideas to contribute and that the collective meaning of the group is enhanced when we each contribute our individual assumptions and opinions.

Groups who adopt the norms develop greater **interdependence.** Using them builds a reciprocity with others and contributes to a sense of community understanding, group meaning, trust, and bonding within members of the group.

Implementing the Norms of Collaboration builds **holonomy.** Discourse occurs between the individual and the group. Through harmony of the individual and the group, the whole moves toward coherence. Thus, in such a group, one can observe both a collective and individual mind; like a stream, the flow moves between them (Bohm, 1990).

Employing the Norms of Collaboration Builds Culture

The Norms of Collaboration assist group members in renegotiating the ways they work together to solve problems and form decisions. Bohm (1990) describes the chaos that frequently occurs in groups when people do not engage in dialogue. He uses the metaphor of a laser to suggest that group power, like a laser, can produce communicative competence. We suggest that the Norms of Collaboration serve as the webbing that produces the same effects that he describes. His account is an excellent description of what occurs when the Norms of Collaboration are in action.

> The power of a group . . . could be compared to a laser. Ordinary light is called "incoherent," which means that it is going in all sorts of directions, and the light waves are not in phase with each other so they don't build up. But a laser produces a very intense beam which *is* coherent. The light waves build up strength because they are all going in the same direction. This beam can do all sorts of things that ordinary light cannot.
>
>   Ordinary thought in society is incoherent—it is going in all sorts of directions with thoughts conflicting and canceling each other out. But if people were to think together in a coherent way, it would have tremendous power. That's the suggestion. If we have a dialogue situation—a group which has sustained dialogue for quite a while in which people get to know each other . . . then we might have such a coherent movement of thought, a coherent movement of communication. (pp. 7-8)

A culture is people thinking together. As individuals share meaning, they negotiate and build a culture (communicative competence through the Norms of Collaboration). As groups become more skillful in employing the Norms of Collaboration, the norms create a renegotiation of the organization by pervading the value system, resulting in the changing of the practices and beliefs of the entire organization. By employing the norms, the group mind illuminates issues, solves problems, and accommodates differences. By using the norms, the group builds an atmosphere of trust in human relationships, trust in the processes of interaction, and trust throughout the organization. The norms facilitate the creation of a shared vision (Senge, 1990).

The Norms of Collaboration promote common communicative behaviors. In school communities, people behave similarly. When one observes an interaction between a secretary and a parent, or a teacher and a student, or a board member and a superintendent, one notices these similarities and can infer from them the basic values of the organization. Wheatley (1992) describes this phenomenon as the organization having a fractal quality. In the best of organizations, one can watch any member to infer the organization's values.

> The very best organizations have a fractal quality to them. An observer of such an organization can tell what the organization's values and ways of doing business are by watching anyone, whether it be a production floor employee or a senior manager. There is consistency and predictability to the quality of behavior. No matter where we look in these organizations, self-similarity is found in its people, in spite of the complex range of roles and levels. (p. 132)

The Norms of Collaboration promote collective thought—thinking together—which is more powerful than individual thought. Schein (1993) refers to this as "metalogue." It is a harmony of the individual and the collective in which the whole constantly moves toward coherence. Collective thought and interaction with others often results from individual thought. Application of the Norms of Collaboration builds coherence of thought and the tacit or unspoken understandings, agreements, or similarities that come from participating in discourse through time (Bohm, 1990). We might refer to this participatory consciousness as *co-cognition*—developing, monitoring, and expressing our thoughts together (Costa & O'Leary, 1991).

The norms contribute to the intellectual growth of the group's participants. Through discourse, ideas are presented and shaped, data are gathered and accommodated, differences in perceptions are understood and resolved, a variety of points of view are interpreted and understood, and differences in values and feelings are accommodated. When the norms are used during dialectical discourse to facilitate explanation, justification, or persuasion, the group grows intellectually. The norms do the same during dialogical discourse to facilitate participants' moving beyond their assumptions, thus creating new connections, new courses of action, and new meaning.

Vygotsky (1978) describes this phenomenon of the group dynamic influencing the growth of individual intelligence by talking about inter- and intrapsychological growth.

> Every function in . . . cultural development appears twice: first, on the social level, and later on the individual level; first between people (interpsychological), and then inside (intrapsychological). This applies equally to voluntary attention, to logical memory, and to the formation concepts. All the higher functions originate as actual relationships between individuals. (p. 156)

The process that Vygotsky describes is a subtle process. The knowledge that results from group interaction is rarely spoken by members of the group. Instead, one infers the knowledge. Sometimes a member does identify a tacit understanding the group has achieved. The group acknowledges that or denies that it has the understanding. The process the member uses to reflect the unspoken, tacit knowledge usually is a group paraphrase—one of the key Norms of Collaboration.

Tacit means that which is unspoken, which cannot be described—such as the tacit knowledge required to dance. Thinking, according to Bohm (1990), is actually a subtle, tacit process—the concrete processes of thinking are very tacit; the meaning is basically tacit. And what we can say explicitly is only a small part of it. Thought emerges from this tacit ground, and any fundamental change in thought will come from the tacit ground. So if we are communicating at the tacit level, then thought may be changing. Truth and enlightenment emerge unannounced.

The Norms of Collaboration contribute to continual learning. Learning to apply the norms together brings integrity and congruence to a learning group or organization. As individuals within a group come to understand, practice, develop criteria for, and assess their continual growth in the skills of discourse, they build a culture of continual learning. We believe they renegotiate their culture. They find that the sharing of mind and consciousness is more important than the content of the opinions. Although the process may arrive at truth, the process is concerned more with developing individual and group meaning. The application of the Norms of Collaboration keeps individuals, groups, and organizations growing, changing, creating, and learning.

Wheatley (1992) suggests that this is the process of *autopoesis*, which groups use to maintain their basic structure while growing.

> *Autopoesis:* (Greek) Self-production. The characteristic of living systems to continuously renew themselves and to regulate this process in such a way that the integrity of their structure is maintained. It is a natural process which supports the quest for structure, process renewal and integrity. (p. 18)

The Norms of Collaboration and Teamwork

As schools and learning organizations work to transform themselves, that is, to renegotiate their culture, collaborative teams need to become skillful in all forms of discourse (i.e., develop communicative competency) and to know when each is appropriate. Collaborative teams need to be able to engage in fruitful, exploratory dialogue—proposing ideas, probing their roots, considering evidence, sharing insights, testing ideas, and moving among various points of view. Collaborative teams also need to develop dialectical reasoning skills so that their thinking moves comfortably among divergent points of view or lines of thought, assessing the relative strengths and weaknesses of the evidence or reasoning presented. They also need to know how to discuss for all to get their ideas into the hopper. They need to converse in a manner that allows for each member's values and feelings to be heard and accommodated.

Collaborative work teams use dialectical and dialogical discourse to achieve two types of decisions:

1. *Focusing-in decisions:* Through dialectical reasoning, a focusing in that seeks a common denominator from among many individual views
2. *Opening-up decisions:* Through dialogue, a way of looking beyond each other's views to agree on something team members might not have arrived at alone

A team performing at peak levels aligns its energies—the group functions as a whole. Collaborative teams reflect on, evaluate, and learn from their activities and keep getting better. Such collective learning from experience has four critical dimensions: the need to gather critical data and information, to think perceptively about critical issues, to act in innovative and coordinated ways, and to attend to individuals' values and feelings to foster the development of peak team performance within the organization.

The power for such generative learning in organizations comes from the synergy between all forms of discourse. We have referred to this synergy as the webbing resulting from the application of the Norms of Collaboration. To capture this synergy, several factors must be present.

- Team members are on the way to mastering the skills that are used in all forms of discourse. They are gaining communicative competency through their use of the Norms of Collaboration.
- Teams can distinguish between the purposes and processes of the different forms of discourse and know when to enlist them.
- Teams can engage the four conditions for communicative competence:
  1. discussing and understanding what is meant by the different forms of discourse and consciously agreeing to engage in them;
  2. suspending assumptions and value judgments at the appropriate times;
  3. regarding one another as trusted colleagues;
  4. assuming the role of facilitative participants or engaging a temporary facilitator who holds the context of dialogue.
- Teams become observers, reflectors, and evaluators of their own thinking and their implementation of the Norms of Collaboration.
- Teams monitor and respectfully divert forces opposing productive discourse.

Productive work teams use skills of talking together (i.e., communicative competence) and can recognize and redirect verbal moves of defensiveness. Defensiveness moves are not in themselves "negative" but are usually employed to protect oneself or others from discomfort or embarrassment or to protect and defend individual opinions and assumptions.

Mental and verbal skills *promoting* productive discourse include the following:

- Choosing appropriate forms of discourse
- Establishing criteria for effective discourse
- Suspending judgments
- Employing the eight Norms of Collaboration
- Accessing holonomous states of mind: efficacy, flexibility, craftsmanship, consciousness, and interdependence
- Working from the balcony: looking down on the interaction—thinking metacognitively about the discoursing
- Recognizing and redirecting forces opposing productive discourse
- Group coaching: planning for, monitoring of, and reflecting on the process
- Self- and group monitoring of the Norms of Collaboration

Forces *opposing* productive team discourse include these:

- Not putting ideas on the table and talking behind the group's back
- Smoothing over situations and avoiding advocacy or inquiry
- Waging abstraction wars—talk for talk's sake—overintellectualizing

- Being patronizing
- Being unwilling to share personal agendas, assumptions, or principles
- Waging abstraction wars
- Saying "that's interesting"
- Sheltering ideas from criticism
- Confronting persons to squash ideas
- Playing a "broken record"
- Changing the subject
- Pulling rank
- Digging in heels
- Intimidating or attacking persons to suppress ideas
- Holding nonnegotiable assumptions
- Referring to rules, traditions, or past experiences ("It didn't work in '77, and it isn't going to work now." "'They' won't let us do that here." "We've never done it that way before.")

Eight Norms of Collaboration

The eight norms, discussed more fully below, serve as standards that are understood, agreed on, and adopted for use by each participant when working as a facilitating and contributing member of a group. They are the glue that enables school and community groups to engage in productive and satisfying discourse. Unlike a rule, which someone else monitors, the norm is a guide that each group member uses to monitor his or her own participation. Once norms are agreed on, each member assumes others will use them as well. Time should be allocated for reflection on the use of these norms by members of the group, for drawing relationships between their use and the group's, and for planning for continued improvement in the use of these norms in the future.

Pausing

In a discourse, space is given for each person to talk. Time is allowed before responding to or asking a question. Such silent time allows for more complex thinking, enhances all forms of discourse, and produces better decision making. Pausing is the tool that facilitative group members use to respectfully listen to each other.

Paraphrasing

Paraphrasing lets others know that a group member is listening, that the member understands or is trying to understand, and that the member cares. An effective paraphrase expresses empathy by reflecting both the feelings and the content of the message. A paraphrase sends four messages:

1. I am listening to your ideas.

2. I understand your thinking.
3. I am trying to understand your thinking.
4. I care about your thinking.

There are many types of paraphrases. We think they can be categorized into four basic types, each having a slightly different intention, although they often blend into one another. The paraphrase is important because it is one of the most critical tools to use to gain understanding. Our colleague, Bob Garmston, has introduced the concept that the paraphrase is the tool that a competent communicator uses to gain permission to ask a question of others.

Four Types of Paraphrase

1. *Empathy:* An acknowledgment and reflection of emotions
   Original statement: "Taking care of Joan has been a difficult situation for me, what with all the other work I have to do! It gets in the way of many other tasks. I just feel so fragmented, trying to handle everything! I'm at the point of quitting!"
   Example: "You're really frustrated with taking care of Joan!"
2. *Summary:* A shortening of a longer communication in your own words
   Example: "So, taking care of Joan has been hard for you what with all your other tasks!"
3. *Clarifying:* A statement ending with an inflection indicating a question
   Example: "You're saying that taking care of Joan is a real problem for you?"
4. *Synthesizing:* A statement that lifts or lowers the logical level of the original
   Example: "So, taking care of Joan has taken you to an extreme position for you of getting out of the obligation!"

Reflection Stems to Consider

"You're suggesting . . ."   "You're thinking . . ."
"I understand that you . . ."   "You're wondering . . ."
"You're feeling . . ."   "You're hoping . . ."
"So your idea is that . . ."   "Your goal is to . . ."

Group paraphrase

In groups, the power of the group paraphrase is a skill to be nurtured. A group paraphrase infers the intent of most people in the group and is stated concisely with the appropriate intonation. When a group paraphrase captures the spirit of the group, it most likely helps the group move to a next stage or into its desire action. When it misses, individuals, often more than one at the same time, offer additional information, which suggests a next step for the group or just falls on deaf ears and the group continues doing what it has been doing.

Classic Group Paraphrases

(Note the punctuation that is an attempt to capture the intonation)

"Time for a break?!"   "Time to move on?!"
"What we seem to be agreeing   "Looks like most of us here
 on is . . ."   would . . ."
"I guess we've just about beaten   "I guess we're ready for a vote?!"
 that one to death?!"   "What seems to be coming through
"Are we agreeing to . . . ?!"   is . . ."
"In other words, we're . . ."   "What we seem to be saying is . . ."

Probing

The use of probing and clarifying is an effective inquiry skill when the speaker expresses vocabulary, uses a vague concept, or employs terminology that is not fully understood by the listener. The purpose of clarifying is to invite the speaker to make clearer, to elaborate, and to become more precise in their meaning. Probing and clarifying are intended to help the listener better understand the speaker. In groups, probing and clarifying increase the clarity and precision of the group's thinking by clarifying understandings, terminology, and interpretations.

Examples of Probing and Clarifying

"Help me understand what you   "What will the participants be doing
 mean by . . ."   if we take this course of action?"
"Which students specifically?"   "When you say this class is better,
"When you say 'the   better than what?"
 administrators,' which   "What do you mean by *appreciate*?"
 administrators do you mean?"

Putting Ideas On and Pulling Ideas Off the Table

Groups are most productive when all members share their thoughts, dreams, mistakes, assumptions, and opinions. Facilitative members engage in productive discourse when they are clear about the intentions or goals of the group and what the group is attempting to accomplish. They offer ideas, opinions, information, and positions. They attempt to keep their suggestions relevant to the topic at hand. There are times, however, when continuing to advocate a position might block the group's functioning. Most of us can remember a time when we were advocating a position and our advocacy was falling on deaf ears. Had we been using the next norm, Paying Attention to Self and Others, we would have known it was not flying. Yet we continued to advocate. Knowing when to pull ideas off the table may be as important as getting them on the table.

The Greek word *koinonia* (fellowship) means to participate—partaking of the whole and taking part in it—not merely the whole group but the *whole* (Bohm, 1990). It is important for everyone to be heard!

Paying Attention to Self and Others

Significant dialogue is facilitated when each group member is sensitive to and conscious of themselves and of others—being aware of and watching all the subtle cues of what's happening inside and what's happening in the group, being aware of the stance of others' bodies, body language, postures, gestures, and language. This develops automatically in dialogue because it is all part of communication—verbal as well as nonverbal (see checklist p. 136).

When group members pay attention to themselves, they are aware of what they are saying, how it is said, and how others are responding. Paying attention to learning styles, modalities, and beliefs when planning for, facilitating, and participating in a group meeting enhances group members' understanding of each other as they converse, discuss, deliberate, dialogue, and make decisions. Managing emotions is a critical part of paying attention to self and others. Being sensitive to one's own and others' emotions and discovering underlying causes that produce those emotions enhance group work and decision making.

Presuming Positive Intentionality/Positive Presuppositions

People operate on internal maps of their own reality, and therefore we assume that they act with positive intentions. This assumption promotes and facilitates significant dialogue. Using positive presuppositions assumes and encourages positive actions.

Our language contains overt and covert messages. The deeper meanings we interpret from the language of others are not always communicated by the surface structure of our words and syntax. The embedded presuppositions in our language can be hurtful or helpful to others in subtle (and often not so subtle) ways (Costa & Garmston, 1994; Elgin, 1980).

Example: "Even Bill could get an A in that class."
Presupposition: Bill is no great shakes as a student.
Presupposition: The class is not difficult.

Limiting Presuppositions

"Do you have an objective?"   "Why were you unsuccessful?"
"What two things went well?"   "If only you had listened!"

Empowering Presuppositions

"What are some of the goals that you have in mind for this meeting?"

"How will you know whether the meeting is successful?"

"As you consider your alternatives, what seems most promising?"

"What personal learnings or insights are you carrying forward to future situations?"

Providing Data

Groups exercising high levels of communicative competence act on information, rather than hearsay, rumor, or speculation. Data serve as the energy sources for group action and learning. Seeking, generating, and gathering data from group members, as well as from a variety of other primary and secondary sources, enhance individual and group decision making. Some examples might be

Using secondary sources: "Let's look up the definition in the dictionary to make certain we all understand what we mean when we use this term."

Using the group as a database: "Let's take a straw poll and find out how the group is feeling about this issue at this point."

Conducting research: "Let's design and conduct an interview to gather data from a random sample of community members about this issue."

Experimentation: "If our hypothesis is correct, then students' performance on tasks of higher-level thinking should increase through the years. How might we collect such evidence?"

Turning to experts: "Let's pose these questions to Judge Smith, who has worked with these cases for many years."

Drawing on research: "According to the research report number 589-3 by the National Center for Teaching Thinking, such forms of higher-level questioning do enhance these types of students' performance on tests of reasoning by as much as 9 percentage points."

Providing Nonjudgmental Feedback: Our colleague Marilyn Tabor says that nonjudgmental feedback is a process whereby concrete and specific factual information about a group's thinking, decisions, and actions is provided so that the group can use the information for self-validation, self-correction, or self-modification. Nonjudgmental feedback is essential and unique in that it represents the setting aside of judgment. Critical characteristics of nonjudgmental feedback are these:

- Based on observation
- Nonjudgmental
- Concrete
- Specific

- Honest
- Relates to strengths
- Relates to needs
- Invites self-correction
- Useful for self-validation
- Useful for self-modification

Examples: "Everyone in our group offered an opinion today. Mary paraphrased three times. Jerry clarified Ralph's assumptions twice. Our dialogue continued for 27 uninterrupted minutes. We stayed on track except for one time when we talked about . . .!"

Pursuing a Balance Between Advocacy and Inquiry

Advocating a position, as well as inquiring into another's position, assists the group to continue learning. Senge, Ross, Smith, Roberts, and Kleiner (1994) suggest that balancing advocacy and inquiry is critical for an organization to perform, grow and learn. When advocating their views, group members should

- Make their reasoning explicit, explaining how they arrived at a view and what it is based on
- Encourage others to explore their views, asking questions such as, "Are there any gaps in my thinking?" "Does this make sense?"
- Invite others to provide different views: "Are there different conclusions?" "What other data should be gathered?" "Are there other ways of viewing this?"
- Actively inquire into others' views that differ: "What is your view?" "How did you arrive at your view?" "What data are you using to support your view?"

When inquiring into other members views, facilitative participants should

- State their assumptions clearly when making assumptions about others' views
- State the data on which their assumptions are based
- Not ask questions if they're not genuinely interested in the others' responses (Senge et al., 1994, pp. 200-201)

Following is the Norms of Collaboration Checklist (Table 8.2) for assessing individual and/or group performance of the eight Norms of Collaboration. The intent of the checklist is to record indicators of the performance of each or several of the Norms of Collaboration by individuals during team meetings (How am I doing?). Individual group members might wish to identify one or more of the norms for self-improvement, then seek feedback from group members about how they did on that particular norm.

Table 8.2 Norms of Collaboration Checklist

How Am I Doing? Or How Are We Doing?

NORM	OFTEN	SOMETIMES	NOT YET
PAUSING:			
• Listening attentively to other's ideas with mind and body			
• Allowing time for thought after asking a question or making a response			
• Rewording in my own mind what others are saying to further understand their positions and points of view			
• Waiting until others have finished before entering the dialogue			
PROBING:			
• Posing questions which invite self and others to recall ideas and past experiences, to describe facts, to express opinions and positions			
• Seeking clarifications, explanations, interpretations, implications or consequences			
• Asking for predictions, postulations, extrapolations, imaginations and new connections			
• Inviting personal connections or relationships; expressing personal values/beliefs; identifying likes and dislikes; making choices and commitments.			

Table 8.2 Continued

How Am I Doing? Or How Are We Doing?

NORM	OFTEN	SOMETIMES	NOT YET
PRESUMING POSITIVE INTENTIONALITY:			
• Assuming that other's intentions are positive and acting as if others mean well			
• Restraining impulsivity under emotional and stressful situations			
• Using positive presuppositions when inquiring and responding to others			
PROVIDING DATA:			
• Asking for and proving information, data, facts			
• Substantiating ideas and opinions with data, facts, and rationale			
• Referring to secondary sources of information			
• Setting up experiments and action research to test ideas			
• Basing actions on best available research			
PURSUING BALANCE BETWEEN ADVOCACY AND INQUIRY:			
• Monitoring the equity of opportunities for participation by all group members			
• Respecting the rights of individual's level of participation in the dialogue			
• Monitoring the relationship between advocacy and inquiry occurring in the group			
• Presenting reasons, logic, and rationale for holding a position and the decision-making processes that led to that position			
• Referring to agreed on goals, values, and purposes in arriving at decisions			
• Inquiring of others regarding their reasons and values for holding a position and how these were arrived at			

Table 8.2 Continued

How Am I Doing? Or How Are We Doing?

NORM	OFTEN	SOMETIMES	NOT YET
PARAPHRASING:			
◆ Acknowledging another's contribution			
◆ Summarizing another's idea			
◆ Translating another's idea into own words			
◆ Empathizing with other's feelings			
PUTTING IDEAS ON/PULLING IDEAS OFF THE TABLE:			
◆ Being clear about the intentions, goals and outcomes of the group			
◆ Offering ideas, opinions, information, or positions			
◆ Removing, rescinding, or changing own ideas, opinions, points of view, and positions			
PAYING ATTENTION TO SELF AND OTHERS:			
◆ Using visual, auditory and kinesthetic clues expressed by others			
◆ Respecting differences in people's preferences, beliefs, values, culture, ethnicity, etcetera			
◆ Maintaining focus on goals and avoiding straying from the topic or issue at hand			
◆ Viewing a situation from own, other's and global perspectives			

Another use of the checklist might be for group performance ("How Are We Doing?"; Costa & Kallick, 1995). The group begins by appointing a group process observer (i.e., coach) and identifying which of the norms it wishes to practice during the meeting. The group process observer then clarifies to ensure he or she and the group understand which behaviors group members have agreed on and what they would look like or sound like. During the meeting, the group process observer records indicators of the agreed-on norms. On completion of the meeting, the group process observer gives feedback to the group about the performance of the norms. These data are discussed, the effects of their use on group effectiveness are illuminated, and strategies for individual and group improvement are planned.

Using the Norms of Collaboration Checklist results in clear feedback. Individuals grow intellectually. Trust grows within the group. Members understand their level of participation in the group. As participants increase their knowledge of communicative competency in groups, there is an increased likelihood that they will transfer these norms to other life situations.

We believe that all forms of discourse, including dialectical and dialogical discourse, must occur if school and community deliberating bodies are to proceed productively and with member satisfaction. We believe that groups talk with each other in at least four different ways. Each of these ways of talking is important for good decision making to occur, yet each way of talking has a different intention.

1. Groups hold *discussions* for the primary intent of each member presenting data, knowledge, positions, ideas, or issues.
2. Groups hold *deliberations* with the primary intent of analyzing and understanding the data, knowledge, positions, ideas, or issues to determine the best course of action. The predominate characteristics of these two modes of group talk can be located in the dialectical discourse column described in Table 8.1.
3. Groups hold *dialogues* with the primary intent of expanding the permutations and possibilities of the ideas, knowledge, and issues to discover new solutions.
4. Groups hold *conversations* with the primary intent of relating personally to the data, knowledge, positions, ideas, or issues to arrive at decisions that are congruent with their values and feelings. The predominate characteristics of these two modes of group talk can be located in the dialogical discourse column described in Table 8.1. Again, the Norms of Collaboration will enhance these forms of discourse.

All groups talk in these four ways to agree on courses of action. All four types of talk occur simultaneously, without differentiation. When members are unaware of this phenomenon, chaos, confusion, conflict, fragmentation, and discord results. When groups consciously employ the Norms of Collaboration and are aware of the type of discourse that is occurring, we believe that harmony, productivity, and satisfaction will result. Because the different types of talk have different intentions, the Norms of Collaboration are used differently, depending on the type of discourse taking place. We believe that groups

Table 8.3 Four Ways Group Members Talk Together

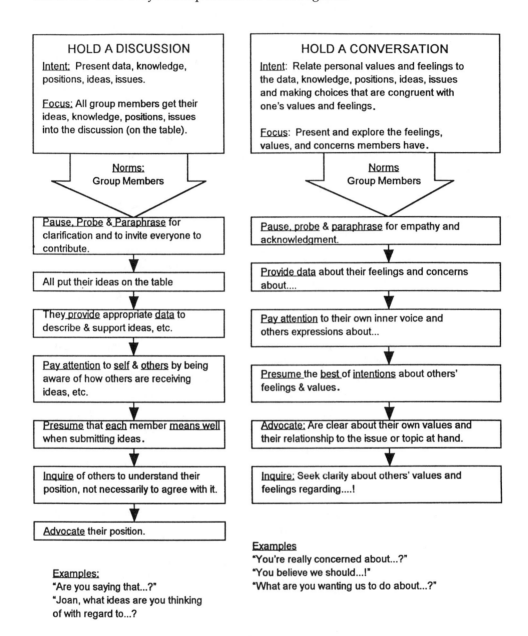

HOLD A DISCUSSION	HOLD A CONVERSATION
Intent: Present data, knowledge, positions, ideas, issues.	Intent: Relate personal values and feelings to the data, knowledge, positions, ideas, issues and making choices that are congruent with one's values and feelings.
Focus: All group members get their ideas, knowledge, positions, issues into the discussion (on the table).	Focus: Present and explore the feelings, values, and concerns members have.

Norms:
Group Members

Norms
Group Members

Pause, Probe & Paraphrase for clarification and to invite everyone to contribute.	Pause, probe & paraphrase for empathy and acknowledgment.
All put their ideas on the table	Provide data about their feelings and concerns about....
They provide appropriate data to describe & support ideas, etc.	Pay attention to their own inner voice and others expressions about...
Pay attention to self & others by being aware of how others are receiving ideas, etc.	Presume the best of intentions about others' feelings & values.
Presume that each member means well when submitting ideas.	Advocate: Are clear about their own values and their relationship to the issue or topic at hand.
Inquire of others to understand their position, not necessarily to agree with it.	Inquire: Seek clarity about others' values and feelings regarding....!
Advocate their position.	

Examples
"You're really concerned about...?"
"You believe we should...!"
"What are you wanting us to do about...?"

Examples:
"Are you saying that...?"
"Joan, what ideas are you thinking of with regard to...?

can become aware of these different ways of talking. By paying attention to the intentions of individuals and using the Norms of Collaboration most appropriate at the moment, their decision making and group interaction will become more productive and satisfying. Table 8.3 outlines these four types of talk and the ways in which individuals might employ the Norms of Collaboration.

Table 8.3 Continued

HOLD A DELIBERATION	HOLD A CONVERSATION
<u>Intent</u>: Analyze and understand the data, knowledge, positions, ideas, issues. Make sense of things! <u>Focus</u>: Find the truths and falsehoods, balance and weight, compare the pros and cons, identify the advantages and disadvantages.	<u>Intent</u>: Expand the permutations, possibilities, the what if's; find the new and untried! <u>Focus</u>: Explore new ideas, make new connections, create something new, go beyond the tried and true!

Norms:
Group Members

Norms
Group Members

<u>Pause, Probe & Paraphrase</u> to invite explanation, to identify consequences, costs & benefits, and to encourage disequilibrium.	<u>Pause, probe & paraphrase</u> to invite shifts of thought, raise or lower logical levels, seek new ways of thinking, reframing the situation.
They <u>provide data</u> by gathering evidence, showing justifications for, presenting arguments for and against....	They pay attention to others to build on other ideas, add to and to support—they view the situation from many perspectives.
They <u>pay attention</u> to <u>self</u> & <u>others</u> to determine the degree of conflict present and judge how to respond.	They seek <u>information</u> or <u>data</u> that will expand their thinking. They generate many ideas.
They actively pursue <u>inquiry</u> as they <u>advocate</u> the pros and cons of a specific course. They focus on finding out why something will or won't work.	They wait until the new is fairly well formed before applying <u>advocacy</u> and <u>inquiry</u> to the situation.

<u>Examples:</u>
"How is what you are saying related to what Jim is saying...?
"Why is that important to do?"
"As we think about next steps, which are the most critical to do well?"

<u>Examples</u>
"What if we were to...?"
"If we take 'X' and 'Y' and put them together, where might that lead us?"
"If we were the parents in this situation, how might we be viewing it?"

These ways of talking together are not mutually exclusive. One way of talking can lead to another way. They can occur simultaneously. Facilitative members of a group can use them to invite the group into different modes of thought. As group members become more aware of these four ways of talking together, at the appropriate time they can decide to focus on one specific way of talking to meet a specific intention.

References

Bohm, D. (1990). *On dialogue.* Dayton, OH: Institute for the Development of Educational Activities.

Bowers, C. A. (1987). *The promise of theory: Education and the politics of cultural change.* New York: Teachers College Press.

Costa, A., & Garmston, R. (1994). *Cognitive coaching: A foundation for renaissance schools.* Norwood, MA: Christopher-Gordon.

Costa, A., & Kallick, B. (1995). *Assessment in the learning organization: Shifting the paradigm.* Alexandria, VA: Association for Supervision and Curriculum Development.

Costa, A., & O'Leary, P. W. (1991). *Co-cognition: The cooperative development of the intellect.* In N. Davidson & T. Worsham (Eds.), *Enhancing thinking through cooperative learning.* New York: Teachers College Press.

Elgin, S. H. (1980). *The gentle art of verbal self-defense.* New York: Prentice Hall.

Isaacs, W. (1993). Dialogue: The power of collective thinking. *The Systems Thinker, 4*(3), 1-4.

Paul, R. (1991). Dialogical and dialectical thinking. In A. Costa (Ed.), *Developing minds: A resource book for teaching thinking.* Alexandria, VA: Association for Supervision and Curriculum Development.

Schein, E. H. (1993, Autumn). On dialogue, culture and organizational learning. *Organizational Dynamics, 22*(2), 40-51.

Senge, P. (1990). *The fifth discipline: The art and practice of the learning organization.* New York: Doubleday/Currency.

Senge, P., Ross, R., Smith, B., Roberts, C., & Kleiner, A. (1994). *The fifth discipline fieldbook.* New York: Doubleday/Currency.

Vygotsky, L. (1978). *Mind in society.* Cambridge, MA: Harvard University Press.

Wheatley, M. (1992). *Leadership and the new science.* San Francisco: Berrett-Koehler.

9

The Process of Coaching

Mediating Growth Toward Holonomy

Arthur L. Costa
Robert J. Garmston

This chapter has three main purposes. One is to describe those outcomes on which fully functioning, self-actualizing human beings exert tremendous energy during their lifetimes striving to achieve. The others are to describe a process of coaching (*cognitive coaching*) that is intended to mediate growth of other individuals and organizations toward those desired outcomes and to identify the capacities of skillful coaches who employ this process.

Holonomy: Life's Universal Paradox

As we develop soul in our work we need to recognize our dual identity: we are both individuals and members of a group. Indeed, finding the soul of work involves the balance and integration of apparent opposites,

AUTHORS' NOTE: Portions of this chapter were taken from Cognition and Instruction and Achieving Holonomy in Cognitive Coaching: A Foundation for Renaissance Schools. Copyright © 1994. Christopher Gordon Publishers, Inc. Used with permission. The evolution of this chapter is a result of long deliberation and refinement through time by the authors and the Senior Associates of the Institute for Intelligent Behavior: Bill Baker, John Dyer, Laura Lipton, Peg Luidens, Marilyn Tabor, Bruce Wellman, and Diane Zimmerman. For their insights and assistance, we are deeply appreciative.

such as head and heart, intellect and intuition, and self and group. This process is not so much based on the "shoulds" but upon "what is." It is my belief that as we attend to the soul of work we will find we feel more complete. (Paulson, 1995, p. 20)

All human endeavors are framed by an overarching quest toward holonomy. Holonomy may be a new concept for many. Although it was explained in the first book of this trilogy (see *Envisioning Process As Content: Toward a Renaissance Curriculum*), let us describe it here: *Holonomy* is a combination of two Greek words, *holos*, or whole, and *on*, meaning part. Thus, holonomy means that an entity is simultaneously both an autonomous unit *and* a member of a larger whole.

Holonomy may be oxymoronic because it implies a combination of opposites—being both a part and a whole simultaneously; acting autonomously and, at the same time, working interdependently. Holonomy is probably the most pervasive and universal paradox because all life forces are simultaneously independent and interdependent, self-assertive and integrative—whole unto themselves yet always a part of systems larger than themselves. An oxymoron implies conflict, and it is this duality that gives rise to certain tensions or conflicts between these internal and external opposing forces. These tensions can occur intrapersonally—within the individual; interpersonally—between individuals; intraorganizationally—within an organization; and interorganizationally—between organizations. The source of tensions might stem from the search for balance between

- *Ambiguity and certainty:* The human passion for certainty and the simultaneous need for doubt
- *Knowledge and action:* The striving for congruence between what we know and believe and how we behave
- *Egocentricity and allocentricity:* The amelioration of our own perspective with others' perspectives
- *Self-assertion and integration:* The striving to become autonomous, self-initiating, unique individuals and, at the same time, holding membership and allegiance to the larger community
- *Transparency between inner and outer lives:* What we think and feel inside is presented on the outside in our behavior (Paulson, 1995)
- *Solitude and interconnectedness:* The desire to be alone and introspective and the basic need to be interactive and reciprocal with others

The internal capacities for responding to these tensions can be found in five mind states that may be thought of as catalysts, energy sources, or passions that fuel human behaviors. Taken together, they are forces that human beings access as they strive for increasingly authentic, congruent, ethical behavior—the touchstones of integrity. They are the tools of disciplined choice making that guide the human actions needed to resolve the tensions listed above. They are the primary vehicles in the lifelong journey toward integration. These basic human forces drive, influence, motivate, and inspire human intellectual capacities, high performance, and productive thought and action. We categorize and define them as follows (Costa & Garmston, 1994):

1. *Efficacy:* Humans quest for mastery of their environment, control, self-empowerment, and continuous, lifelong learning.
2. *Flexibility:* Uniquely, humans possess the capacity to perceive situations from multiple perspectives and endeavor to change, adapt, and expand their repertoire of response patterns.
3. *Craftsmanship:* Humans yearn to become clearer, more elegant, precise, congruent, and integrated.
4. *Consciousness:* Humans uniquely manage to monitor and reflect on their own thoughts and actions.
5. *Interdependence:* Humans need reciprocity, belonging, and connectedness and are inclined to become one with the larger system and community of which they are a part.

Believing these five mind states to be the generators of effective thought and action, we will elaborate each by describing their intellectual and behavioral manifestations. Although each is described separately, we realize that they operate in combination with each other and that the boundaries between them are amorphous.

Efficacy

Efficacious people have an internal locus of control. They produce new knowledge. They engage in causal thinking. They pose problems and search for problems to solve. They are optimistic and resourceful. They are self-actualizing and self-modifying. They are able to operationalize concepts and translate them into deliberate actions. They establish feedback spirals and continue to learn how to learn.

Efficacy means knowing that one has the capacity to make a difference and being willing and able to do so. Efficacy is a particularly catalytic state of mind because the sense of efficacy is a determining factor in the resolution of complex problems.

If persons feel little efficacy, then blame, withdrawal, and rigidity are likely to follow. With robust efficacy, people are likely to expend more energy in their work, persevere longer, set more challenging goals, and continue in the face of barriers or failure. Efficacious people regard events as opportunities for learning. They believe that personal action produces outcomes, they control performance anxiety by accessing personal resources, and they recognize and draw on previous experiences. They are aware of what they do not know and actively seek other resources to complement and enhance their knowledge.

The more efficacious people feel, the more flexibly they can engage in critical and creative work. Developing effective thinking requires becoming increasingly self-referencing, self-evaluating, self-initiating, and self-modifying.

Flexibility

Flexible thinkers are empathic. They are able to see through the diverse perspectives of others. They are open and comfortable with ambiguity. They create and seek novel approaches and often have well-developed senses of humor. They envision a range of consequences. They have the capacity to change their minds as they receive additional data. They engage in multiple and simultaneous outcomes and activities, draw on a repertoire of problem-solving strategies, and can practice style flexibility—knowing when it is appropriate to be broad and global in their thinking and when a situation requires detailed precision.

Flexible people can approach a problem from a new angle using a novel approach (deBono, 1991, refers to this as *lateral thinking*). They consider alternative points of view and deal with several sources of information simultaneously. They are able to sustain a process of problem solving through time and, therefore, tolerate ambiguous situations. Their minds are open to change on the basis of additional information and data or reasoning that contradicts their beliefs. They can state several ways of solving the same problem and can evaluate the merits and consequences of two or more alternate courses of action. Working in groups, they often resolve conflicts through dialogue, express a willingness to experiment with another person's idea, and strive for consensus.

Flexible people know that they have and can develop options to consider about their work and are willing to acknowledge and demonstrate respect and empathy for diverse perspectives. They are able to work within rules, criteria, and regulations and can predict the consequences of disregarding them. They not only understand the immediate implications but also are able to perceive the bigger purposes that such constraints serve.

Flexibility of mind is essential for working with social diversity, enabling individuals to recognize the wholeness and distinctness of other people's ways of experiencing and making meaning. Flexible thinkers are able to shift their attention at will through multiple perceptual positions:

- *Egocentric:* perceiving from our own point of view
- *Allocentric:* perceiving through another person's orientation (We operate from this second position when we empathize with others' feelings, predict how others are thinking, and anticipate potential misunderstandings.)
- *Macrocentric:* perceiving the big picture (This is similar to looking down from a balcony at ourselves and our interactions with others. Macroattention is intuitive, holistic, and conceptual. It is the bird's-eye view, useful for discerning themes and patterns from assortments of information. Because we often need to solve problems with incomplete information, we need the capacity to perceive general patterns and jump across gaps in present knowledge. The macrocentric view allows this.)
- *Microcentric:* examining the individual and sometimes minute parts that make up the whole (A micromode is the worm's-eye view without which science, technology, and any complex enterprise could not function. Microattention involves logical analytical computation searching for causality in methodical steps. It encompasses attention to detail, precision, and orderly progressions.)

Flexible thinkers display confidence in their intuition. They tolerate confusion and ambiguity and are willing to let go of a problem, trusting their subconscious to continue creative and productive work on it. Flexibility is also the cradle of humor, creativity, and repertoire. Consciousness informs the need for a fluidity of flexible perspectives. Although there are many possible perceptual positions—past, present, future, egocentric, allocentric, macrocentric, visual, auditory, and kinesthetic—the flexible mind is activated by knowing when to shift perceptual positions. High degrees of craftsmanship require many of these.

Craftsmanship

Craftspersons seek perfection and pride in their work. They strive for precision and mastery. They seek specificity in oral and written communications and work constantly for refinement, exactness, and accuracy in thought, language, and deed. They generate and hold clear visions and goals. They employ critical thinking processes. They use precise language for describing their work. They make thorough and rational decisions about actions to be taken. They test and revise, constantly honing strategies to reach goals.

Embodied in the grace and the strength of a ballerina—or a shoemaker—craftsmanship is about striving for mastery, elegance, and economy of energy to produce exceptional results. To be craftsmanlike means knowing that one can continually perfect one's craft by working to attain the highest possible self-initiated standards and pursue continual learning to bring a laserlike focus of energies to task accomplishment.

Craftsmanship includes exactness, precision, accuracy, correctness, flawlessness, faithfulness, and fidelity—but not in all things. Craftspersons also work flexibly. Craftsmanship without flexibility is perfectionism.

Because language and thinking are closely entwined, precision of language is an important characteristic of craftspersons. Language refinement plays a critical role in enhancing persons' cognitive maps and their ability to think critically, which is the knowledge base for efficacious action. As humans acquire more exact language for describing their work, they begin to recognize concepts, identify key attributes, distinguish similarities and differences, and make more thorough and rational decisions. Developing craftsmanship, therefore, enriches the complexity and specificity of language and simultaneously produces effective thinking.

Consciousness

Conscious thinkers metacogitate. They monitor their own values, intentions, thoughts, feelings, and behaviors and the effects of these on others. They are aware of their own and others' progress toward goals. They articulate well-defined value systems. They generate, hold, and apply internal criteria for their decisions. They practice mental rehearsal and the editing of mental pictures in the process of seeking improved performance. Consciousness means knowing what and how one is thinking about one's work in the moment and being willing to be aware of actions and their effects on others as well as on the environment.

Consciousness is the central clearinghouse in which varied events processed by different senses can be represented and compared and, therefore, has particular catalytic properties for the other mind states. It is *the* state of mind prerequisite to self-control and self-direction. Consciousness means being aware that certain events are occurring and being able to direct responses to the events.

The function of consciousness is to represent information about what is happening outside and inside the organism in such a way that it can be evaluated and acted on. Without consciousness, people would still "know" what is going on but would have to react to it in a reflexive, instinctive way. Because individuals have consciousness, they can daydream, change perceptual positions, write beautiful poems, and develop elegant scientific theories.

Consciousness provides a distinctive characteristic of the nervous system in that humans are able to affect their own emotional or mental states. Individuals can make themselves happy or miserable, regardless of what is actually happening "outside," just by changing the contents of their consciousness.

Intentionality keeps information in consciousness ordered. To have intentions and to be conscious of one's intentions is to live in two different worlds. To be conscious of one's intentions is to have choice to focus attention at will, to be oblivious to distractions, to concentrate for as long as it takes to achieve a goal and to align thoughts, feelings, and behaviors with that intention. Developing effective thinking, therefore, requires the development of this priceless resource, consciousness.

Even the most effective, self-modifying, self-authoring autonomous individual, however, is still a member of a larger community. The second component of holonomy, therefore, and that which gives it the paradoxical conflict, is about the human capacity and proclivity to work collaboratively in and to learn from collegial groups engaged in continuous cycles of self-improvement.

Interdependence

Interdependent people have a sense of community, regarding "we-ness" as important as "me-ness." They are altruistic. They value consensus and are able to hold their own beliefs and actions in abeyance to lend their energies and resources to the achievement of group goals. They contribute themselves to a common good, seek collegiality, and draw on the resources of others. They regard conflict as valuable, trusting their abilities to manage group differences in productive ways. They continue to learn on the basis of feedback from others and from their conscious attending to their own actions and their effects on others. They seek engagement in holonomous part-whole relationships, knowing that *all* of us are more effective than any *one* of us.

Interdependence means knowing that individuals will benefit from participating in, contributing to, and receiving from professional relationships and being willing to create and change relationships to benefit their work. The human intellect grows in reciprocity with others. Russian psycholinguist Lev Vygotsky (1978) suggests that intelligence grows in two ways. One is the intelligence that develops through individuals' own experiences. But intelligence also gets shaped through reciprocity with others. Justifying reasons, resolving differences, actively listening to another person's point of view, achieving consensus, and receiving feedback actually increase individual intelligence.

As humans develop cognitively, they value and, with increasing consistency, view situations from multiple perspectives. As stated earlier, flexibility is prerequisite to the state of mind of interdependence because flexibility allows persons to see others' points of view as well as being able to change and adapt on the basis of feedback from others.

Interdependent people interpret conflict as valuable with the potential benefits of solving problems or finding new ways of solving problems. Endowed with the passion for interdependence, people can focus on ways to let a conflictual relationship transform the parties, rather than on the parties resolving the conflict.

As persons become more interdependent, they may experience a sense of interconnectedness and kinship that comes from a unity of being, a sense of sharing a common community (class, school, neighborhood, etc.), and a mutual bonding to common goals and shared values. Interdependent individuals' sense of self is enlarged from a conception of *me* to a sense of *us* (Sergiovanni, 1994). They understand that "as we transcend the self and become part of the whole we do not lose our individuality but rather our egocentricity" (p. 10).

As interdependence develops, it is characterized by altruism, collegiality, and the giving of self to group goals and needs. Just as interdependent persons contribute to a common good, they also genuinely value and draw on the resources of others. They value dialogue and lend their energies to the achievement of group goals. Interdependent people envision the expanding capacities of the group and its members.

Interdependence facilitates systems thinking, in which many variables are constantly interacting. Each variable affects another, which affects another, and so on. Families, weather systems, and national economies are examples of systems. In these dynamic systems, tiny inputs can reverberate throughout the system, producing dramatically large consequences. Because of this, interdependent thinkers realize the potential to significantly influence the direction of the community of which they are a part.

Interdependence, along with the other four mind states—efficacy, flexibility, craftsmanship, and consciousness—makes possible more complete and effective functioning of human beings.

Becoming Intentionally Holonomous

We believe these five mind states to be the generators of effective thought and action when humans are confronted with problems, tensions, and conflicts. Self-modifying, self-authoring autonomous individuals are members of a larger community. It is through interaction with the larger universe—the environment, the organization, and other people—that the states of mind are disclosed, exercised, and expanded. Through interaction with others, humans develop efficacy, mastery, and control. Consciousness emerges as a social phenomenon from encounters with others. Craftsmanship grows as a result of feedback from others and from the environment. Flexibility is expanded as a result of repeatedly encountering the diversity of other humans and situations. What begins as a source of conflict, therefore, can result in a form of continuous learning. The processes of resolving the tensions are the very processes that produce growth.

To be intentionally holonomous, therefore, is to consciously and continuously draw on these five mind states as resources in resolving these personal and organizational tensions. Holonomous persons learn to

- Balance solitude and togetherness, action and reflection, and personal growth and professional growth
- Draw from prior knowledge, sensory data, and intuition to guide, hone, and refine actions
- Pursue ambiguities and possibilities to create new meanings
- Explore choice points between self-assertion and integration with others
- Seek perspectives beyond self and others to generate adaptively resourceful responses

We believe that when confronted with problematic situations, the human capacity to draw on the resources of the five states of mind and to continually learn from the experience can be mediated and habituated through the process of coaching.

The Process of Coaching: Mediating Growth Toward Holonomy

The next goals of this chapter, therefore, are about developing the identity and capacities of persons to assume roles as mediators of other individuals and organizations and describing the coaching process. We refer to persons who adopt this mediational stance as *cognitive coaches* (Costa & Garmston, 1994). Their focus is on cognition, not behaviors; decision-making capacities, not techniques; and states of mind, not external resources. Coaches cause individuals and organizations to engage in continuous cycles of learning and self-improvement by accessing the five states of mind while engaging in the duality of acting autonomously and, at the same time, working collaboratively.

The role of coaches becomes one of enhancing the resourcefulness of their own, other individuals', and the organization's capacity to access these states of mind to function more autonomously and effectively in resolving and learning from conflicting and problematic situations. The mediational role of cognitive coaches may be played in many relationships: parent-child, teacher-student, teacher-teacher, administrator-teacher, employee-manager, and so forth.

Continually mindful of the five states of mind described above, persons who mediate

- Assess the state of mind in which they and their colleagues are presently operating
- Envision increasingly holonomous states of mind for themselves and others; apply tools and strategies to facilitate others in becoming intentionally holonomous by constructing and using clear and precise language in the facilitation of others' cognitive development

- Devise an overall strategy through which individuals will move themselves toward desired states
- Maintain faith in the potential for continued movement toward more holonomous states of mind and behavior
- Believe in their capacity to serve as empowering catalysts of others' growth
- Purposely structure the environment to enhance growth in the five states of mind and collect evidence that indicates growth toward holonomy

We shall describe four main functions of coaches who perceive themselves as mediators of another person's or an organization's development of those attributes of holonomy described earlier. Mediators

1. *Establish and maintain trust.* Mediators strive to enhance trust in four areas:
   - *Trust in themselves as competent coaches:* All organizations would profit from a sign posted somewhere that said "Trust starts with me." When coaches trust themselves, they can build trust with others. Coaches consciously plumb their own motives and intentions to ensure that they are honorable and altruistic; they place faith in their own abilities to mediate others' growth; and they trust their own capacities (consciousness, efficacy, flexibility, and craftsmanship) to learn from their own experiences—to self-monitor, self-evaluate, and self-modify.
   - *Trust in the relationship with each other:* Wise coaches assume the other party is trustworthy without needing a demonstration of trust first. This facilitates both parties in the coaching relationship to trust and respect each other. Both realize that neither person needs to be "fixed." Coaches believe that people have the inner resources to achieve excellence.
   - *Trust in the process of coaching:* As coaches and their colleagues work together in a nonthreatening and reciprocal relationship, they increase their faith in the coaching process. They realize the intent of this process is to grow intellectually, to learn more about learning, and to mutually increase their capacity for self-improvement.
   - *Trust in the environment:* The culture of the workplace often signals norms and values that are more influential on staff performance than are the skills, knowledge, training, staff development, or coaching (Frymier, 1987; Rosenholtz, 1989). Thus, effective cognitive coaches also work to create, monitor, and maintain a stimulating, mediational, and cooperative environment deliberately designed to enhance continued intellectual growth.
2. *Envision and assess states of mind and generate and apply a repertoire of strategies to enhance states of mind.* Mediators realize that the five states of mind are
   - *Transitory:* Like any other form of energy, they come and go; they peak and plateau. A person's state of mind varies, depending on a variety

of factors including experience, knowledge, fatigue, emotion, and so on.

- *Transforming:* Dramatic increases in performance accompany heightened states of mind. Just as a person's current state of confidence will affect his or her in-the-moment competence, the states of mind access the personal resources required for peak performance. To be effective, to make things happen, in other words, first think efficaciously.

- *Transformable:* The states of mind can be mediated by individuals themselves or by others. Colleagues can cheer each other up or encourage each other, changing in that moment others' states of mind and capacities. Similarly, individuals' own conscious awareness of states of mind allows them to choose and change them.

The five states of mind, therefore, serve coaches as diagnostic tools or constructs through which the cognitive development of other individuals and groups can be assessed and, therefore, interventions planned. But assisting others toward refinement and expression starts first with the self, a person's own states of mind. From there, it emanates to others with whom the person interacts and to the system of which the person is a part.

3. *Interact with the intention of supporting others in producing self-directed learning.* Mediators hold the clear intention of causing others to become increasingly more self-aware, self-directed, self-referencing, self-analytical, self-evaluating, and self-modifying. Mediators of these processes operate on certain fundamental beliefs or assumptions about human growth and learning. Mediators believe

- All human beings are capable of change—that humans continue to grow cognitively throughout their lifetimes and that all possess a vast reservoir of untapped potential.

- The performance of any craft—teaching students, managing corporations, welding a seam, or extracting an appendix—cannot be reduced to a formula or a recipe. There is an enormous amount of information today about the invisible mental processes in which professionals engage while performing their craft. Another fundamental assumption, therefore, is that a person's observable performance is driven by certain internal, invisible skills—thought processes that drive the overt behaviors (Joyce & Showers, 1988).

- Any type of goal-directed endeavor may be described as a four-phase cycle of decision making in which people engage before, during, and after the event. The first phase comprises all the thought processes that are performed prior to the event—the planning phase. The second includes those mental functions performed during the event—the interactive phase. The third is the reflective phase in which persons reflect on the event to compare, analyze, and evaluate the decisions that were made during the planning and execution phases. Finally, there is an applicative phase, in which persons abstract from what has been learned during their critical self-reflection and then project those learnings to future activities. They then cycle back to the planning phase. (See Costa & Garmston's chapter, "Teaching as Process," in *Supporting the Spirit of Learning*, the second book of this trilogy.)

- Learning requires an engagement and a transformation of the mind. To learn anything well—a golf swing, a poem, a new computer program, or a different way of teaching—requires thought. Coaches, therefore, are skillful in engaging their colleagues' intellect, in maintaining access to their higher cognitive functions, and in employing tools and strategies that will enhance perceptions and transform their colleagues' frames of reference.

4. *Maintain faith in their ability to mediate their own and others' capacity for continued growth.* Enlightened, skillful coaches maintain faith in the human capacity for continual intellectual, social, and emotional growth. They possess a belief in their own capacity to serve as empowering catalysts for others' growth. They not only engage but significantly enhance and modify (mediate) others' cognitive processes, perceptions, decisions, and intellectual functions that are prerequisite to and determiners of overt behaviors.

As coaches become increasingly skillful in mediating others' growth, there is a reciprocal effect on themselves. In recognizing states of holonomy in others, coaches recognize states of efficacy, consciousness, flexibility, craftsmanship, and interdependence in themselves. The *external* language used by coaches to empower others becomes *internal* in the coaches, thus mediating themselves to higher states of holonomy. Coaching, then, not only means mediating others but also means self-mediating, self-transforming, and self-modifying for coaches themselves. As Erich Fromm (1956) wrote,

> In thus giving of his life, the mentor enriches the other person; he enhances the other's sense of aliveness. He does not give to receive; giving is in itself exquisite joy. But in giving he cannot help bringing something to life in the other person, and this which is brought to life reflects back to him; in truly giving, he cannot help receiving that which is given back to him. (p. 62)

Coaching Competencies

Mediators are *not* the solvers of others' problems. The critical distinction between mediators and "fixers" is that coaches provide these experiences not to "teach behaviors" but to move persons toward more holonomous states. With the intention of building holonomous individuals and organizations, coaches employ certain nonjudgmental mediational competencies. Coaches must remain nonjudgmental throughout the coaching process so that others can think without fear of being judged. When people feel judged, their thinking shuts down. Following are five nonjudgmental coaching competencies that are intended to produce self-directed learning.

1. The **intentional** coach poses carefully constructed questions intended to cause the coach's partner to access one or more of the states of mind. For example,

   Flexibility: "If you were Barbara, how would you react to this situation?" "What are some alternative strategies for accomplishing this goal?"

   Efficacy: "When you have been faced with similar situations in the past, what has worked for you that you could apply in this situation?"

   Efficacy and Consciousness: "What were you aware of in your own behavior that caused the students to be successful?"

   Consciousness: "As you envision this lesson, what will you see students doing as indicators of success?"

   Flexibility and Consciousness: "How do your questioning strategies take into account your students' various learning styles?"

   Consciousness and Interdependence: "What will you be aware of in your own decision making during your interaction with these students?"

   Craftsmanship: "When you say you want the students to enjoy the music, how specifically will they exhibit their enjoyment?"

   Craftsmanship and Efficacy: "What learnings will you carry forth from this experience and apply to future events?"

   Interdependence: "To whom might you turn for help with this problem?" "How might we secure the other staff members' thinking about this policy change?"

   For additional questions related to the states of mind, see also Luidens's chapter, "Paper Thinking: The Process of Writing" in *Envisioning Process As Content*, the first book in this trilogy. For applications of states of mind to mediating group development, see Garmston and Wellman (1996).

2. The **caring** coach paraphrases. According to Carl Rogers, the paraphrase is probably the single most important communication tool and yet is the most undcrused. Paraphrasing communicates that "I am attempting to understand you, therefore I value you." Because it conveys such powerful empathy, its use permits deep and tenacious probing.

3. The **precise** coach probes for specificity, clarity, and elaboration. For example, "Which students specifically?" "What criteria will you be using to assess the accuracy of student responses?" "What else were you considering when you reorganized the assignment?" Clarifying invites and promotes deeper, more detailed thinking that results in greater consciousness, craftsmanship, and more analytical, productive decision making.

4. The **patient** coach uses silence. Wait time has been found by Rowe (1986) and others to be a significant linguistic tool leading to more complex, creative, and reflective thinking.

5. The **observant** coach collects data and presents them objectively. The skillful coach assists others in designing strategies for data collection or draws from personal repertoire of data-gathering techniques relevant to the teacher. The coach and partner can then examine the data in a literal

and nonjudgmental way (Costa, D'Arcangelo, Garmston, & Zimmerman, 1988).

The Coaching Process

The coaching process is much like a Socratic dialogue. The better thinkers coaches are, the more capable they are of producing and stimulating thinking in others. Our model of coaching includes a planning conference, an observation, and a reflective conference, making the format of the coach's role compatible with the four phases of thought that effective, competent, thoughtful problem solvers perform. (See Costa & Garmston's chapter, "Teaching as Process," in the second book of this trilogy; see also Costa & Garmston, 1994.)

Planning: We attach great importance to planning and find that coaches may mediate planning in a variety of informal ways—in the hallway, on the phone, in meetings with groups and individuals, and in casual conversations with parents, colleagues, students, and others—and in more formal settings when a planning conference, an observation, and a reflective conference can be scheduled.

Winning athletes mentally rehearse what they will be doing to produce desired results prior to performance (Garfield, 1986). We, too, believe that planning is the most important of all the thought processes. The quality of the plan affects the quality of all that follows. Coaches, therefore, engage their colleagues in mental rehearsal. Through well-structured dialogue, coaches invite colleagues to

- Identify outcomes and goals and describe the strategies to be used that are intended to achieve those outcomes
- Anticipate what decisions and actions will be needed to achieve those outcomes
- Envision the desired behaviors and performances of the participants as indicators that the strategy is achieving the desired outcomes
- Design a mental method of monitoring the performance of those indicators

In more formal planning conferences, when the coaches are to be present during the forthcoming events, the planners may request that the coaches serve as additional sets of eyes. The planners direct the observation of the coaches by identifying what they should pay attention to and collect data about in the event that will support the planners' reflection and enhance meaning making from the data collected. Skillful coaching assists the teachers in imagining, elaborating, and designing strategies to monitor such formative cues indicating success during the event.

Monitoring: During the event itself, the coaches collect only those data their colleagues requested during the planning conference. Such observations may focus on individual or groups of participants' performance, indicating goal achievement and on-task behavior. The coaches may also be requested to collect data about techniques that their colleagues are striving to perfect: wait time, questioning strategies, proximity, movement, clarity of directions, and so forth.

Reflecting: The reflective conference frequently begins with an open-ended question such as, "How do you feel it went?" We say *frequently* because although coaches have certain conferencing objectives they intend to meet, the dialogue is more individualized and Socratic than it is a recipe. An open invitation allows the reflectors to decide how they will enter the conversations and begin self-assessment. The next question may be one such as, "As you reflect on the event, what are you recalling that leads you to those inferences?" This question focuses on another important cognitive function—monitoring and recalling what happened during the event. Because the ultimate goal of coaching is self-modification, coaches strive to develop the conscious capacity to monitor their own and the participants' behaviors and to recall what happened during the event. Data collection is fundamental to their self-analysis and self-coaching. Processing the data from the event enables reflectors to reconstruct and analyze what went on while they were conducting the plan and to make the experience intelligible.

Mediators shine a flashlight of awareness on data in the environment and interact to support self-directed learning. Reflectors may be asked to interpret the data—to compare desired with actual outcomes: "How did what happened during the event compare with what you planned?" The reflectors may also be asked to infer what they observed in the lesson in cause-effect relationships.

Applying: On the basis of this analysis, the reflectors are asked to project and apply what has been learned: "How will you use these insights in future situations or in other aspects of your work?" Notice the positive presuppositions that are embedded in these questions. This is a process concerned with self-motivation and self-directed growth. The job of the coaches is to support their colleagues in this natural mental journey.

Cognitive coaches not only work in reciprocal relationships but also structure the environment to enhance individual and collective growth. Two types of structuring are possible.

In *organizational structuring,* tasks and goals are timed and defined purposely so that people from diverse backgrounds, cognitive styles, levels of maturity, content expertise, and philosophical beliefs must collaborate with each other to accomplish the task. The confluence of these multiple perspectives enriches the flexibility and thoughtfulness of all participants. Similar diffusion of knowledge and of assumptions about learning occurs when teachers from different grade levels and disciplines are paired in peer coaching partnerships, when they observe in each other's classroom, when they share responsibilities for student learnings, and when they are assigned the same students for multi-year periods.

Logistical structuring occurs when the environment is deliberately constructed to produce certain forms of interactions. One high school in Edmonton, Canada, for example, constructed one departmental science laboratory to serve the entire school and to be shared by all the science teachers and students to purposely make connections between the sciences. In the Community High School District 155 in Crystal Lake, Illinois, the superintendent's team of architects and educators purposely structured the new high school to embody the five mind states. They built flexibility into the very walls and passages of the edifice. They made it necessary for the staff, students, and community to function in interdependent ways. They even interviewed and selected their architectural team on the basis of their display of these five mind states. (See Saban's Chapter 11 in this volume.)

Outcomes of Coaching

Several studies report increases in such factors as cognitive development, job satisfaction, and inferred increases in student learning (Garmston & Hyerle, 1988). In her studies in several locations during the past 5 years, Edwards (1992) generally and consistently found teacher efficacy enhanced by this coaching process. Both Foster (1989) and Edwards found that it takes repeated experiences through time for teachers to begin internalizing the process as self-awareness and self-modification. Higher frequency of practice yielded higher ratings of efficacy.

As a result of cognitive coaching, teachers and coaches report that they are deriving enormous satisfaction from using this process. A teacher who had not been reflective reports that he now is watching himself teach, almost as if he had a camera on himself, and that when he catches himself in old patterns, he now employs alternatives. Administrators describe how they use the coaching process with each other as they talk through plans for staff development training or a crucial parent meeting. Teachers report that the process is enjoyable and exciting, that it makes them think, *and* that as a result of the coaches' modeling higher-level questions, probing, and paraphrasing, they are using those same nonjudgmental behaviors with students! Many participants in coaching have remarked on the transference of these nonjudgmental behaviors to other settings: with parents, in counseling sessions, in problem-solving groups, and at home with their own spouses and children.

Changes in policy become increasingly apparent as the principles of mediation are internalized and applied. Policy change does not happen quickly and usually occurs after there is a critical mass of staff members who are experimenting with the coaching process. We have observed a shift in district practices from teacher evaluation to alternative forms of assessment, including teacher portfolios and coaching; from competition to cooperation; from conformity to creativity; and from control to empowerment of leadership in all. We have observed a dissatisfaction with existing curriculum and a shift from acquiring more content to a focus on developing students' intellectual processes. We believe that coaching can be the impetus for developing the school as a home for the mind—an intellectual ecology wherein all the school's inhabitants' intellects are mediated. We believe coaching can provide a foundation for developing and achieving schools as generative and adaptive learning organizations (Costa, 1991; Garmston & Wellman, 1995; Senge, 1990). (See also Chapter 7 by Garmston & Wellman in this volume.)

References

Costa, A. (1991). The school as a home for the mind. In A. Costa (Ed.), *Developing minds: A resource book for teaching thinking*. Alexandria, VA: Association for Supervision and Curriculum Development.

Costa, A., D'Arcangelo, M., Garmston, R., & Zimmerman, D. (1988). *Another set of eyes: Conferencing skills* [Videotapes and trainer's manual in ASCD's supervision series]. Alexandria, VA: Association for Supervision and Curriculum Development.

Costa, A., & Garmston, R. (1994). *Cognitive coaching: A foundation for renaissance schools.* Norwood, MA: Christopher-Gordon.

deBono, E. (1991). The CoRT thinking program. In A. Costa (Ed.), *Developing minds: Volume II. Programs for teaching thinking.* Alexandria, VA: Association for Supervision and Curriculum Development.

Edwards, J. (1992). *The effects of cognitive coaching on the conceptual development and reflective thinking of first year teachers.* Unpublished doctoral dissertation, Fielding Institute, Santa Barbara, CA.

Foster, N. (1989). *The impact of cognitive coaching on teachers' thought processes as perceived by cognitively coached teachers in the Plymouth-Canton Community School District.* Unpublished doctoral dissertation, Michigan State University, Detroit.

Fromm, E. (1956). *The art of loving.* New York: Harper & Row.

Frymier, J. (1987, September). Bureaucracy and the neutering of teachers. *Phi Delta Kappan, 69*(1), 9-14.

Garfield, C. (1986). *Peak performers: The new heroes of American business.* New York: William Morrow.

Garmston, R., & Hyerle, D. (1988, August). *Professor's peer coaching program: Report on a 1987-88 pilot project to develop and test a staff development model for improving instruction at California State University.* Report prepared for California State University, Sacramento.

Garmston, R., & Wellman, B. (1995, April). Adaptive schools in a quantum universe. *Educational Leadership, 52*(7), 6-12.

Garmston, R., & Wellman, B. (1996). *Adaptive schools: Developing and maintaining collaborative groups.* El Dorado Hills, CA: Four Hats.

Joyce, B., & Showers, B. (1988). *Student achievement through staff development.* New York: Longman.

Paulson, D. (1995, January-February). Finding the soul of work. *At Work: Stories of Tomorrow's Workplace, 4*(1), 18-20.

Rosenholtz, S. (1989). *Teachers' workplace: The social organization of schools.* New York: Longman.

Rowe, M. B. (1986, January/February). Wait time: Slowing down may be a way of speeding up! *Journal of Teacher Education, 23*, 43-49.

Senge, P. (1990). *The fifth discipline: The art and practice of the learning organization.* New York: Doubleday.

Sergiovanni, T. (1994). *Building community in schools.* San Francisco: Jossey-Bass.

Vygotsky, L. (1978). *Mind in society.* Cambridge, MA: Harvard University Press.

10

Developing a Scoring Rubric for a Process School

Charles Lavaroni

In the past, Phaedrus' own radical bias caused him to think of Dynamic Quality alone and neglect static patterns of quality. Until now he had always felt that these static patterns were dead. They have no love. They offer no promise of anything. To succumb to them is to succumb to death, since that which does not change does not live. But now he was beginning to see that this radical bias weakened his own case. Life cannot exist on Dynamic Quality alone. It has no staying power. To cling to Dynamic Quality alone apart from any static patterns is to cling to chaos. He saw that much can be learned about Dynamic Quality by studying what it is rather than futilely trying to define what it is.

Persig, R., 1993, p. 139

And the Lists Go On

How do educators study what *dynamic quality* is in relation to a process-oriented school? Persig (1993) suggests that we look at what "it" is. We describe it, not define it. Many of our collective efforts of the past concentrated on its definition. We have used phrases such as "outcome based," "inquiry centered," "personal meaning," and "participatory management" in trying to define "it." We have assumed that everyone has the same mental construct of these and thousands of other concepts used as we try to define that which we consider *quality*.

Table 10.1 Evidence of School Board Problems

- Boards are not providing far-reaching or politically risk-taking leadership for education reform.
- Boards have become another level of administration, often micromanaging the school district.
- Boards, particularly in diverse communities, are so splintered by their attempts to represent special interests or board members' individual political needs that boards cannot govern.
- Boards have broad goals but lack the capacity for strong goal setting and planning to give direction to school systems.
- Boards are not spending adequate time on educating themselves about the issues or on education policy making.
- Boards have not provided leadership with other agencies and organizations necessary to meet the human and social needs of students.
- Boards do not exercise adequate policy oversight, nor do they have adequate accountability processes and processes for communicating about schools and the school system with the public.
- Boards' actions are less impressive than their rhetoric in devolving decision making to schools.
- Boards exhibit little capacity to develop positive and productive lasting relations with their superintendents.
- Boards pay little or no attention to their governance performance and to their needs for ongoing development of their capacity to govern.
- Boards in conflicted communities tend to make decisions in response to the "issue of the day," whereas boards in more stable communities tend to govern to maintain the *status quo*.

SOURCE: From *Governing Public Schools: New Times, New Requirements*, pp. 62-63, by J. P. Danzberger, M. W. Kirst, and M. D. Usdan, 1992, Washington, DC: Institute for Educational Leadership, Inc. Used by permission.

For years, educators have been exposed to a variety of "lists" either describing what is "wrong" about educational practices currently in vogue or describing what "should be" if education is going to meet its responsibilities in a free, democratic society. Such lists frequently punctuate pieces that speak to the challenge of the future. Sometimes, they describe all the wondrous elements that someone has decided have been lost from the past. At times, they are compilations of observations or impressions about a particular issue (Table 10.1). The one attribute all such lists have in common is that they represent a particular perspective or point of view. Each list, by its nature, is prejudicial. I use the term *prejudicial* in a most positive sense. The purpose of such lists is to offer the clearest picture possible of what the presenter wants the recipient to know, believe, or feel.

Other lists are those under the title or organizational format of "From—To" (Table 10.2). They, along with the "wrong" and/or "should be" lists, appear in textbooks, professional magazines, and, on occasion, statements of purpose from organizations. Sometimes, they contain elements of agreement when they are compared with one another; often, they do not. As should be expected, when they agree, it is because of the underlying values from which the particular lists emerge.

Table 10.2 The Quality Paradigm Shift in Education: From Teaching and Testing to Continuous Learning and Improvement

Old Paradigm of Teaching and Testing	New Paradigm of Continuous Learning and Improvement
Success is artificially limited to a few "winners." All others are made to consider themselves and their work as mediocre or inferior.	Unlimited continuous improvement and successes are the objectives of schooling.
Competition-based.	Cooperation-based.
Lessons are linear, consecutive segments of one-way communication.	Learning is like a spiral with off-shoots, with energy directed toward continuous improvement. Assessments are used for diagnostic and prescriptive purposes.
Product-oriented; focused solely on results, without acknowledgment of their short-term nature. Grades and rankings are important in themselves.	Process-oriented. Goals are important, but the process of getting to the goal is at least as significant. Assessments are used for diagnostic and prescriptive purposes.
Life, including schooling, is only worthwhile if you reach goals. The process has little or no intrinsic merit, and must be abbreviated whenever possible so the goals can be reached sooner.	Life is a journey, and has intrinsic merit if lived with a zest for life, love, and learning. Developing a "yearning for learning" is most important of all.
The system and its processes don't matter as long as the ends are achieved.	The integrity and health of the system, its processes, and its people must be maintained, or the system will be suboptimized and will eventually fail.
Work is a task, not intended to bring joy to the worker.	Work should be challenging, invigorating, and meaningful. Everyone in the school should take pride and joy in the products and processes of the work.
School as a place where teaching is done to (at) students. Students are passive, teachers are active.	School is a true community of learners in which administrators, teachers, and students learn how to get better and better at the work they do together, so that everyone succeeds optimally.
Teachers are isolated from each other by time and space.	Teachers work together to build success with each other and with a manageable number of students in a cohort group.
Administration is viewed as the teachers' natural adversary (perhaps as enemies).	Administrators are viewed as teammates and partners in removing the obstacles to student and teacher successes.
Tayloresque factory model: Rule by compliance, control, command. Authoritarian, hierarchical. Management based upon fear.	New model: Lead by helping and by providing vision and support toward the aim and mission of the school, making it possible for teachers and students to take greater and greater pride in their work together and to have joy in the processes and products of continuous improvement. (In Japan this is called *kaizen*.
Centralized control over resources curriculum, teaching methods, length of class periods, school day, school year, and so on.	Site-based management of resources, curriculum, methods, time considerations, and so on.
Single-discipline instruction.	Multi- and cross-discipline learning.
External validation of truth and the "one right answer" for every question asked by teacher, text, and test.	External and internal truths discovered through students' and teacher's questioning together.
Testing as primary means of assessing the results of the learning process.	Testing, when appropriate, to help modify (improve) the teaching/learning process. Other modes include process portfolios, exhibitions, student-led teacher-parent conferences, performances, and so on.
Instruction is set up to generate (right) answers.	Instruction is set up to generate better and better questions, followed by student inquiry into some of the areas of those questions. Student performances demonstrate improved understanding of the nature of the questions and some of the ways they might be solved.

Table 10.2 Continued

Old Paradigm of Teaching and Testing	New Paradigm of Continuous Learning and Improvement
Teachers are expected to know everything about their subjects. They give students data and information; students memorize it, then promptly forget most of it. Competency demonstrated in exams is short-lived, though this is not reflected in the durable nature of the grades representing that supposed competency.	Teachers are experts in their field. But more importantly, they are the most enthusiastic and dedicated learners in the classroom. Students learn from teachers, other students, community, and other sources, and incorporate those learnings into their lives, applying their insights as appropriate to real-life challenges.
Parents are outsiders, often made to feel unwelcome, even if unintentionally.	Parents are partners, suppliers, and customers. They are an integral part of the student's progress from the very beginning through the end of the schooling process.
Businesses are sometimes welcome to "adopt" a school; kept at arm's length.	Businesses are invited to become partners (secondary suppliers and customers) in the students' continuous progress, not for direct commercial gain.
People of the community are not encouraged to take part in the life of the school, or in the education of the community's young people. Not encouraged to have pride in the community schools.	People of the community are brought into the school and made welcome, encouraged to contribute time and talents to the betterment of their school and their community's children.
Ultimate Goal: Students as products of the school.	Ultimate Goal: Students as their own products, continually improving, expanding their interests, improving their abilities, and developing their character—getting better and better every day and helping others to do the same.

SOURCE: From *Schools of Quality: An Introduction to Total Quality Management in Education,* by John Jay Bonstingl. Association for Supervision and Curriculum Development, Alexandria, VA. Second edition, 1996 (Appendix 4, pp. 101-104). Copyright © John Jay Bonstingl, 1996. Used by special permission of the author. For information, contact The Center for Schools of Quality at (410) 997-7555 or e-mail: Bonstingl@aol.com.

Yet another structure for this type of presentation is one in which two or three similar concepts are described side by side (Table 10.3). The purpose of this type of organization is to present similarities and/or differences between those concept(s) under consideration. These lists provide a guide, usually designed to help the audience quickly clarify a personal understanding of the concepts presented. That they appear in list form with similar subconcepts juxtaposed next to each other simplifies the comparison process for the user.

These methods of organizing data or ideas have some distinct and important positive attributes:

- They are easy to read and use.
- They summarize a great deal of information in a small space.
- They are "cost-effective" in their time-to-function ratio.
- They are easy to reproduce for discussion purposes.
- They quickly present a point of view.
- They can be used to concretize some rather abstract notions.

I have found any one of these presentations interesting and stimulating because they are designed for ease in communication. They have often provided a focus for discussion with peers, parents, students, and the general public. Such

Table 10.3 Standardized Testing Versus Authentic Assessment

Standardized Testing	*Authentic Assessment*
Reduces children's rich and complex lives to a collection of scores, percentiles, or grades	Gives the teacher a "felt sense" of the child's unique experience as a learner
Creates stresses that negatively affect a child's performance	Provides interesting, active, lively, and exciting experiences
Creates a mythical standard or norm which requires that a certain percentage of children fail	Establishes an environment where every child has the opportunity to succeed
Pressures teachers to narrow their curriculum to only what is tested on an exam	Allows teachers to develop meaningful curricula and assess within the context of that program
Emphasizes one-shot exams that assess knowledge residing in a single mind at a single moment in time	Assess on an *ongoing* basis in a way that provides a more accurate picture of a student's achievements
Tends to place the focus of interpretation on errors, mistakes, low scores, and other things that children *can't* do	Puts the emphasis on a student's *strengths;* tells what they *can* do and what they're *trying* to do
Focuses too much importance on single sets of data (i.e., test scores) in making education decisions	Provides *multiple* sources of evaluation that give a more accurate view of a student's progress
Treats all students in a uniform way	Treats each student as a unique human being
Discriminates against some students because of cultural background and learning style	Provides a *culture-fair* assessment of a student's performance; gives everyone an equal chance to succeed
Judges the child without providing suggestions for improvement	Provides information that is *useful* to the learning process
Regards testing and instruction as separate activities	Regards assessment and teaching as two sides of the same coin
Answers are final; students rarely receive an opportunity to revise, reflect, or redo a testing experience	Engages the child in a continual process of self-reflection, mediated learning, and revision
Provides results that can be fully understood only by a trained professional	Describes a child's performance in common-sense terms that can be easily understood by parents, children, and other noneducators
Produces scoring materials that students often never see again	Results in products that have *value* to students and others
Focuses on "the right answer"	Deals with *processes* as much as final products
Places students in artificial learning environments that disturb the natural ecology of learning	Examines students in *unobtrusive* ways within the context of their natural learning environments.
Usually focuses on lower-order learning skills	Includes higher-order thinking skills and important subjective domains (e.g., insight and integrity)

(continued)

Table 10.3 Continued

Standardized Testing	*Authentic Assessment*
Encourages extrinsic learning (e.g., learning to pass a test or to get a good score)	Fosters learning for its own sake
Has time limits that constrain many pupils' thinking processes	Provides students with the time they need to work through a problem, project, or process
Is generally limited to reading, listening, and marking on a piece of paper	Involves creating, interviewing, demonstrating, solving problems, reflecting, sketching, discussing, and engaging in many other active learning tasks
Generally forbids students to interact	Encourages cooperative learning
Promotes unhelpful comparisons between children	Compares students with their own past performances

SOURCE: From *Multiple Intelligences in the Classroom* (pp. 117-118), by T. Armstrong, 1994, Alexandria, VA: Association for Supervision and Curriculum Development. Used by permission.

lists sometimes caused personal moments of revelation, often periods of anxiety, an occasional pang of guilt, and, on especially relevant and personally important issues, a sense of excitement and celebration, especially when my values have been reinforced and validated.

On reflection, however, I have also found that these lists have frequently left much to be desired. Their simplicity makes it possible for misunderstanding to occur. A list without clarification assumes that the person reading it is coming to that experience with the same or similar background, knowledge, values, and beliefs as the person who prepared the list. The easy reproducibility of these types of presentations is certainly a strength. It is also, however, a possible weakness. Reviewing a list without thought, consideration, and reflection might well lead to nothing more than an exercise in memory. The list, regardless of how it is organized, conceivably could help a person derive a rather shallow understanding of the concepts or points of view it is intended to explore, develop, or perpetuate.

Although these lists do help focus on a particular issue and/or concept, they have also been used as a means to develop a sense of direction for those people looking to evaluate where they are or where they are going. For example, Table 10.1 might easily be used by individual school board members to assess how well they measure up to some of the apparently observable criticisms of how boards perform their duties. If they collect data that suggest that they, as a board of education, are not experiencing many of these "problems," they might use the data to suggest they are functioning effectively and efficiently. To conduct such assessments, there has to be some type of agreement that these specific behaviors are in fact "wrong" and "observable." This refers to the earlier statement that lists, by their very nature, are prejudicial. If there isn't agreement, then board members could use the same list to determine how well they are doing by showing that they *are not* experiencing many of those listed "problems" considered inappropriate and harmful by the authors of the list. Either way, that list can be used to help determine success when it is compared with the reality of the actions of the school board being studied.

Tables 10.2 and 10.3 could readily be used to help people evaluate their current status in relation to the concepts rooted in the lists. Table 10.2 assists those of us who want to see whether or not we are moving toward Bonstingl's (1996) description of *quality*. Table 10.3 helps educators who are interested in having a better understanding of the relationship between authentic assessment and standardized testing (Armstrong, 1994) to assess their adherence to any of his interpretations of those differences, especially as they are related to Gardner's (1990) theory of multiple intelligences.

Although each of those applications or uses of the list might be legitimate and helpful, there are at least three concerns. First, looking at any of these lists in isolation ignores that none of them represent the reality that education is a system made up of many related and interrelated parts. Every classroom, school, district, intermediate unit, state department of education, college, university, and so on throughout the United States is part of that system. Public schools as well as independent schools must be included. Charter schools, home instruction, and tutorial programs are all part of the system. To review those lists without identifying the specific environment to which the list is being applied is making the assumption that there is universal agreement as to the values and beliefs underlying that part of the system being reviewed.

Lists tend to be all or nothing. Table 10.2, for example, is a complete, comprehensive, and impressive list of many of the changes that would have to be in place if quality principles were to become part of the system—part of a learning organization. As Bonstingl (1992) states, "There would have to be a significant paradigm shift for those changes to take place" (p. 31). Certainly, many ideas he suggests as descriptors of that paradigm shift are consistent with those found throughout the three volumes of this Process as Content trilogy. Although Bonstingl does not suggest it in the remainder of the text, his list assumes first that to bring about change, we are probably all starting from the same place. To get to the new paradigm implies we are initially locked into the old. Thus, the second concern is that lists, although they effectively describe what the system will look like *when* it achieves quality, do not provide any indicators or benchmarks as to what the system would look like *while* it moves toward that end.

A third concern is that these lists are designed to focus on only one or two issues, concepts, or concerns at a time, often completely separate from the other elements directly influencing them. This is one of their strengths, and, as is often the case, it automatically becomes one of its weaknesses. Revisit Table 10.3. There is no question that Armstrong speaks directly and effectively to the differences between standardized testing and authentic assessment when considering the effect of Gardner's (1990) theory on classroom programs. It must be observed, however, that this list, as in the case of most such lists, reviews its content in isolation from and between the many related and interrelated concepts, concerns, or issues that make up the totality of what or how the child learns according to Gardner. Nor does the list reflect the many other ingredients that make up the system in which the student learns. It does not speak to questions of how the curriculum is to be delivered or organized; how the classroom, school, or district is governed; the role of the administration or the board in relation to assessment and evaluation; and why the changes described should be institutionalized. These and many more questions and ideas are reviewed throughout Armstrong's writing. They appear both before and after the presentation of the list. Yet by the very nature of listing, those other elements take on a lesser place in relation to all the other patterns that make up the totality—the system.

These and the literally hundreds of such lists already existing might be helpful as educators analyze and plan for the necessary elements that make a process-oriented school. Certainly, they remind us that many separate and yet interrelated concerns must be studied. As the three previous examples indicate, a process-oriented school recognizes the importance of how the school is governed, the relation of organization to the idea of quality, as well as the roles of assessment and evaluation. And, there are more!

Revelations in Rubrics

All the preceding is designed to help set the foundation for the introduction of yet another style of list: the *rubric*. A *rubric* is defined as a scoring system used to evaluate performance. Rubrics consist of a fixed scale, a list of characteristics that describe criteria at each score point for a particular outcome, and sample responses (anchors) for the various points on the scale (adapted from the Maryland School Performance Assessment Program, 1991).

Rubrics have many of the same strengths and weaknesses of the other types of lists previously reviewed. They are simple and easy to use. They present particular points of view and provide a great deal of information organized in a relatively small space. They assume that there is general agreement as to the values represented in the rating scale, from low to high.

The rubric format has some advantages over other lists. It is designed specifically to help in the evaluation process. It recognizes that several levels of "achievement" are involved when trying to evaluate where we are and where we are going. The particular rubric described in this chapter also acknowledges that many interrelated parts make up the whole.

Table 10.4, "A Rubric for a Process-Oriented School," is presented for review with the following disclaimers:

1. This rubric is my product and is based on the work of a group of teachers and administrators from several independent schools throughout Africa. The original rubric on which this is built was developed as a part of a workshop co-led by Dr. Arthur Costa and myself in the spring of 1995 in Nairobi, Kenya. That workshop was sponsored by a professional organization, the Association of Independent Schools of Africa (AISA).

   As in all lists, it is important to know not only why the list was developed but by whom. Lists and rubrics, by their very nature, are prejudicial.

This one is no different. It proudly offers a visual way to look at a school, a quick way to focus attention on the collection of assessment data, a quick way to diagnose where the school is in relation to the data, and a quick way to determine some possible problem areas in relation to this particular point of view.

2. This rubric is most useful to the workshop participants who were active in its development. It will not and should not be transferred to another group, school, or district. As is always the case, the process of developing the rubric must become the responsibility of the people using it. This one might be used as a model to offer some ideas, some suggestions, and some notions of import.

3. This rubric reflects many of the ideas and concepts about the importance of process found throughout the Process as Content trilogy. It is hoped that there is nothing in violation with those ideas and concepts. On the assumption that there are no significant and serious discrepancies between the rubric and the ideas presented by other contributors, it must be recognized that if another author had the responsibility to prepare this chapter, the rubric would be different. Not only would different people offer different rubrics, but if I were asked to prepare a similar rubric sometime in the future, it, too, would be different.

4. This rubric does not have any "anchors." Those are up to the reader-user to identify. Think of the school that has some of the descriptors or indicators of the characteristics described in each level of the scale and in each category of the rubric. Remember, there are many parts that make up the whole. Any anchor, to be of value, should be discreet enough to be useful—it is unlikely that any one anchor will be used for the identification of all the qualities described. There will be differences between the various categories as well as differences between the levels represented within any one category.

5. This rubric recognizes five possible categories of indicators of the school of process: governance, organization and climate, instruction, curriculum, and assessment/evaluation. One might want to look at others, such as community involvement, students' rights and responsibilities, the role of technology, budget and finance, and so on. The issue is the recognition of and response to the multiple influences on the development of the school as a learning organization.

Rubrics as Instruments of Change

Those of us interested in moving toward a process-oriented school need some type of instrument and/or process that provides the vision, direction, and a means to communicate movement. The rubric is such an instrument. The process of developing and interpreting this instrument (rubric) can function as the communication focus for continuous movement.

Rubrics exist because people created them. This rather simple and obvious statement might at first reading appear to be silly. Yet I include it here to make

Table 10.4 A Rubric for a Process-Oriented School

Level	Governance	Organization/Climate	Instruction	Curriculum	Assessment/Evaluation
Level 4 The Process School Vision held by everyone	Shared ownership and responsibility Problems identified at any level and solutions sought by all levels Bottom-up decisions Student involvement valued and encouraged Site-based management system in place Individuals are the focus Change is seen as growth	Student choice and control of learning and scheduling Authentic learning activities in all classrooms Minimal time constraints Total integration of content Teacher as mentor Flexible grouping Flexible scheduling Students pose own questions/answers Risk taking assumed	Process based Emphasis on whole person Integrated approach Student directed Collaborative learning emphasized Critical thinking processes infused Instruction not limited to the classroom	Cross-cultural Inquiry driven Fluid, organic, and serendipitous Teacher as facilitator and resource Concept and process focused Recognition of unlimited sources of knowledge, including the student Values explored Focus on learning about learning	Student centered Focus on self-evaluation Multiple tools and strategies used Partnerships: parent-student-staff Focus on quality products Continuous process Purposes made clear and public Assessment and instruction intertwined
Level 3 The Transitional School Vision held by principal and some staff	Attempts at shared ownership evident Change is encouraged Recognized school community links in place Administration seeks input from staff and others Individuality somewhat encouraged	Entire school community has input Faculty and students share in classroom decisions Students have some choices Opportunities for many alternative activities Some multiaged grouping and other alternative grouping Risk taking allowed	Teacher learning to be facilitator Evidence of more student involvement Some individualized learning strategies Cooperative learning encouraged Instruction defined by curriculum and student needs Emphasis on process along with content Students encouraged as active learners	Recognition of changing needs of students Pragmatic curriculum Some piloting of innovative programs Attempt to match curriculum materials with instructional materials Integrated curriculum introduced Recognition of the individual's role in personal meaning	Some attempts at authentic assessment Recognition of the differences between assessment and evaluation Use of more than one form of assessment Grades often a mix of traditional and newer methods of evaluation External norms still in place

Level 2 The Traditional School Vision held by principal and those above	Principal implements policy rigidly Policies are determined externally Policies are imposed Principal ownership ("my school/my staff") Staff role seen as one of conformity Much insecurity with change Focus on the status quo	Some flexibility in scheduling Some teacher input for schoolwide decisions Some student input for classroom decisions Some opportunity for alternative learning activities Ability groups in place Much independent silent work Risk taking discouraged	Teacher centered Lecture main instructional strategy Emphasis on texts and work sheets Instruction focused on recall and memorization Limited student interaction Some group work in place Some independent thinking encouraged Some encouragement of risk taking	Limited resources in place Content tried-and-true Defined by textbooks Syllabus "must be covered" Skills and content taught in isolation Frequent external values imposed Little encouragement of creativity in the academics Emphasis on mechanics and detail	Reliance on standardized tests Reliance on external norms Students compared with each other Bell curve is used Self-evaluation introduced Percentages serve as major criteria for success "Grades" are valid with little public criteria Dominated by letter grades and symbols
Level 1 The Archaic School Vision held only at top levels	All decisions from the board and/or superintendent External control of all details Absence of freedom for all participants Very little change evident or possible Centralized structure/authority Focus on specific procedures Obedience is expected and required from all	Decision making hierarchical Inflexible schedules Subjects taught in isolation Dominated by rules Limited or no choice Silence is valued above other school attributes Children "seen, not heard"	Teacher dispenses all knowledge Recall of the Three Rs as primary goal of learning No deviation from syllabus/textbook Student independent thought discouraged Student risk taking discouraged and often punished Little or no student interaction	Personal and cultural values presented as universal Attempt at total uniformity of pacing of information Content rigid by age and grade Very few resources available or used Presented as linear and sequential Assumes a finite body of knowledge	No consideration of individual strengths or weaknesses Skills and knowledge assessed/evaluated in isolation from instruction Routine tests No recognition of self-assessment, even as a concept Used as rewards and punishments Teacher infallible

SOURCE: Based on a rubric developed as part of a workshop co-led by C. Lavaroni and A. Costa, Spring 1995, in Nairobi, Kenya, sponsored by the Association of Independent Schools of Africa.

a point! Rubrics are most beneficial to the people who design and use them. A process-oriented school certainly recognizes and incorporates the function of process in the creation and re-creation of any such rubric. As learning is continuous and always changing, so is any viable rubric. The process-oriented school recognizes the relationship between what is and what could be—as does a rubric. And, as indicated above, many people must be involved in the development and implementation of that rubric. Teachers, administrators, students, parents, and community members are all stakeholders in the change process. They all have roles to play throughout the system. They all must have the opportunity to participate in the evolution of a rubric that will be used to evaluate any progress, change, and/or problems in the movement toward the ultimate goal.

Obviously, one of the more important results of the development of any rubric is the opportunity that process provides for open communication between all the participants. That communication requires clarity. The process necessitates precision of language. It makes clear as to what is dynamic—and what is static. It makes public what needs change and what needs to be maintained.

A rubric, by its nature, is an interesting instrument. Any truly useful rubric is, and should be, a living instrument. It is never complete. It provides a target toward which various participants in the system can collect assessment data. To collect those data, we must be able to clearly identify what indicators are consistent with what we are studying. For example, if, as in the model rubric introduced earlier, we were agreed that in a Level 4 school, "students pose own questions/answers," a system must be in place to collect evidential data as to who is involved in the identification of questions and answers and how often. Observations, videotapes, audiotapes, journals, reflective essays, and personal checklists might be some of the means that could be employed to collect those types of data. As those data are studied further, clarification of the rubric will occur.

Rubrics also serve as a means to evaluate progress. Data can be interpreted in relation to the agreed-on goals as indicated in the various levels of that rubric. Each level in each category under study helps identify where "we are" as we move toward the highest level of that rubric. That level, the highest, is the goal. The highest level of the rubric does more than specify or define. It serves as a means of study—to collect a wide range of appropriate and authentic data, as well as to describe and communicate anchor examples of, as Wiggens (1993) might say, a world-class process-oriented school. It offers focal points and direction for our creativity.

The Process-Oriented School: A True Learning Organization

This, then, is the basic meaning of a "learning organization"—an organization that is continually expanding its capacity to create its future. For such an organization, it is not enough to merely survive. "Survival learning" or what is more often termed "adaptive learning" is important—indeed necessary. But for a learning organization, "adaptive learning" must be joined by "generative learning," learning that en-hances our capacity to create. (Senge, 1990, p. 14)

References

Armstrong, T. (1994). *Multiple intelligences in the classroom.* Alexandria, VA: Association for Super-vision and Curriculum Development.

Bonstingl, J. J. (1992). *Schools of quality: An introduction to total quality management in education.* Alexandria, VA: Association for Supervision and Curriculum Development.

Bonstingl, J. J. (1996). *Schools of quality: An introduction to total quality management in education* (2nd ed.). Alexandria, VA: Association for Supervision and Curriculum Development.

Costa, A. (1991). *The school as a home for the mind.* Palatine, IL: Skylight.

Danzberger, J. P., Kirst, M. W., & Usdan, M. D. (1992). *Governing public schools: New times, new requirements.* Washington, DC: Institute for Educational Leadership.

Gardner, H. (1990). *Frames of mind: Theory of multiple intelligences.* Cambridge, MA: Harvard University Press.

Lavaroni, C. (1994, Winter). Self-evaluation: A learned process. *Inquiry: Critical Thinking Across the Disciplines, 14*(2). (Newsletter of the Institute for Critical Thinking, Upper Montclair, NJ)

Lavaroni, C., & Costa, A. (1995, November). Promoting self-evaluation, not self-defense. *Critical Linkages, 2*(5). (Newsletter of Sager Educational Enterprises, Chestnut Hills, MA)

Maryland school performance assessment program. (1991). Baltimore: Maryland Department of Educa-tion.

Persig, R. M. (1993). *Lila: An inquiry into morals.* London: Transworld.

Senge, P. (1990). *The fifth discipline: The art and practice of the learning organization.* New York: Doubleday.

Wiggens, G. (1993). *Assessing student performance.* San Francisco: Jossey-Bass.

11

Capturing the Spirit

Process Pervades the Organization

Joseph M. Saban

This chapter is a story about process beginning to pervade an organization. The introduction of the chapter is no more than an invitation to you to take a journey. On the journey, you will be asked to immerse yourself in thought about organizations, learners, and change. Begin only when you are ready to do what you are asked. The following pages are inspired by Mr. Outlaw's words and process-centered learning. The journey leads you through an experience of a school district in Illinois that has "captured the spirit." The journey also exposes a process through which thoughts become destiny.

The story begins with an Illinois school district's attempt to capture the "process spirit" in an unusual but significant way. The school district needed to design and build its fourth high school because of overcrowding. A referendum, brought before the community for $32 million, passed.

The new school had to reflect in brick and mortar what the community valued for its children. We (the school district community of learners) saw the brick and mortar as an opportunity to "capture the spirit" of, and to engage our constituency in, the skills, operations, and dispositions of process-centered learning.

During your journey through this chapter, insights are shared about the theoretical frameworks influencing the school district's blueprints for action. Three major constructs are unfolded for your examination. The constructs are related to the district's experience and promoted as invitations through which you may find your own ways to "capture the spirit." The three major constructs are (a) the systems operating in typical schools today, (b) the value system underlying process-centered learning, and (c) five disciplines of learning organizations.

You are invited to analyze (and synthesize) personal experience, process-oriented theory, and your own reflective thoughts. This chapter concludes with a challenge for you to think about reconstructing your school into one that promotes process-centered learning everywhere.

Capturing the Spirit: An Illinois Experience

A Process Envisioned

We had big decisions to make. We wanted the best architect team we could find. After all, an opportunity to design a new high school from the ground up isn't a common happening. We thought we knew what we wanted in a high school building, but we also knew that translating our vision into actual brick and mortar would require architects with great personal and technical skill. We determined that our architects needed to be open to learning and to be professionals who would honor the collective intelligence of the school design team we had assembled. Our architects would need to accept the challenge of designing a space in which learners could gather and find a place where their thoughts, feelings, and actions blend in powerful ways. This architect team had to be one that could capture, in brick and mortar, the spirit of process. Finally, our architect team needed to find how that spirit could operate pervasively within the building through numerous subtle and not so subtle features.

If our architects possessed the process orientation we valued (i.e., the spirit), we knew that the school would be not solely a place for the purveying of information but also a place in which learners gathered to be coaches and to be coached. We felt certain that the spirit would allow those who assembled here to be innovators, collaborators, and researchers. The spirit would ensure that the physical plant supported the positive faith that humans are natural and continual inquirers who are internally motivated, curious, and passionately driven to resolve problems. In short, our architects needed to be translators of our process-oriented value system.

We published a request for proposals and got to the task at hand. Firm after firm came to us, each representing itself in different ways. Some presented us with written recommendations from former or current clients. Others had polished, canned presentations that included combinations of photographs, blueprints, recommendations, videotapes, and even miniature representations of buildings they had designed.

All these factors were informative but did not capture our interest. We wanted to see *how* the architects developed their representations, not *what* they had brought with them as relics of past action. We wanted to know (a) how they intended to structure the process of building design, (b) how their thinking might influence the design of our school, (c) how they would attend to our process-oriented values, (d) how they would gather and process information, and (e) how they would translate process values into brick and mortar. We were most interested in their process skills, their use of process operations, and their process dispositions. Our professional judgment held that process-oriented architects would build process-oriented schools.

The Process of Searching for a Process Orientation

Our interview process was designed to be a filtering mechanism that, in the end, would convince us that the firm we selected could indeed "capture the spirit." Ultimately, we wanted to feel confident that when we inked the contract, the selected team of architects possessed and was congruent with the values we held. Using our values and our undergirding vision, we developed a three-stage screening process. Stage 1 was traditional and consisted of soliciting written proposals from architectural firms. These proposals were screened and rated for evidence of a process orientation. Stage 1 filtered out 26 of 32 proposals! Stage 2 featured a face-to-face meeting at which a short list of six firms were allowed to present anything they pleased for the first 15 minutes and the last 5 minutes. We required the architects to react to questions formulated around process-oriented values and the cognitive coaching model's states of mind (Costa & Garmston, 1994). Table 11.1 offers sample questions, sorted by the states of mind, that the architects were asked to answer.

The interview committee assessed each firm by ranking the firm's oral answers. Stage 2 further culled the hopefuls to three finalists. In Stage 3, the finalists were given a list of questions to which they were to prepare written answers within a specified period of time (see Table 11.2 for representative questions). The answers were then analyzed by looking for innovation, flexibility, creativity, logic, and research. The responses were rated numerically. To close the architect selection process, the interview team looked, in total, at the assessments made in Stages 1, 2, and 3. Following all this, a decision was made to concentrate on one firm.

What We Learned

We checked references and visited a number of buildings designed by our chosen firm. We talked to the educators in these buildings about the processes the architects used in design. We wanted to know if the architects exhibited process skills, operations, and dispositions in practice. After our numerous visits and inquiries, we felt satisfied that our process had identified the type of architectural firm we envisioned for our important project. The successful architect team was the one whose professional portfolio of completed projects most closely matched what we valued for our community's children and the process-oriented vision we held for our school. We learned that the architects'

Table 11.1 Architects' Values/States of Mind Questions: Oral Interview

State of Mind: **Interdependence**

> Given the task of designing an 1800 seat high school, describe in detail:
>
> a.) who (by name or by job description) should be on the project design team as well as what function they would serve,
>
> b.) lines of communication that need to be established for the timely completion of this project.
>
> In order to ensure that equitable opportunity for students is secured, explain which design team member's expertise would be most utilized in the quest for sex and educational equity within the new building.

State of Mind: **Flexibility**

> As technological and instructional advances in education unfold so will the space utilization demands on our buildings. Detail how you will guarantee the building will be designed to:
>
> a.) incorporate flexibility within the physical structure to accommodate changing technologies and teaching.
> b.) support reflective professional practice and innovative thinking.

State of Mind: **Craftsmanship**

> Discuss how your architectural firm can assist us in developing;
>
> a.) realistic financial targets and budgets for the project,
> b.) checks and balances to limit over-design or construction excess,
> c.) school district confidence that existing budgetary limitations are adequate for the architect to oversee the successful completion of this endeavor.

State of Mind: **Consciousness**

> Suppose for a minute that your children were going to attend this school. What design/construction elements of the school would you advocate for that world:
>
> a.) maximize your student's learning and achievement while engendering a deepened sense of responsibility for their own education,
> b.) insure that the school be a place that your child and the district's staff want to attend.

State of Mind: **Efficacy**

> As our community grows, social issues will further alter the school environment. Predicting what the social trends and pressures are likely to develop in this area of the state, discuss how the campus design can:
>
> a.) contribute to an environment that is physically safe for students to attend,
> b.) allow for an environment that is psychologically safe for students in which to learn.
>
> In order to ensure that equitable opportunity for students is secured, explain design features you would incorporate in the building that would support equitable student opportunities.

Table 11.2　Architects' Values/States of Mind Questions: Written Interview

State of Mind: **Interdependence**

a.) In an effort to hold down misunderstanding and conflict on the job, what provisions, understandings or job related realities must be in place before construction actually begins?
b.) From your experiences on job sites, which trades, professionals, or bureaucrats have been most difficult to work with?　How do you describe your own communication style when working with these people?
c.) What can an architect contribute that will help ensure that the school they are working on will be safe for the tradesmen, owners, partners, community, staff and student?

State of Mind: **Flexibility**

a.) If you were the owner of this project. describe what specific kinds of on the job flexibility you would expect from an architect.　Give specific examples and how an owner could insure that creativity and flexibility exist on this job.
b.) You have just had a valuable engineering idea that would allow for the boys who will attend this school to have an improved athletic locker room at no extra cost. Let us know how you would inform the owner and the architect of your idea and options the owner and architect should now consider.

State of Mind: **Craftsmanship**

a.) You have an idea that will save the owner money, but the contractor disagrees with the merit of your idea.　What do you do? How might a contract with the owner read to prevent this occurrence and why?　Should others mediate?　Who? (no attorneys please!)
b.) Identify one duty contained with your job responsibilities that gives you the most satisfaction. One that gives you the least satisfaction.

State of Mind: **Consciousness**

a.) Briefly describe your duties on your last job site.　Identify something that you learned about construction on that job and how what you learned will improve your ability on this job.
b.) What attitudes does your company have towards improving your skills?　Give specific examples of opportunities you have been given to learn by your company and how you will use what you have learned on this job site.
c.) What provisions do you make for time to look back on a day's work, a week's work, a month's work, a year's work and a completed project with your team? With contractors? With the owner?

State of Mind: **Efficacy**

a.) Suppose your children were going to attend this school.　What one aspect of the school's design, engineering, or construction are you going to be most interested in?　Each team member should answer this.
b.) Compare and contrast the following statements then give your opinion of the statement with which you are most closely aligned.
　　　This is a building for education.　　　　　This is a building for children.
c.) The owner intends to award a bid to a local contractor on a particularly difficult aspect of the job but another contractor you have successfully worked with on a number of occasions has an identical bid. What do you do?

answers to our questions were true representations of the architects' quality of work and, perhaps more important, of the architects' professional values. We discovered this partially by examining the buildings they built but more so by examining the process the architects had used in designing them.

As our school building project progressed, we delighted in the way our architect team purposefully engaged individuals, small groups, and large groups. Parents, educators, students, neighbors, agencies, utilities, engineers, contractors, and various experts were assembled and challenged to assist us in our learning about how to design and construct our new school. We were pleased to witness the architects consider the human element and how learners would feel in the new building as they participated in activities there. We were excited about the way space was designed to promote human interaction for all learners and the easy manner with which resources could be accessed. We were gratified with the way the design promotes the general public's use as a way to promote lifelong learning in our community. We were impressed with the architects' planning when designing the exterior walls as weight-bearing walls so the inside of the building might easily change and evolve when professional practice dictates internal modification. We were tantalized with the potentials for a truly integrated process-oriented curriculum by the placement of centers for learners to innovate, research, assess, and grow. We were appreciative of the prospect of drawing together the external site environment and the learning experience through the considerable attention to natural light, internal courtyards, and alignment of learners' sight lines with the natural beauty of the site. In all, the architects, as a result of our interview process and subsequent team-centered learning, knew what we valued. More important, they were able to translate the values, by way of their technical skills, an array of process-oriented operations, and process-centered dispositions, to brick and mortar.

Educators as Architects: Construct 1:
The Systems of a School

In many ways, educators are architects. They are architects in the sense that they assist in designing and building climate and programs that define teaching and learning in schools. Although it is rare that educators have the opportunity to assist in the design of a school from the ground up, they are involved on a daily basis in designing, monitoring, and fine-tuning internal learning systems. These systems are not the heating and cooling, electrical, and plumbing aspects about which professional architects are concerned. Instead, these are the systems of curriculum, staff development, personnel management, building climate, instructional program, public relations, special population services, leadership, planning for change, supervision, problem solving, decision making, service to learners, research, assessment, technology, and finance. This list identifies many (perhaps not all) of the internal systems a typical school possesses. Operating within each of these systems are process skills, operations, and dispositions that give each system its identity and purpose.

Our challenge as educators is to seek out and change processes now operating in the systems that are not congruent with the tenets of process-oriented education. We must toil to eliminate regimented and convergent thinking in all systems of a school. As educators, we understand the school organization and its internal workings just as architects understand the internal mechanics of a school building. Moreover, like architects, we influence the organization by adjusting the processes that operate within the systems.

We must ask ourselves, reflect on, and seek the answers to these questions: Should our passion for process influence all school systems? Or does the spirit live only in curricular arenas? Could a process-centered, value-driven approach pervade a learning organization? Or is the spirit's bounded space confined to specific systems and not inclusive of all the organization? Individually and collectively, are we capable of influencing the systems of education with which we interact? Or might these systems be so entrenched in tradition that they cannot be changed? Those who lead will be the architects for the practical translation of these questions into organizational reality.

The Spirit of Process-Centered Learning: Construct 2: Process-Oriented Value System

To move an organization, system by system, to a process-centered orientation, one must first be in touch with process-centered values. Current learned thinkers—Collins and Porras (1994), Covey (1989, 1991), Land and Jarman (1992), Senge (1990), and others—tell us that organizations will change only when *individuals* shift to living with a new set of values. These values represent the spirit of the process-centered school. Our experience with changing the traditional school design to a highly process-centered approach may serve as an example. We consciously applied a set of process-centered values in an attempt to hire a process-centered architectural firm. In this way, we applied process-centered values and techniques to influence and modify the physical building and all its systems.

Coursing through, and undergirding each of the preceding chapters, seven distinct process-centered values manifest themselves in elegant and diverse ways. They appear and reappear as fractals throughout this trilogy, *Process as Content*. They surface over and over again within the bounded space of school systems. These values are listed below. Take a moment to study them. Then reflect on what you have read in the previous chapters. You will be able to identify the presence of the process values—the spirit—in each chapter. Often, they reside in the chapters in quiet, subtle ways. These seven values constitute the architectural framework on which grows the passion for process-centered schools. Moreover, they are the educator-architect's structural framework on which to rebuild the school organization system by system.

The Seven Values

The seven values below serve as scaffolding in the reconstruction of our craft, our systems, and our organizations. Those who dream of building process-oriented schools value

1. promoting humans to become lifelong learners who possess the necessary process skills;

2. honoring the collective intelligence of the group as well as the individual intelligence of the learners;

3. seeking congruence between what learners are thinking, feeling, and doing;

4. structuring schools as learning societies in which educators are not merely dispensers of information but coaches, catalysts, innovators, researchers, and collaborators with learners;

5. fostering the development of learners' unique abilities while recognizing that each is in a constant process of growth and change;

6. striving for a significant process-oriented curriculum as the passion that binds the organization; and

7. believing that humans are natural inquirers and learners who are internally motivated, naturally curious, and driven to resolve problems.

Process-Centered Schools: Construct 3: The Five Disciplines of Learning Organizations

Senge (1990) characterizes elegant learning organizations as places in which individuals actively engage in five distinct disciplines:

1. *Shared vision:* Creatively seeking to unearth shared "pictures of the future" that foster genuine commitment among people

2. *Systems thinking:* Integrating the thinking of others and fusing those thoughts into a coherent body of theory that seeks out interrelationships

3. *Mental models:* Recognizing internal patterns in our world, scrutinizing those patterns, and making them open to the influence of others

4. *Personal mastery:* Willingly clarifying and deepening our individual skills in pursuit of improved practices

5. *Team learning:* Thinking, discovering, and planning together through mastering the practice of dialogue and discussion

Senge's disciplines become useful as a model in reconstructing our schools as value-driven, process-centered, learning organizations.

Discipline 1: Shared Vision

Our reconstruction process began by developing a clear shared vision of what a process-centered organization looks like. Authors of other chapters in the books in this trilogy initiate the visioning process by having us look at process orientations in many of the systems found within schools. As an example, Marilyn Tabor and Fred Wood challenge us to envision staff development as a process approach, whereas Bena Kallick, Charles Lavaroni, Art Costa, and Rosemarie Liebmann draw our attention to envisioning assessment in a process-centered organization. Their vision acts as a guide for us. Their vision becomes even more powerful when aligned consciously with values. Similar to architects attempting to construct a new building around a clear set of values, so must we reconstruct the school clearly knowing the values that drive our vision. Shared vision and undergirding values provide the framework to reflect on our decision making.

Moreover, reflection (Schon, 1987) ensures that our decisions are truly aligned with our vision and values. Argyris (1982) tags the reflective process involving the review of values *double loop feedback*. In double loop feedback, decisions are evaluated on how they promote the values and vision of the organization. Shared vision and a commonly held value system allow us to acknowledge common ground to which we can retreat for dialogue when disagreement arises. On these grounds, problems and confusion can be dealt with respectfully, rather than in belligerent encounters. Disagreement can be dealt with as a positive element, rather than avoided and swept under the carpet.

Discipline 2: Systems Thinking

As we continue to reconstruct our organizations to be truly process-centered, we engage in systems thinking. We consider all systems in operation in the organization and attempt to integrate a process approach when making decisions about each system. We must remember the Peking butterfly effect, that is, tinkering with one system will in some way affect the others. For example, when we institute process-centered staff development, we may also consider (a) process-centered hiring and induction practices that select staff members who value and have dispositions toward personal growth and lifelong learning, (b) process-centered budgeting practices that involve the budgeter as a collaborator in staff development, and (c) process-centered building decisions that are creative and ensure that physical space will not limit what is learned in staff development activities. This type of systems thinking promotes process throughout the organization and gives us a way to create a definition of what we want to be.

Discipline 3: Mental Models

Progressing in the reconstruction, we seek to integrate all the systems in our schools by engaging in dialogue about them in relation to jointly accepted processes known as mental models. These models are commonly held, widely known, tried-and-true procedures and understandings of how we go about our organizational business. With these models, we challenge tradition and follow process-centered change schemes such as those proposed by Fullan (1990) and Bridges (1991). Ideally, each of a school's systems is scrutinized using these models. In this analysis, the systems are transformed to capture the spirit nested in the seven process values.

In advancing our reconstruction, we must relish being problem posers and problem solvers while we operationalize the ideas proposed in this book. We organize commonly accepted feedback models to inform us of our progress and to keep us aligned with our values. Feedback spirals as proposed by Costa and Kallick (1995) serve as an example of a useful mental model to assist our thinking and reflection, both as individuals and as a group. We attempt to engage these commonly accepted models in a fractal manner across the entire organization and within each system of the school. We find that commonly held models provide us with a common language through which we communicate our inspirations, successes, and failures. The models, we discover, help us learn and change. As an example, we learned that feedback spirals allow us to adopt a common language and a commonly accepted means to monitor change in systems we are reconstructing. The model is useful whether we are talking about reconstructing personnel operations, custodian's responsibilities, finance, supervision plan, or any system found within the organization. We further notice that the model is useful in thinking about changes occurring at the classroom level, the building level, and the district level. The feedback model works horizontally across levels of the organization and vertically through the organization. The feedback model also engages those who use it in various process skills and operations.

Discipline 4: Personal Mastery

While we engage in the process of changing the organization, we must also personally change. We must deepen and clarify our personal understanding of process-centered education. For example, the superintendent and all others who lead must be willing to expand their own understanding of what a process orientation means in science, reading, history, and so on. Leaders must also show willingness to learn about how exceptional children, communication networks, staff development, and so forth operate in a process-oriented organization. By learning these things, a superintendent may artfully engage in planning the support of process endeavors across all the district's systems. Knowledge allows the superintendent (analogous to architects assisting in the translation of values to brick and mortar) to position resources so that process values have a chance to be implemented in practical ways. Process-centered leaders must continuously work toward personal mastery of the skills, operations, and dispositions of process-centered education. In doing so, leaders may better mesh in the process-centered culture and indeed even model it. As leaders of a process-oriented organization, it is the engagement in continuous learning that is the very essence of leadership.

Discipline 5: Team Learning

Process-centered orientation in education values the collective growth and intelligence of the group as well as the abilities and growth of the individual. Team learning is structured into ordinary routine tasks as well as the extraordinary task of reconstructing all the systems of a school. To do this, the open discussion of process values and how the values relate to and influence team tasks initiates every team meeting. This is routinely done when any team assembles to think and learn. Teams are led to use dialogue, "metalogue," and discussion to gain a deeper understanding of (a) the team's shared vision, (b) the mental models employed in the organization, (c) one's own personal mastery of process-centered education, (d) what the team needs to learn, and (e) the "big picture" via systems thinking. Team meetings are engaging activities through which team members are consciously and unconsciously contributing to learning through the use of their own process skills, operations, and dispositions. As members of the team, the superintendent and other leaders continually work at developing comfort with reliance on the collective intelligence of the group and engage freely in team learning. Essential to the success is the willingness to abandon traditional thinking that holds leaders as ones who know the right answer and have the final authority in favor of process orientation, which holds these leaders as ones who (a) facilitate, (b) engage others in visioning, (c) promote the quest for understanding, (d) seek values clarification, and (e) are continuous learners. In other words, the superintendent or any other leader does not operate as the architect who knows all there is to know about designing a school building to the exclusion of those who have not benefited from an architect's training and experience. Instead, the leader operates similar to the architects described earlier who seek a team of thinkers with whom they are able to learn, grow, and achieve.

Five Disciplines, Seven Values, and a Whole Bunch of Systems

Three overarching mental models (constructs) are being promoted to "capture the spirit" in this chapter. In review, they are (a) the multiple interrelated systems found operating in all schools and school districts, (b) the seven values of process-centered education, and (c) the five disciplines of learning organizations. To capture the spirit of process education, these models are harnessed to operate together (Figure 11.1).

When educators-architects consider systems within schools as arenas to capture the spirit, the three model constructs form a framework for redesigning our schools. Whenever teams of educators-architects assemble to consider any system within the school, the teams (a) dialogue around process values to establish guideposts and (b) engage actively to develop the five disciplines. These educator-architect teams deepen dialogue in this endeavor and seek to clarify their tasks by drawing in other models (feedback loops or other models promoted in these books) to augment the emerging structural framework of their process-centered school.

Value-Driven Shared Vision

Engagement in constructing a process-centered learning organization via Senge's (1990) five disciplines immerses educators-architects in process-centered activities. In so doing, the educators-architects become active translators of the very changes they espouse. As they dream about process-centered schools, they transform themselves into living and breathing embodiments of the values of process-centered change.

Shared vision emerges from the dreaming, and the educators-architects recognize and accept that they are cloaked in responsibility for the practical

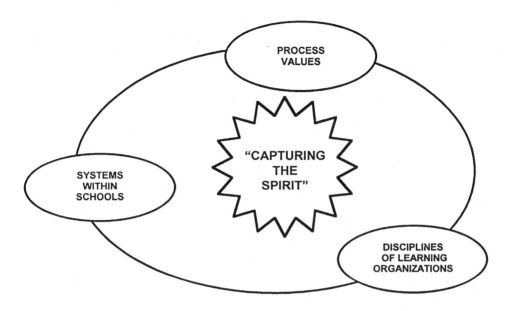

Figure 11.1. Capturing the Spirit of Process Education

translation of process-centered values. For example, "structuring schools as learning societies in which educators are not merely dispensers of information but coaches, catalysts, innovators, researchers, and collaborators with learners" (Value 4) becomes a potent and practical visionary guideline for reconfiguring various systems within the school. This value may suggest that block scheduling be instituted as a means to support a school in which learners are given adequate time to further their process skills and operations. It may suggest that cognitive coaching be incorporated into the staff's supervision plan so that process dispositions may be advanced. It may suggest that places where individuals can go to meet with one another or to do research must be designed into school space to promote the skills of process learning. Through these value-driven explorations of systems within the school, educators-architects become generative of ways to capture the spirit.

For the school leader, this exploration serves as a path to a shared vision steeped in a commonly held core set of values. A value-driven shared vision is basic to and extremely important for change. Furthermore, creating the value-driven shared vision allows the leader to elegantly model process-centered leadership.

Value-Driven Systems Thinking

In the facilitation of systems thinking, educators-architects are encouraged to analyze the entire school as a complex organization of interrelated systems. Leaders urge them to search for systemic relationships that can assist in the practical translation of process-centered values across the organization. For instance, the value "seeking congruence between what learners are thinking, doing, and feeling" (Value 3) begs systemically thinking educators-architects to consciously look for, then incorporate into practice, the integration of the mind, body, and spirit across traditional configurations. *Strange attractors*, that is, systems not ordinarily associated with one another, can be grouped, then explored, for places for the spirit to be captured (Wheatley, 1992). As an example, can the spirit be caught by teaching all learners ballet as a means to integrate French language, physical education, Russian culture, kinesiology, and art? Bringing these somewhat isolated and disparate disciplines together may serve up potentials within curriculum systems in ways not yet imagined.

Integrating these attractors together as thematic components of the curriculum system may somehow influence the system of instructional program and how we teach. This influence might trigger the research system of the school to search out all the interrelationships these attractors have to one another and how teachers may effectively use the interrelationships. The assessment system of the school might be called on to design the means through which the curriculum change is assessed for effectiveness. Assembling these strange attractors together may also cause us to communicate, through the public relations system, the value of such a union to the parents and community.

The reverberations travel, system by system, in often odd and unpredictable ways. School leaders allow this to happen and are tolerant of chaos and ambiguity. Leaders examine chaos and ambiguity through the lens that value-driven shared vision provides. Leaders ensure that orientation to the guiding vision is adhered to when chaos or ambiguity reign. Systems thinkers automatically enter feedback loops when their idea's application causes repercussion in systems other than for which they initially intended the idea. Their reflective thinking helps them understand the relationships between systems that are not normally associated with one another. While thinking systemically, educators-architects discover challenges to create frameworks that course throughout the organization's systems and job responsibilities.

Systems thinking creates the unifying structure of the organization and promotes efficiency. "Striving for a meaningful process-oriented curriculum as the passion that binds the organization" (Value 6) is a call for creating fractally applied mental models throughout the curriculum system of a school. It is a value closely associated with systems thinking.

Value-Driven Personal Mastery

As educators-architects apply process-centered values to systems within the school, they begin to discover new understanding of the process-centered orientation. These understandings cause them to stretch and grow and are the seeds of personal mastery. Personal mastery is fluid and ever changing. Its structure is influenced when colleagues attempt to create a shared vision of their school or when teams gather to think systemically.

During personal mastery building, at least two values operate within and on educators-architects. The values are (a) "fostering the development of learners' unique abilities while recognizing that each is in a constant process of growth and change" (Value 5) and (b) "believing that humans are natural inquirers and learners who are internally motivated, naturally curious, and driven to resolve problems" (Value 7). As educators-architects engage in the reconstruction of their schools, they become personally engaged in the reconstruction of themselves. They confront the uncertainty of change as well as personal renewal as they sense exhilaration about their own growth. Educatorsarchitects experience what they espouse and are able to metacogitate, reflect, and self-adjust.

Educators-architects become part of the framework of the process-centered school by striving for and achieving personal mastery over as many systems within the school as possible. Process-oriented school leaders cultivate the climate for this to happen by modeling continuous learning and welcoming problem posing and solving. Leaders also model reflective and metacognitive practices. In pursuit of personal mastery over how to infuse the values into the systems of the school, the people of the organization infuse the values into themselves. This too captures the spirit.

Value-Driven Team Learning

Earlier in this discussion, I referenced educator-architect teams assembling to hammer out a shared vision. In the shared visioning process, team members expand personal mastery and engage in team learning. Engaging in team learning is a real-life manifestation of the process value "honoring the collective intelligence of the group as well as the individual intelligence of learners" (Value 2). Team discussions center on process values and process education within systems of schools. The shared understandings that develop give the team common ground and language on which teams may (a) clarify goals and purposes, (b) take action and experiment, (c) assess and gather evidence, (d) study and reflect, (e) modify actions, and (f) revisit and redefine goals (Costa & Kallick, 1995).

Discussion and dialogue on each system of the school generates varying points of view, some of which conflict. These points of view are addressed by the team, and information is imported into the discussions as needed. Typically, conflict among team members occurs when actions or people are not in alignment with group values, visions, models, and/or understandings. When conflict occurs, common values, shared visions, accepted mental models, and mutual understandings allow team members to address conflicting viewpoints through the use of double loop feedback.

Value-Driven Mental Models

Using mental models results in "promoting humans to become lifelong learners who possess the necessary process skills" (Value 1). In the processoriented school, patterns emerge. People and procedures begin to fit into expected models of behavior. They use process skills (comparing, inferring, listening, questioning, etc.), process operations (problem solving and posing, decision making, intuiting, etc.), and process dispositions (flexibility, craftsmanship, interdependence, etc.) in everything they do. These patterns are noticed at all levels of the organization and within the systems of the school. For example, as we drive through cities, we may recognize architectural patterns in buildings. We observe that buildings in these cities are both the same and different. They may look different, and perhaps house different clientele, yet they each have internal systems (plumbing, electrical, etc.), they each have structural frameworks, and they each have some sort of human operating system in place to make them useful.

As time and reconstruction go on, the patterns will be the same with process-oriented schools. They will be different, yet the same. Their addresses will be different, and they will house different people, yet they will each have similar supporting systems (assessment, special populations programming, staff development, public relations, etc.). They will each have structural frameworks (process-centered values), and they will each have a human operating system in place to make them efficient (disciplines of learning organizations). The patterns found among all schools will be different, yet the same, as process skills, operations, dispositions, and passions will manifest themselves in myriad ways within and across the systems of the school. Ideas put forward in this book will be applied differently in each school locale under reconstruction, yet the ideas and their process orientation retain their integrity. The process values described in this chapter will generate different plans of action within different systems and within different schools, yet the spirit remains the same. Learning organization principles will play out in a rich and diverse array of educational strategies as teams and individual harness their talents, yet the five principles remain the same. Various mental models will be introduced to aid reconstruction in different ways, yet the models remain the same while demonstrating exportability and importability in their original form.

The value-driven mental model's role is to assist us in capturing the spirit by introducing strategies to do so. The strategies embedded in these models are process skills, operations, dispositions, and passions that engage us in process-centered learning. Leaders of the process-centered school seek out these models, employ them judiciously, and engage individuals and groups in their use. In doing so, the leaders and the model embody the process spirit.

Process Pervades the Organization: Capturing the Spirit in Illinois

In our school district, we had big decisions to make. We wanted our new school to be a physical manifestation of what we value. So we set about the task of creating a value-driven shared vision of how this building would become a school in which process-centered learning was the norm and thereby would pervade the organization. We selected a team unafraid to engage in process-centered learning. We used value-driven visioning as our guideline. We engaged in value-driven systems thinking to learn how the school could support process learning—system by system and value by value. We adopted appropriate mental models for our analysis, including feedback loops, change models, value clarification techniques, learning organization theory, and the like. These models helped us personally and collectively deepen our understanding of the task at hand and generate a blueprint for action.

In the process, we all learned. But more than this, we experienced the power of process-centered learning. And by living the experience, process-centered learning pervaded our building, our people, and our organization.

Capturing the Spirit: A Formula

Is there a way to quantify a formula for capturing the spirit? Mathematically, we can't think of one. Instead, our district's experience humbly forwards ideas and models to consider when undertaking your reconstruction. Perhaps our experiences, insights, and musings will help you develop your recipe for success.

Each school is different, as are the learners who inhabit them. Diversity is energy and supplies a magic through which your school will ultimately be transformed. The magic resides with your people. Challenge them to participate in your reconstruction efforts. They alone can unlock their personal magic and will do so through involvement. Try to involve everyone.

Hold true to process-centered values, that is, "the spirit." Search out ways to ensure their presence in your curriculum. But don't stop there. Search out ways for process values to be incorporated in every system operating in your school. Assess and refine their application continuously. Revisit the values frequently.

Draw people into experiencing the five disciplines that so potently contribute to elegant learning organizations. Have your community of learners experience dialogue about value-driven, process-centered learning. Nurture them. Let them build personal mastery over process skills, operations, and dispositions. Let them attain mastery over the process values. Let them forge mastery over the systems already in place in schools. In doing so, they build personal mastery over their profession.

Create the climate for teams to meet and learn. Supply the resources that teams require for significant change. Ultimately, it is the people—the learners— who make curriculum and all other systems become process oriented.

Take a moment to dream of a school in which the vision of process-oriented learning lives—a place that evidences process values everywhere you look. Imagine value-driven, process-centered learning happening everywhere—all the people, and all the systems, immersed in process. It can be so. Dream of it.

Allow your process-centered thoughts to become words.
Your process-oriented words to become actions.
Your process-centered actions to become habits.
Your process-oriented habits to become your character.
And your process-centered character to become your destiny.

References

Argyris, C. (1982). *Reasoning, learning and action: Individual and organizational.* San Francisco: Jossey-Bass.

Bridges, W. (1991). *Managing transitions.* Reading, MA: Addison-Wesley.

Collins, J., & Porras, J. (1994). *Built to last: Successful habits of visionary companies.* New York: HarperCollins.

Costa, A., & Garmston, R. (1994). *Cognitive coaching: A foundation for renaissance schools.* Norwood, MA: Christopher-Gordon.

Costa, A., & Kallick, B. (1995). *The role of assessment in the learning organization: Shifting the paradigm.* Alexandria, VA: Association for Supervision and Curriculum Development.

Covey, S. (1989). *The seven habits of highly effective people: Powerful lessons in personal change.* New York: Simon & Schuster.

Covey, S. (1991). *Principle-centered leadership.* New York: Simon & Schuster.

Fullan, M. (1990). Staff development, innovation, and institutional development. In B. Joyce (Ed.), *Changing school culture through staff development* (pp. 3-25). Reston, VA: Association for Supervision and Curriculum Development.

Land, G., & Jarman, B. (1992). *Breakpoint and beyond: Mastering the future—today.* New York: HarperBusiness.

Schon, D. (1987). *Educating the reflective practitioner.* San Francisco: Jossey-Bass.

Senge, P. (1990). *The fifth discipline: The art and practice of the learning organization.* New York: Doubleday.

Wheatley, M. (1992). *Leadership and the new science.* San Francisco: Berrett-Koehler.

12

Searching for Evidence

Toward a Renaissance Community

Arthur L. Costa
Rosemarie M. Liebmann

People don't need to be forced to grow. All we need is favorable circumstances: respect, love, honesty, and the space to explore.

Ellen Bass

A renaissance community is neither a destination to be reached, nor a place to be located, nor a state of being to be achieved. Rather, it is a process of becoming. It is a vision in the making. To gather evidence of its qualities, therefore, we must search for indicators in the emerging vision itself, in the processes that are producing that vision, and in the interaction between the two. Charles Lavaroni, in Chapter 10, this book, referred to this as static quality—the quality of product—and dynamic quality—the quality of process.

The most memorable and significant experiences of our lives cannot be reduced to numerical interpretations. The engagement of the body, mind, and spirit simultaneously holds more learning in a short time than immersion in weeks of study at the cognitive level alone. Learning is derived from reflection on experiences not only at the cognitive level but also at the affective and behavioral levels before, during, and after the experience. Searching for evidence, therefore, is a paradoxical process that is both personal and interpersonal, in-the-moment and reflective, emotional and cognitive, immediate and cumulative.

Learning organizations converge on three domains of inquiry: *organizational purpose*—the struggle to explain why we exist, what our mission is, and how we will assess progress toward that vision; *organizational people*—explorations of who I am, what I value, to what do I aspire, what is expected of me, and how I contribute to this organization; and *organizational culture*—investigations into what the organization needs, how business is conducted around here, how decisions are made, how it feels to be here, how things work in this organization, and how the people in the organization interact with each other and with the organizational purposes.

Using these domains as organizers, we will revisit the seven paradigm shifts underlying the renaissance school described in Chapter 3, "Shifting Paradigms From Either/Or to Both/And," in the first book of this trilogy, *Envisioning Process As Content*. The intent is not to present an assessment design but to encourage a search for evidence of that shift toward process. Such evidence is to be used as feedback and guide and quest toward a process-oriented community.

The Search for Evidence

Old Paradigm #1: The school's mission is to produce educated, literate persons who have mastered basic skills and have acquired significant concepts.

New Paradigm: The school's mission is to produce lifelong learners who continue their personal development and who promote the well-being of the larger community.

Organizational Purpose

Renaissance communities hold an ever unfolding and evolving vision of educated persons and the type of education that will develop those capacities. As the needs of learners and society change, so does the vision. All members—teachers, administrators, children, parents, custodians—are open to new thoughts and ideas. The school's mission is in constant development because its authors are aware that the world is continually shifting and that they are learning more about learning. Its authors renew and refresh their vision by incorporating thoughts and perspectives that have evolved from new learnings. As a result, the vision applies to those who are here now and not to a world that once was. On the basis of this evolving mission, goals are continually clarified and objectives are established. Aligning the goals and the outcomes, establishing the purposes of the renaissance school, and creating a personally and collectively significant vision of the future are artifacts of a process orientation.

The envisioning process is valued because it produces discomfort, anxiety, and frustration when the mission statement is used as a basis for decision making: policy formation, instructional planning, and resource allocation. Such continuing task analysis, problem solving, curriculum development, and curriculum modification to make them more consistent with the vision cause the stakeholders to derive personal and collective meaning from the experience.

Organizational People

> The soul would rather fail at living its own life than to succeed at living someone else's.
>
> *David Whyte*

Increasing numbers of renaissance community members are engaging in continuous development of a range of intellectual capacities and resources. Each member of the community is developing additional strengths and is valued for his or her continued learning.

There is a shifting toward greater interdependence—from *me* to *we*. There is movement away from competition with others toward greater craftsmanship and competition with self. There is increased valuing of diversity—recognizing that a group of unique individuals working together brings greater knowledge than each one working individually. (See also Liebmann & Colella's Chapter 11, "Processes for Diverse Voices," in the second book of this trilogy, *Supporting the Spirit of Learning.*)

Organizational Culture

In the renaissance culture, the world is seen as limitless—not limited to what is known or to what is safe. New thoughts and ideas are the result of adventure and "inventure." Continuous learners seek out new lands (adventure) and travel to new frontiers (inventure). Inventure, nurtured by the valuing of process, is the inward journey to the heart, the mind, and the soul.

"Inventurers" celebrate the mysterious. They appreciate the unconscious wilderness in their own spirit and recognize and accept their unique path. They enjoy the process of exploring uncharted land because this is where life gains much of its vitality and meaning. An "inventuring" spirit finds aliveness at the edges of discovery and growth (Leider & Shapiro, 1994).

Further, individuals are coming to accept personal responsibility for preserving the intellectual environment of the community at large. What is becoming valued in the school is also becoming valued at home, at work, and by the influential groups within the community. The result is increased involvement by students, parents, support staff, and community members in the strategic planning, problem solving, and development of goals, values, and beliefs for the learning organization. This co-cognition (thinking together) empowers members to recognize the whole of which they are a part and moves them toward a more complete expression of the will of the community in their individual actions (Leavitt, 1995).

The organizational structure is becoming more collegial. Greater numbers of stakeholders are sharing the decision making, problem solving, and identification, as well as implementation and assessment. The culture increasingly allows for continuous experimentation, reflection, and modification on the basis of the needs of the individual and community.

Old Paradigm #2: It is the responsibility of the schools to educate the child.

New Paradigm: It is the responsibility of all community agencies to contribute to the development of the potentials, continued growth, and lifelong learning of all members of the community.

Organizational Purposes

Janov (1994) addresses the inventive organization that goes beyond the fixed organization and the adaptive organization. The inventive organization must continually "rethink what we create, the process by which we produce, the principles by which we organize ourselves, and the means by which we engage our customers" (p. 28). This spiraling need for renewal comes from an awareness that we live in a chaotically harmonious world in which everything is in constant evolution. Premises and theories designed months ago may no longer be valid. The renaissance community is open to new and evolving stimuli while keeping positive outcomes for learners in perspective. Political institutions, churches, families, businesses, and the media, along with schools, are beginning to view themselves as part of and contributing to their constituents', their employees', and their community's continued learning.

Organizational People

In the renaissance organization, everyone at one time or another shares the acts of leading and following, rather than being assigned the roles of leaders and followers. Partner relationships are preferred to dependency; invention is encouraged over maintenance.

In the renaissance community, there is movement between shared decision making and bureaucratic decision making. The position along the continuum depends on the nature of the problem or challenge. Members of the renaissance community care about what their colleagues and community members (parents, board of education, and others) think and do. Increasingly, honest and open feedback and communication are expressed. Individuals begin exercising personal responsibility for their work. Suggestions, regardless of origin, are being listened to, considered, and acted on.

Organizational Culture

In the renaissance culture, there is an increasing investment of the total person—intellectually, physically, and emotionally. Educators tap into the natural, inherent strengths and propensities of individuals. Teachers and administrators intrinsically believe every student has exceptional skills, talents, and intelligence. Each learner has expanding opportunities to contribute significantly to the community as learning opportunities are provided that enhance the giftedness of each student.

This process of reaching on a personal level for high quality involves an emotional commitment, as well as growth, change, and learning. The result is the development of self-esteem and pride. Learners—adults and children—require nurturance—that important demonstration that someone cares. A greater sense of community, combined with significant learning and caring, produces students who are more persistent, creative, and flexible in solving real-life problems and conflicts. There will be, therefore, a decrease in the number of students who resort to substance abuse, suicide, or dropping out as a means of avoiding difficulties.

Old Paradigm #3: Those in the educational setting are to check their deepest personal selves on the steps of the school and should be the passive recipients of those with greater knowledge.

New Paradigm: Learners are active participants in the learning process, in which relationships, creativity and innovation, authenticity, diversity, self-expression, and the human spirit are valued.

Organizational Purpose

In a renaissance community, the richness of a learning experience is integrated with personal beliefs, values, and prior experiences. Students become more willing to experience disequilibrium caused by the discrepancy between old ways of thinking and new information. As a result of the internal conflict caused by disequilibrium, community members are motivated to make personal changes. The processes involved for the change to occur are based in the constructivist principles of accommodation and assimilation. Students are spontaneously integrating their own linkages, bridges, and connections to new learning.

Members of a renaissance community are striving to become more resourceful in the five mind states addressed by Costa and Garmston in Chapter 9 in this volume. Community members act as coaches for each other in the development of efficacy, flexibility, interdependence, craftsmanship, and consciousness and are seeking out each other because of their coaching skills. The intent of the coaching dialogue is to help each other grow toward greater holonomy.

Organizational People

Community members are learning to be nonjudgmental—probing to learn from each other in their attempts to reach consensus or conclusions. Their goal is to digest, synthesize, and reflect on what they are hearing and/or doing. They are learning the skills of paraphrasing and clarifying each other's ideas, terminology, and intentions.

Community members are learning to accept each other as equals as they practice the skills and strategies of collaboration: dialogue, compromise, consensus, and mutual respect. Members are self-regulating and self-determining. Conflicts are substantive, rather than being over hidden issues, and are coming to be viewed as opportunities to learn about self, others, and the organization. Members are learning to be honest with each other, assessing the openness of their communications and taking ownership of responsibility for their feelings.

Formalized structures become dissipated and are replaced by informal groups. Masks and protective facades are dropped, resulting in a freer flow of feelings, thoughts, ideas, and perceptions; a visible increase in empathy; and an increase in cooperation and shared responsibility. Members of a renaissance community experience intense joy and pleasure not only with self but with each other. They share a sense of pride in their community and are eager to tell their story to others. They have

- *Hope:* Community members are learning to expect positive outcomes and attainment of new goals.
- *Effort:* The holistic connection within our mind and our bodies is increasingly evident. Community members are learning to exhibit physical, emotional, mental, and behavioral actions. When one domain is activated—cognitive, affective, or psychomotor—the other domains are also awakened.
- *Trust:* Individuals are learning to exhibit confident reliance and appropriate dependence on others and on themselves. They demonstrate a willingness to trust their own abilities, which is a fundamental outcome of process learning—the awareness of one's strengths and weaknesses. They are learning to use resources that compensate for their own weaknesses.
- *Constructive level of anxiety:* There is a balancing of constructive levels of anxiety—knowing and accepting that humans feel vulnerable when there is too much anxiety or disequilibrium. To change, old structures have to be dissipated and new structures built in their place. Anxiety and disequilibrium are welcomed because they cause people to get out of their comfort zone and try new behaviors to lessen the anxiety. There is, therefore, an increasing acceptance and valuing of each other's capacity to cope with and learn from ambiguity.
- *A sense of the unknown or unpredictable:* Individuals are developing and increasing their sense of awe or mystery regarding what they are learning. They raise questions in a search to make meaning and sense out of a learning experience. Teachers help students make predictions and search for their own solutions. Everyone is learning to metacogitate, to examine personal thinking, and to begin to identify their own strengths and weaknesses. Quiet time for reflection is increasingly available, and all are encouraged to share when appropriate what they are learning—not only about content but also about their thoughts and feelings concerning their thinking and/or processing skills. It is through such sharing that others are encouraged to take risks and are invited to wander into strange new territories.

Organizational Culture

Community members are becoming increasingly interdependent, collaborative individuals who are continually practicing autonomy, proactivity, empathy, intuitiveness and creativeness, transformation, and political skillfulness. As process intertwines with content, individuals begin to answer four key questions: (a) Where do I best fit in? (b) How can I develop my desires, abilities, temperament, and assets? (c) What networks should I be a part of? and (d) How can I get to know myself better? Going deeper into ourselves and connecting with the right people represent the growth and development not only of the individual but also of the organization.

Old Paradigm #4: Evaluation of learning is a summative measurement of how much content the learner has retained. It is useful for grading and segregating students into ability groups. It is useful in predicting success in later life and indicates aptitude for profiting from more advanced academic instruction.

New Paradigm: Evaluation is neither summative nor punitive. Rather, assessment is a mechanism for providing feedback to the learner and to the organization as a necessary part of the spiraling processes of continuous renewal: self-analyzing, self-evaluating, and self-modifying.

Organizational Purpose

Mindful attention is increasingly paid to the "soul of learning/educating." As different members of the community are embraced, we become inspired by the artistic nature revealed through their beliefs. The artist in each of us is our opening to an infinite variety of lenses that lead to a sparkling picture of a renaissance school. Because all learning is part art and part science, the renaissance school will begin seeing evidence of:

- Growth in all forms of human energy—physical, mental, emotional, social, aesthetic, and spiritual—are welcomed, validated, and viewed as a contribution to the organization.
- Joyfulness and the pleasure intrinsic to the teaching-learning process are monitored.
- Commitment is the norm.
- The degree to which individuals are provided with the needed resources to become holonomous is assessed.
- Spirit and soul are observed, and the meaning gained from these observations influences the direction of the future activities.
- Decisions are made on the basis of intuition, inspiration, and intellect, as well as logic.

- Openness and the free flow of communication are continually monitored and assessed.
- Community members strive to be perceptive, receptive, and expressive.
- People are actively engaged in, proud of, and committed to the renaissance school.
- People within the renaissance school understand that the organization must continue to learn, grow, and change.

Organizational People

Parents, teachers, and school board members understand that what is inspected is what is expected. Therefore, assessment in a renaissance school provides learners with feedback that not only values inventure and adventure but also is designed to assist them in their own learning, risk taking, and thoughtful behavior.

Organizational Culture

In a renaissance school, success and failure become mutual parts of the learning experience. Edison's coworkers once complained after trying 1,000 times to develop the filament for the light bulb without success. In response, he said, "Well, at least we now know 1,000 ways that don't work which we didn't know before."

Edison was displaying in the extreme a characteristic that is common to most Americans—the unconscious desire not to succeed on the first try. Overcoming "failure" is seen as part of the process of improving. How often do we hear, "Without some pain, there is no gain." We accept that making mistakes and learning from them are how we get better. Our society believes, rightly so, that not doing things right gives us the opportunity to assimilate new knowledge, acquire new skills, and become better persons.

So, it appears we enjoy eliminating our safety nets to engage in the search for unorthodox solutions or groundbreaking approaches to solving problems. In schools that value the teaching of process, rigid job descriptions are replaced with flexible descriptors. The morale of the staff is higher because the culture is now compatible with the needs of the students and the adult learners. The freedom to be creative leads educators to higher levels of energy, more thoughtful behavior, and greater personal involvement.

Old Paradigm #5: The understanding of the whole can be achieved only as a result of studying the smallest unit (reductionism).

New Paradigm: Nothing can be truly understood unless we study it in isolation as well as in connection (holonism).

Organizational Purpose

There is a shifting from episodic learning that is quickly forgotten to the celebrating of learning as an important experience, never to be forgotten. There is a widening acceptance of the principle that nothing can be truly understood unless we study it in isolation as well as in connection (holonism).

Organizational People

An increasing number of renaissance community members are expressing a need to be part of a grand vision that meshes with their personal visions. In the process as content paradigm, the vision remains clear while simultaneously unfolding and shifting. It is not static but is part of the evolving culture. It begins to be seen in publications, to be heard in conversations, and, most important, to be internalized and modeled by those in the community.

Organizational Culture

In the renaissance school, decisions are made with a systemic perspective, understanding the importance of looking not only at a single unit but also at how that unit interacts with all other units within the organization. When an individual considers a change, thought is given to its impact on the person, the classroom, the school, the district, and the community.

Old Paradigm #6: The intent of objective, linear, scientific/mechanistic inquiry is to establish causality, laws, truth, and how to control and make accurate predictions.

New Paradigm: The quantum paradigm of process intends to continue seeking greater understanding of multiple causalities, nonlinear and chaotic systems, interactions, and connections and to continually discover hidden meanings.

Organizational Purpose

The purposes of the renaissance communities that are adopting the process paradigm are clearly articulated: to develop the skills, operations, dispositions, and mind states. These processes are leading to an understanding of a way of being that affects not just how we think but also who we are. The organizational purpose strives to develop the whole of each person by integrating head, heart, and body.

Organizational People

The members of the community (teachers, administrators, students, and support staff) are freely choosing to develop and improve their own innate abilities. Growing numbers of community members are involved in unpacking and repacking themselves. They are open to new experiences and new relationships—taking risks, facing new challenges, and seeing life as an ever unfolding dream, much as they did when they were young.

Organizational Culture

> If we could only learn to laugh at ourselves, we would never cease to be amused.
>
> *Anonymous*

Learning is becoming more fun before, during, and after the experience. Making learning fun is key to building trust, energy, and interdependence. Laughter helps us see things through a positive set of lenses. Experiencing a "learner's high" stimulates the brain to produce endorphins. Endorphins renew people physically, mentally, and emotionally; they contribute to feelings of relaxation and refreshment (McGee-Cooper, 1994; see also John Dyer's chapter, "Humor as Process," in the first book of this trilogy, *Envisioning Process As Content*. When learners can laugh at their mistakes and have fun in searching for solutions, they feel enthusiastic about their work and acquire a sense of ownership for their ideas. The community values the stimulation that is provided by healthy fun, recognizing greater and increased enjoyment for learning.

Old Paradigm #7: Only knowledge that is discovered through the use of sensing and thinking is worthy of acceptance and recognition.

New Paradigm: The processes of knowing through the use of feeling and intuition are valid and result in greater depth of understanding.

Organizational Purpose

> We worry constantly about making a living but rarely about making a life.
>
> *Richard Leider and David Shapiro*

As the processes of knowing through the use of feeling and intuition are validated, the result is greater depth of understanding. As process and content interact, strategies and techniques for solving problems shift. Schools witness fewer physical disagreements when students engage more in dialogue, discussion, and debate. Valuing of differences leads to less fractionalization of the population; greater intrigue, wonderment, and curiosity about peers; development of empathy and flexibility; and more openness to new thoughts and ideas.

Organizational People

Because newly acquired knowledge allows learners to stretch and grow in uncharted territory, they discover new patterns and unique outcomes. Their feelings influence what they are thinking, and their thoughts influence their feelings. They own their own projections. They become conscious of self-limiting beliefs. They are more willing to take risks, make new contacts, ask for feedback and support, and reevaluate and assess their own behavior. They are more willing to play with new thoughts and ideas, listen to and express intuitive insights, and communicate clearly with others.

Organizational Culture

In the renaissance community, love is spreading—love that grows from empathy, altruism, compassion, acceptance, and nurturance. Children are frequently the best teachers of this force, which unites us all.

In communities in which process and content are interacting, individuals are listening to their intuitive guidance systems and trusting their wisdom. By accessing and sharing their own deepest truths, community members are pooling their energies to create a new way of living in the world that expresses not who we should be but who we truly are.

A renaissance school recognizes that learning requires time for reflection on, processing of, and assimilation of new knowledge. During these quiet moments, students are open to receiving guidance from their feelings, thoughts, senses, and intuition. They accept or reject new information on the basis of the integration of the four functions of knowing—intuiting, feeling, thinking, and sensing. When we structure the school's culture around an atmosphere of love and acceptance and look for the positives in everyone, uniqueness is nourished and individuals begin to develop into healthy human beings.

Final Thoughts

Darly Paulson (1995), president and chief executive of Bio Science Laboratories, summarizes the soul in the work of a renaissance community. Paulson identifies five keys to embracing this soul in work: (a) the existence of common goals, (b) open communication, (c) positive regard for coworkers, (d) transparency between one's inner and outer selves, and (e) respect for one's being.

> As we develop soul in our work we need to recognize our dual identity: we are both individuals and members of a group. Indeed, finding the soul of work involves the balance and integration of apparent opposites, such as head and heart, intellect and intuition, and self and group. This process is not so much based on the "shoulds" but on "what is." It is my belief that as we attend to the soul of work we will find we feel more complete. (p. 20)

Renaissance community members are learning to express themselves boldly and passionately, developing an appreciation for content and process and cultivating a willingness to venture into the unknown and accept responsibility for their inspirations and talents. They understand that passion and commitment, as well as innocence and experience, bring inspiration and dedication into the renaissance school. They are learning to embrace the mystery of life with a passion.

We are explorers—and the most compelling frontier of our time is human consciousness. Our quest is the integration of science and spirituality, a vision that reminds us of our connectedness to the inner self, to each other, and to the Earth.

References

Janov, J. (1994). *The inventive organization: Hope and daring at work.* Reading, MA: Addison-Wesley.

Leavitt, C. (1995, January-February). Aiming for organizational gestalt. *At Work: Stories of Tomorrow's Workplace, 4*(1), 9-10.

Leider, R., & Shapiro, D. (1994, July-August). Finding your true vocation or, having a mid-life crisis on purpose. *At Work: Stories of Tomorrow's Workplace, 3*(4), 7-9.

McGee-Cooper, A. (1994, May-June). Fun at work. *At Work: Stories of Tomorrow's Workplace, 3*(3), 7.

Paulson, D. (1995, January-February). Finding the soul of work. *At Work: Stories of Tomorrow's Workplace, 4*(1), 18-20.

13

Change

The Journey Begins

Arthur L. Costa
Rosemarie M. Liebmann

In spring's awakening may I find excitement.
In summer's blossoms may I find wonderment.
In fall's colors may I find courage.
In winter's beauty may I find wisdom.

Change—a gift of everlasting youth.

Maggie Liebmann

Three years ago, a dream was born. For one of us, it had been incubating for a long time; for the other, it was as fresh and novel as the dawn of a new day. Both of us, as editors, along with our many contributing authors, walked the beauty path of our landscapes in slightly different ways. Each of us has grown as a result of the journey in unexpected ways. Each of us has been changed forever.

One of our greatest joys came from the authors as they shared with us the *difficulty* and *joy* of looking inward at their beliefs and formulating clearer

AUTHORS' NOTE: We would like to acknowledge the contributions made to this chapter by Dr. Anthony Colella. Dr. Colella was willing to share his thoughts on the change process with us. As a result of his expertise and insights, this chapter emerged. We are most appreciative of his dedication to the process.

pictures to share with others. Their sharing affirmed that we were all being challenged to continue evolving. Some of the contributing authors revealed the following:

> What a wonderful gift this experience was. My ideas have been fuzzy, and I've not taken the time to think them through. This process really forced me to do so, and I'm so glad I have.

> I knew I had this passionate belief system inside of me, but I wasn't sure what it was all about. Now I can see it so much more clearly.

> In doing the research for my chapter, I discovered a whole new interest that has changed how I see the world.

Inner Self and Change

As winter finally relinquishes its icy grip to spring, we are conscious of the changes that we are eagerly awaiting: changes in the weather; changes in our clothing from overcoats to sweaters or, even better, to shirtsleeves; and changes in our environment. From once lifeless trees now emerge tiny red buds. The ground, once frozen, releases its green anticipations of crocuses, tulips, and lilies. And so there is hope—hope that the warmth of the sun will return and bring dormant life back to our Mother, the Earth.

The universe discloses the inevitability of change and evolution. The four seasons may be analogous to the stages of the change process. Spring signals the anticipated change—intense in color, not quite in full bloom but ready to burst. An air of excitement and eager anticipation prevails. Just as the leaf or flower is struggling to come into sight, so is the new thought, idea, or **desire.** Freshness, hope, beauty, and initiative abound. We are aware of our internal forces: Just as the natural world sets its own schedule, our creative inner selves yearn for the natural movement through the spiral of change.

We awaken to the awareness of the sun's soothing warmth, the humming of the bees, and the blossoming of the flowers. We feel significance within us—a shift in energy. With greater clarity, we see what is blossoming. The desire to embrace the change has stirred from within. We create a scene filled with feelings, tastes, smells, sounds, and sights that will permit us to live change. We move from an urging desiring (spring) to **imagining** (summer).

But the journey is not complete. Fall is on its way. Colorful leaves represent the approach of reflectiveness—the time to harvest the benefits of our spring and summer investments. It is the time when the desired change is internalized. Our energy and thoughts have evolved from desire through imagination to expectation. **Expectation** is accompanied by a strong belief of what is possible. Expectation, much like the sap of the trees, represents a slowing down of the processing of the shift to a deep internalization. As the sap thickens, so do thoughts and ideas take hold.

As winter extends its icy grip, leaves and birds escape. Flowers pull back into the earth. After **assimilating** the first three seasons—desire, imagination, and expectation—we need time to practice, rest, and restore before we begin the

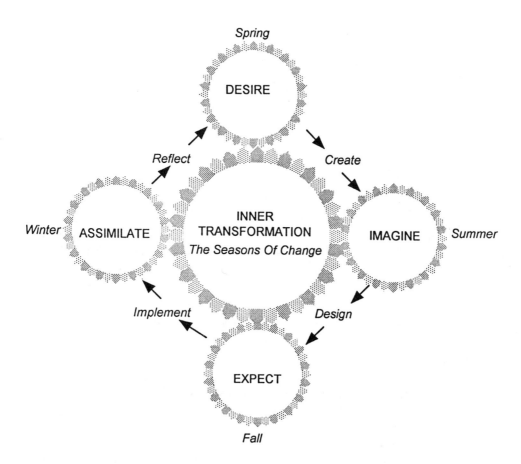

Figure 13.1. The Seasons of Change

cycle anew. Winter provides us with time to assimilate and reflect. Tiny diverse snowflakes glitter an outgrowth in our responses to the desired change. We are continuing to evolve (Figure 13.1).

Numerous researchers have attempted to understand the process of change. Like a stream's continuous flow, it cannot be impounded long enough to reveal its true nature. Never being able to fully understand it, we must be satisfied with a few luminous glimpses of its events. Myths about change—and our resistance to it—abound, especially the myth that resistance to change is negative.

Many of the contributors encourage us to let go of dichotomous, either/or thinking. When we relinquish this type of thinking, we find resistance to be simply a concept by which we describe a current mind state, way of being, or season through which persons pass on their journeys toward enlightenment— sometimes swimming with the current, sometimes against it; sometimes in the center of the rapids, and sometimes floating in a quiet pool. Wherever we are, we see the change forces as complementary relationships (Figure 13.2).

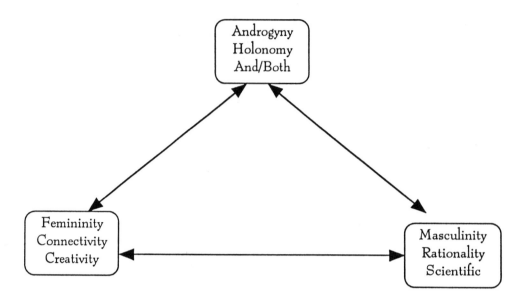

Figure 13.2. Change Forces as Complementary Relationships

We all have internal maps of our own reality and, therefore, not under-standing the source of resistance, we do not have the right to judge others. We can, however, lend a hand. We *cannot* change others. If others change, it is because they have chosen to embark on the journey from within. As Figure 13.3 indicates, people stand at a fork in the road and have to make the choice regarding which way to go. If the choice is to travel down an unfamiliar path, then individuals open themselves up to growth. The willingness to accept the shift in perception indicates a readiness to consider and perhaps internalize a new paradigm. Neither way is right or wrong; we can only honor where persons are. They may need the quiet of the winter to renew themselves before embark-ing on a journey into spring.

Change comes in two ways—internal and external. Internal, or proactive, change is initiated from within. *Proactive* may convey that it is positive. It can be but is not necessarily so. A change that is proactive and negative might be to abandon one's children. This might be positive for the individual but negative for the children. External, or reactive, change, initiated by someone else, shares the same duality. It can be positive or negative. In some cases, benefits accrue from imposed change—such as a teacher who has taught a class for students who are neurologically impaired for 6 years and is reassigned. This might be positive for the teacher while being negative for the students.

Humans constantly respond to energy sources emitted from each other, from the environment, from within, and from the universe. We can choose to respond either proactively or reactively. If we choose to be proactive, we assume an internal locus of control, and we assess whether the desired change is consistent with our self-perception. This can happen only when our self-perception is

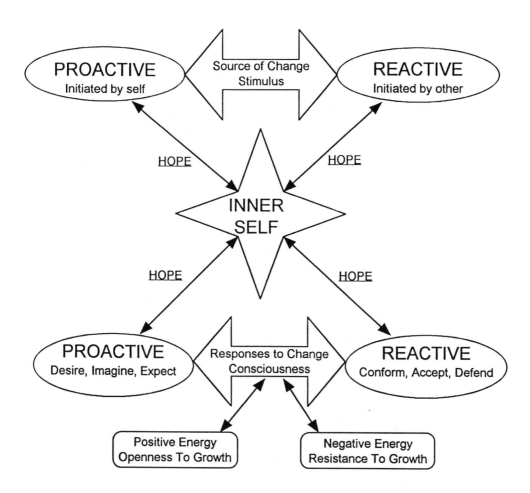

Figure 13.3. The Change Process

consistent with the desired change. If our self-perception and the desired change are compatible, we can begin to bring the shift in paradigm into our repertoire of behaviors.

We believe this is also true as we shift toward a process orientation. We have found that most educators strive for a process orientation, believing that content to be learned is only a vehicle for the processes of continued, lifelong learning. Standing in our way are well-meaning mandates, irrelevant curricula, and standardized assessment practices—all of which constrain professional educators from moving to a more internal and proactive stance.

As we embrace change, it is helpful to remember that acting as if it is real makes it real. Engaging with the shift allows us to be open to alternatives, thereby increasing our ability to articulate, strive for, and accomplish what we desire and feel is right: a cyclical process.

This trilogy, Process as Content, advocates a monumental paradigm shift for some communities and many educators. Support systems for the journey will be needed when the road gets rough. The vision will become blurred as pressures mount to return to the tried and true.

Persistence, flexibility, empathy, networking, and creativity will be essential to withstand the attacks. Total community involvement will be imperative to build understanding and commitment to the new vision. Educational communities will have to align policies, assessment techniques, teacher preparation and certification, curriculum, and testing with the vision of process-centered schools. This paradigm shift also requires the realignment of personal, professional, and organizational philosophies—no small task. Stakeholders in the community need to be reeducated as to the new mission of the schools and the research that supports the change.

An unflagging effort will be needed to communicate that this is not just another fad. For too long, educators have "jumped on bandwagons," relentlessly searching for "quick fixes." Many teachers, parents, and boards of education are jaundiced and jaded by this Band-Aid approach to solving complex educational problems with simplistic solutions.

This trilogy offers a significantly different journey involving clear, long-range, spiraling changes. Furthermore, anyone embarking on this illusive journey needs to be mindful that it is never ending and always evolving; once persons have arrived, they are no longer there!

Although the journey is difficult, we must maintain faith in our mission, sustain hope for a grander vision and a better world, constantly search for multiple solutions to problems, and maintain a state of conscious awareness for each of us on our separate journeys that our paths will take us toward the solutions. The journey is a difficult one—especially in today's turbulent society. Yet if we look for the beauty, love, and hope, we can find them—in our children, in our homes, in our schools, and in our communities. The terror in our world has been provided to heighten our level of understanding and to push us to find cures and/or solutions for problems. It is through discomfort that we grow.

Each of us must model a process orientation, continually learning, growing, and changing. As Mahatma Gandhi said,

You must be the change you wish to see in the world.

The Essence

Process as Content

Louis Rubin

The volumes in this trilogy are rooted in the persuasive conviction that thought serves as the essence of the educational process. Because there are distinct modes of thinking for the accumulation, interpretation, and application of knowledge, each of these warrants due curricular emphasis. Moreover, because students can know without understanding—and understand without perceiving implication or use—good schooling must ensure that acquiring and exploring the powers of insight are significant by-products of learning. In short, learners must know things—know what they really mean—and know how they can be used.

Such arguments are of particular moment at a time of massive ferment and upheaval in the quest for effective reform. Federal initiatives such as Goals 2000: Educate America and the Elementary and Secondary Education Act, for example, aim at high expectations for all students—measured by what they know and can do—and structured, presumably, by sensible conceptions of consequential teaching and worthy subject matter. Much depends, however, on what knowledge and capabilities are deemed worthy and what learning experiences are harnessed to their attainment. It is hardly surprising, therefore, that in the wake of ideological insecurity, an ambiguous curriculum spawns confusion.

Margaret Mead (personal communication, 1965) once noted that "the task confronting today's schools is to teach the young how to solve yet unborn problems, through still unknown solutions." Her point was that students now in school will face an inevitable and immense array of social problems. Without knowing the precise nature of these difficulties, however, we cannot teach their solutions. Our only viable option, then, is to teach youth *how* to solve problems. It is in this spirit, perhaps, that the editors saw fit to organize the volumes around the premise that teaching that (a) generates knowledge and understanding, (b) poses related problems, (c) demonstrates potential steps to their solutions, and (d) integrates direct practice in problem solving not only can increase comprehension and retention but—of even greater consequence—can enhance intellectual capability as well as the capacity to use acquired knowledge constructively. Knowledge is the most useful when it propagates intuition. The distinction between inert and active knowledge, in sum, lies in the degree of functionality.

Furthermore, a growing body of research-based theory suggests that connectivity is central to the construction of meaning and the sense of application. Too often, we tend to break down complex operations, assuming that learning is at its best when discrete conceptual components are taught separately. Psychologists contend, however, that only when the pieces are reconstructed into a workable entity are true meaning and significance grasped. In the absence of such reconstruction, a disjointing of perception occurs. There are instances, for example, when an idea is best comprehended by contemplating the whole rather than the sum of the parts. In piecing together an unassembled table, to wit, some find it easier to form a mental picture of the end product rather than to insert peg A in slot B. Similarly, the child tinkering with the family computer may fathom its intricacies as fast—or faster—than the adult laboring through a manual. Put succinctly, the fracturing of reality has its liabilities.

We are once again, ironically, in the periodic cycle of debate over the relative merits of segregated and integrated curriculum. There are those who maintain that much is gained when concepts from different subject areas are coalesced into a holistic perspective, as well as those who contend that the discipline's unique methods of inquiry and knowledge structure are lost in homogenization. Both views have their validity, and the error may lie in opting for one over the other—rather than exploiting the advantages of each. Generic and universal thinking modes clearly exist. For example, mathematical understanding, literary insight, and historical interpretation require distinct cognitive operations that can be taught in conjunction with knowledge acquisition and use. "Knowing" and "using" are discrete—but corollary—dimensions of learning. The interplay between perception and use, moreover, can also serve as a unifying mechanism for integrating classroom and real-world experience.

Because human minds function in an interlocking sequence of networks through which we meld multiple sources of comprehension, formulate meaning, and grasp significance, events and encounters are meshed, juxtaposed, and counterbalanced in a continuing web of cognitive activity that eventually enables us to make sense of things. For this reason, the aims of education are assumed to be encapsulated in both the subject matter and experiences of schooling. Students are shaped, thus, by the range and complexity of whatever occurs in the classrooms and the consequent interplay with perceptions gained elsewhere. Yet the curriculum does little in the way of orchestrating and consolidating the emotional and intellectual activity such occurrences encompass. Perkins and others repeatedly have reminded us that useful learning evolves when students assemble, analyze, and interpret diverse information and gradually create personal meaning that leads to conceptual applications. But our ways of choreographing learning and instruction typically assume that chunks of this and that can be added, subtracted, or combined willy-nilly.

It also is tempting to assume that if random efforts to raise standards, improve instruction, update content, and enhance curriculum organization are each managed competently, schools will benefit and students will be better served. It has now become plain, however, that such temptation is naive. Disjoined innovation, although advantageous in piecemeal ways, does not circumvent the need for connection and synergy. The degree to which such initiatives attend to linkage, congruence, and common cause is of consummate importance. Policymakers, nevertheless, often approach their task unilaterally; content specialists advocate revisions inspired by their subject matter; textbook manufacturers are guided by marketplace appeal; leadership is geared to one temporal fad of the moment or another; revisions are initiated in response to the clamoring assertions of vested interest groups; opportunists exploit the commercialization of learning; and intelligent cohesion in service of the strengthening of mind has become a lost cause.

Worse, because one aspect of restructuring frequently affects others, single-minded change invariably has a downside. Pedagogical innovations, as a case in point, are governed by the practitioner's adeptness in using them skillfully. Similarly, policy changes—placing greater emphasis on cultural diversity, for instance—necessitate coupling with compatible instructional methodology. Seemingly lacking, however, are viable ways to integrate reform in broad, closely aligned patterns.

In the same vein, much attention during the last decade has been devoted to thoughtful curriculum implementation: using rational theory in a context and manner that enhances organizational cohesion, combining efficient instruction with discerning evaluation, and so on. The aftereffects have not been encouraging. In subsequent efforts to unravel the problem, three significant conclusions emerged: First, good curriculum constructs, used unintelligently, produce little good and sometimes considerable harm; second, disordered attempts to reform and restructure have a short life as well as limited advantage; and, third, implementation difficulties make it plain that good constructs can be perceptibly weakened by artless management. And, in the absence of de facto centric planning, some provision for effective coalescence is essential. The trilogy fashioned by the volumes' editors sets forth the compelling logic that a process curriculum—anchored by modalities of intellection—can provide badly needed unity.

A variety of recent educational policies have sought to resolve current dilemmas by regulating minimum standards, toughening assessment procedures, and intensifying content criteria. Few of these, however, have achieved their intended effect. There is, thus, a growing suspicion that even good improvement policies are difficult to actualize with any degree of success—first, because they are isolated and lack connection with other independent organizational provisions; and, second, because they frequently fail to make due allowance for the pragmatic problems schools confront.

Even when implemented effectively, moreover, they may not accomplish their intent because the reformers often decipher problems inaccurately, neglect to anticipate the barriers in prevailing practice, and ignore the lessons of historical analogy and precedent. Additional hurdles lie in the gulf between curriculum and reform strategies. If process as content is to affect teaching practices, it must address the broad spate of attendant factors involved. Preparation, licensing criteria, performance assessment, instructional objectives, and student evaluation must be tied to the nurture of process capability. A realignment of purpose and focus will also need to cope with vagaries of organizational change, competing concerns, and theoretical divisiveness. And more impediments exist in the possible fallout between means and ends—the aims of process curriculum and the necessary course of action. The restructuring literature provides little in the way of guidance or workable blueprints for dealing with the stumbling blocks of disparate policy, divergent implementation tactics, and the combined overload of excessive school obligations. All this suggests that our greatest need is a shrewder fix on the matters of greatest importance. A major challenge thus arises: How can we best establish new goals within the system, mount a coordinated thrust toward process-based education, and create collaborative forces to energize the changeover?

What sort of networking, for example, would enable schools to take advantage of existing models? How might improvement programs evolve new teaching and learning procedures yielding symbiotic benefit? Can the necessary connective tissue be most effectively accomplished by the architects—or the users—of process-based innovations? Can concurrent attention be focused on a process curriculum *and* its corresponding need for pedagogical approaches?

The significance of these requirements is highlighted by problems stemming from recent reform endeavors. Emphasis has focused on three primary goals: (a) formulating better organizational approaches to professional development; (b) introducing intellectually more demanding content, wherein teachers guide students in constructing cumulative personal meaning as well as a sense of its use; and (c) eliminating restrictive controls that inhibit teachers and administrators from right-minded self-direction. Progress has been uneven. Some teachers, caught up in the promise of the intended reform, stay committed. Others, out of disinterest, disillusionment, or confusion, lose interest. Highly motivated at the outset, they gradually abandon a process approach and return to old patterns of pedestrian teaching and the lures of convenience. Hence, although newer texts reflect a conspicuous leaning toward cognitively oriented curricula, most instruction remains dominated by teacher-talk and didacticism.

What might constitute an optimum melding of subject matter and cognitive development? Skills developed through repetitive drill—such as rote memorization knowledge devoid of understanding—neither provoke thought nor enlarge the intellect. Conversely, skills developed through discerning practice, and comprehension evoked by inferring, interpreting, and organizing meaning that is applied in related problem solving, result in a richer, more functional, knowledge stockpile and a considerably expanded efficacy for productive thinking.

The critical challenge confronting curriculum practitioners, consequently, is to sequence optimally useful subject matter, incorporate process-centered learning activities, integrate a variety of instructional formats in diverse contexts, ensure that all of these experiences extend mental proficiency, and devise assessment measures that verify the accomplishment of process and content objectives. When teachers help students access information and ideas, cognitive processing can occur. But only when learners actually "get it"—relating new conceptual insight to previously acquired understanding—does knowledge becomes functional. It follows, therefore, that content and thinking are best taught and evaluated simultaneously.

New instructional materials and testing prototypes are beginning to embrace a conception of teaching and learning wherein functional knowledge is seen as a blend of knowing and using. The 1994 National Assessment of Educational Progress geography tests are illustrative. Subject mastery was construed not as naming world capitals and rivers but rather as the ability to interpret maps; describe significant physical and cultural features of regions; discuss political, social, and economic characteristics of world areas; and so on. The assessment, in turn, dealt not with simple recall but with the competence to analyze, compare, and generalize—to think.

In a sense, process education lends additional weight to Dewey's convictions regarding activity-centered curricula and what currently is referred to as constructivist learning theory. Reduced to its essence, the theory postulates that concepts within subject areas can be taught in a manner that encourages students to draw on their own social experience in constructing meaning. Such personally constructed understanding can also be used in classroom analysis of social phenomena to inject situated cognition—learning in actual contexts. Teaching that enables students to grasp meaning in their academic tasks, to correlate concepts from different subjects, and to fuse such learning with the outside world creates an impressive repertoire of useful skills.

Viewed in the large, then, the volumes' implications are of considerable consequence—particularly in pointing the way to replace our present leaden approach with boldly invigorated curriculum designs. New frameworks can structure disciplinary concepts and process-linked instruction into a cognate nexus embracing texts, methodology, and evaluation. Teachers, obviously, will need to redefine goals and procedures, as well as adopt a broader range of intentions, but the advantages would be substantial. Once empowered and unfettered, intellectual processes develop a life of their own, acquiring through repeated use cumulative strength, complexity, and applicability. Few reform efforts could make more of a difference.

Index

CORWIN
PRESS

The Corwin Press logo—a raven striding across an open book—represents the happy union of courage and learning. We are a professional-level publisher of books and journals for K-12 educators, and we are committed to creating and providing resources that embody these qualities. Corwin's motto is "Success for All Learners."